The Structures of Love

SUNY series, Insinuations:
Philosophy, Psychoanalysis, Literature

Charles Shepherdson, editor

The Structures of Love

Art and Politics
beyond the Transference

James Penney

SUNY
P R E S S

Cover photograph courtesy of David G. Mills.

Published by State University of New York Press, Albany

For information, contact State University of New York Press, Albany, NY
www.sunypress.edu

Production by Eileen Meehan
Marketing by Fran Keneston

Library of Congress Cataloging-in-Publication Data

Penney, James, 1971–
    The structures of love : art and politics beyond the transference /
James Penney.
        p. cm. — (SUNY series, insinuations: philosophy, psychoanalysis, literature)
    Includes bibliographical references and index.
    ISBN 978-1-4384-3973-0 (hbk. : alk. paper)
    1. Psychoanalysis—Philosophy. 2. Love. I. Title.

    BF175.P4157 2012
    150.19'5—dc22   2011009759

10 9 8 7 6 5 4 3 2 1

Contents

List of Illustrations

Acknowledgments

An earlier version of chapter 3 was published as "Passing into the Universal: Fanon, Sartre and the Colonial Dialectic," *Paragraph: Journal of Modern Critical Theory* 27, no. 3 (2004): 49–67; reprinted with permission of Edinburgh University Press. An earlier version of chapter 4 was published as "Genet among the Palestinians: Sex, Betrayal, and the Incomparable Real," in *Comparatively Queer: Interrogating Identities across Time and Cultures,* ed. Jarrod Hayes, Margaret R. Higonnet, and William J. Spurlin (New York: Palgrave Macmillan, 2010), 193–213. An earlier version of chapter 5 was published as "The Failure of Spectatorship," *Communication Theory* 17, no. 1 (February 2007): 43–60; reprinted with permission of John Wiley & Sons, Inc.

Diagrams from Lacan's seminar are from *The Four Fundamental Concepts of Psychoanalysis* by Jacques Lacan, translated by Alan Sheridan. Copyright © 1973 by Editions du Seuil. English translation copyright © 1977 by Alan Sheridan. Used by permission of W. W. Norton & Company, Inc.

A Standard Research Grant from the Social Sciences and Humanities Research Council of Canada provided the resources necessary to complete this project. Special thanks to Beaverbrook Art Gallery and Lucian Freud for permission to feature reproductions of his stunning work. My research assistants Susanna Ashley and Jacob Potempski provided invaluable help. Trent University students too numerous to name expressed views that contributed to my thinking about the transference and forced me to invent new ways of talking about psychoanalysis and Lacan. Finally: hello Ian and Violet! And thanks, Dave, who likely wouldn't want me to go on.

Preface

The premise of this book is that transference is the concept with which psychoanalysis thinks through the unconscious demands that circumscribe and can sabotage our creative initiatives in the arts and politics. I aim to demonstrate that transference theory, derived from Freudian clinical experience, allows the critic of literature and culture to radicalize the disappointing poststructuralist understandings of agency as, on the one hand, performativity and resignification (Judith Butler, Derrida) and, on the other, the redirection of existing relations or vectors of power or force (Foucault, Deleuze). The method of analysis that transference theory suggests allows us to recognize the transformative potentialities of genuine artistic and political *acts*.

The transference's interpretation divulges our collective subjective capacity to unfurl the invigorating consequences of such events in specific social, historical, and cultural circumstances. By interpreting the transference we can remain faithful to the work of singular artists and thinkers who take up the challenge of moving beyond the ego's claims to social recognition, and therefore beyond the treasonous ambivalences and compromises that arise when we fail to pursue desire beyond the limits policed by fear and anxiety. Though no form of artistic or political practice can precisely reproduce the course of analytic treatment, the texts of culture leave discernible traces of a sort of psychical *work* that runs strikingly parallel to the analyst's work of interpretation. The chapters that follow aim to discern these traces, formulating in precise but accessible terms the philosophical, literary, cinematic, and painterly stratagems that have allowed the creators of concern to accomplish their challenging and inspiring innovations.

Specifically, *The Structures of Love* explores the aesthetic, political, and ethical ramifications of the transference idea through detailed analyses of five objects of culture from an eclectic, and no doubt idiosyncratic, range of genres and media: Plato's *Symposium* (via Jacques Lacan's reading), Frantz Fanon's body of work, Jean Genet's *Prisoner of Love* and political essays, Chantal Akerman's cinematic Proust adaptation *The Captive*, and the nudes of Lucian Freud in painting. The seemingly haphazard quality of this group of objects is not the result of mere whimsy. It is intended, rather, to help liberate literary and cultural studies from the moribund historicisms and contextualisms that have gained ascendancy during the last couple decades or so.

I don't think as a rule that it's the author's business to tell readers how to read his book. Given its eclecticism, however, a brief introductory comment may be in order. Chapter 1 offers a thoroughgoing analysis of the development of the transference concept in Freud and Lacan, focusing on how Lacan's teaching suggests a fresh reading of Freud's technical writings that foregrounds the improperly acknowledged social and political implications of psychoanalysis. Not infrequently, the remaining chapters make reference to this theoretical discussion, aiming to specify exactly how transference theory can be put into practice in the arena of cultural interpretation. Yet these chapters are written in such a way that they can be read independently of chapter 1. The critic of postcolonial culture, for instance, may want to focus on chapters 3 and 4 (on Fanon and Genet respectively), which together aim to suggest a reformulation of the tenets of postcolonial theory. Alternatively, the student of visual culture may decide to proceed directly to chapters 5 and 6, curious about what there could possibly be left to say about psychoanalysis and film theory, or else about Lacan's sweeping and neglected pronouncements on the function of art. Though I tried consistently to make the connection between the theoretical and cultural aspects of the project as explicit as possible, links which I have not foreseen can and no doubt will be made. This, surely, is one of the things that readers are for.

I

The Refusal of Love

Love in the Social

It's not too much to claim that the entire project of psychoanalysis was set in motion by Freud's remarkable discovery at the outset of his investigations that the patient never fails to fall in love during treatment. Baptizing this phenomenon transference love, Freud argues that such a love cannot *not* occur in analysis; that the rules of the game— patient lying on the couch, analyst seated behind, law of free association imposed—guarantee that it will occur without fail. The event of love revealed in the transference is the underlying condition of possibility of psychoanalysis. My initial aim in this chapter will be to show that, despite some terminological confusion and symptomatic ambivalences, two distinct ideas of love can be discerned in the pioneering Freudian texts. There is first the enigmatic power of resistance of the transference love that initiates Freud's analytic desire to solve the riddle of his patients' symptoms. But there is another kind of love as well, and the transference concept as Lacan formalizes it in his teaching is in my view the key to distinguishing between the two.

There is a love "beyond" the transference, that is to say, but it emerges only on condition that we come to terms with a paradox. Though, as Freud consistently maintains, the transference functions objectively as a form of resistance against unconscious desire, perpetuating thereby the symptom's nagging neurotic agency, its manifestation remains an efficient condition of the cure. In other words, the transference reliably points the way toward its own elusive beyond. The occurrence and proper interpretation of the transference are therefore necessary prerequisites for the setting in motion of our inherent capacity to love in the ethical, and therefore political, way that this book sets out to explore in some detail.

I will argue moreover that these statements hold true as firmly outside the specific concrete "situation" of analysis as they do within it. The scare quotes signal how the idea of the analytic scene differs from the phenomenological, existentialist, and sociological understandings of the term developed by Jean-Paul Sartre and Pierre Bourdieu, for example. We can distinguish the psychoanalytic understanding from its rivals by pointing to its acknowledgment of an unconscious psychical agency—desire—that cannot be charted onto the terrain of a situation through reference to either the phenomenon in any of its aspects or its determination by "concrete" or "material"—socioeconomic, most often—factors. This is not to say that the socioeconomic has no role to play in the psychoanalytic theory of love. Indeed, I will argue in this chapter that it leaves its mark on Freud's thought, though in a resolutely psychical guise. For this reason, as I will aim to show, the very category of the socioeconomic must be viewed as always and necessarily inflected by unconscious desire as it is made manifest in the transference.

Historically, the discipline of psychoanalysis writ large, perhaps especially in the Anglo-American region, has had tremendous difficulty relating its apparently subjective or person-based concepts to the collective, the social, and the political. By cutting down to size the formidable discursive wall that for many separates the intimacy of the clinic from the vagaries of its outside, I mean to suggest that no legitimate line of demarcation in theory or in practice can be drawn between our relation to the analyst as determined in the transference and our relation to the wider social world—to the Other, as I will prefer to say after Lacan. The latter relation is equally and identically determined by this very same transferential dynamic. Indeed, the only basic difference between what occurs inside and outside the analytic chamber with regard to the event of transference is that the analytic commitment to "neutrality"[1] has the benefit of making tangible the inauthentic, indeed illusory, foundations of the demand that lies at its root. As Freud clearly knew, the fact that the patient should address a strong passion to someone about whom he knows essentially nothing has the illuminating effect of isolating the psychical sphere, thereby making it amenable to intervention. What is all too rarely acknowledged, however, is that this clinical event uncovers how the transference necessarily mediates our relation to the social world as such, how in fact it has a crucial role to play in the structuring of the social relation in its various forms.

One of this book's underlying premises is therefore that the ambiguities and contradictions that mark Freud's usage of our term of concern have far-reaching consequences for a wide range of fields of inquiry that, with precious few exceptions, have been perfectly happy not to take account of the unconscious; that are even sometimes invoked, especially on the political left, as ways of compensating for the allegedly individualistic or subjectivist shortcomings of Freudian psychoanalysis both as theory and practice. Indeed, the transference concept holds crucial implications for any field of study that sets itself the task of tackling—or reframing through alternative concepts—the thorny, age-old question of the relation between the subject and society, or between the psychic and the social, to use Judith Butler's formulation.[2] Foremost among these consequences is the fact that only muddled abstractions can result from any method of analysis that fails to acknowledge that the social acquires its properly human dimension through its inflection by the subject's desire—that of not just any old subject, mind you, but specifically that of the unconscious subject as Freud defines it.

I will take the risk of hazarding some reckless generalizations to illuminate this contested social-theoretical terrain in preparation for my intervention. As I present this brief theoretical survey I will attempt the perhaps impossible task of doing so at once in the technical terms familiar to specialists as well as in an ordinary idiom which I hope the general reader will find more accessible. Despite the considerable pressure exercised by a variety of self-styled postmodernist and poststructuralist discourses throughout the latter half of the twentieth century, numerous qualitative and quantitative social-scientific methodologies continue to approach the question of the social as if it were a self-sufficient entity requiring no consideration of its means of presentation or representation, regardless of whether or not such means are viewed as informed or determined by something of the order of the subject, be this either the psychological subject of sense perception or consciousness or the epistemological subject of knowledge. Through their precritical empiricism, these approaches fall short of acknowledging the problematic of the transference by simply approaching the social as if it were already there, ready-made and fully transparent to thought, untouched by the faculty of desire. Though these methodologies persist unquestioned in the less theorized enclaves of the social sciences in all their vastness, they are clearly not the ones that have gained ascendancy in cultural and literary studies over the last three or four decades.

Contrary to received wisdom, however, the more current and avowedly sophisticated discourse theories that strongly posit the constructed nature of the social fail to alter the approach considerably. Though they are explicitly recognized as contingent in their status as representations or vectors of desire, power, or force, social arrangements in these discourses are imagined as fabrications, however multiform and heterogeneously conceived, which remain ultimately consistent—accessibly positive (even in their radical difference), fully knowable or closed—in their inconsistency. More simply, not only does the construction of the social leave nothing unconstructed by discourse, nothing unproduced by power, but this construction is all-pervasive, leaving no empty pockets of negativity or non-knowledge. Remaining unexamined in such approaches is our collective libidinal investment in this construct of seamlessly consistent heterogeneity; in other words, how "the social" is propped up and totalized by both our narcissistic demand for personalized meaning and our submissive fascination with power. The result is that, on the rare occasion when these discourses try to account for (the possibility of) transformational or thoroughgoing change, they must resort to tortuously convoluted formulations and disorienting conceptual gymnastics. There is no space for the act, for the event: happenings that are not already immanent with respect to existing significations, logics, or relations of force. This remains the case even when these happenings are explicitly qualified as oppositional—deterritorializing or micropolitical, for example.

Alain Badiou's more consequential work does not lie vulnerable to these accusations. To my mind, the refreshing conceptual break that his system forces with respect to today's dominant cultural-theoretical orthodoxies is what accounts for the highly welcome, though no doubt improbable, ascendancy of Badiou's work in Anglophone theory circles during the past decade or so. His avowedly Platonist outline of a social world of appearances amenable to logical formalization and subordinated to a mathematical ontology of pure inconsistent multiplicity not only recognizes the objective possibility of unforeseeable and undetermined events, but also attributes to these events the hallowed but unfashionable status of truths, positing moreover that thought is capable of tracing the consequences of these truths in specific contexts through acts of militant fidelity. In other words, in contrast to the theories of discourse production and biopower, Badiou's framework privileges what does *not* appear in discourse. Put in more positive terms, Badiou aims to

The Refusal of Love 5

think the evanescent event that is all too easy to ignore or to dismiss as never having taken place.

However, Badiou's recent and laudable effort to define specific world-situations through logical formalization, amounting to a kind of non- or antisubjectivist phenomenology, rests on what I consider an aseptic transcendental conditionality that is troublingly severed from its link with human libidinal investment. Put in less philosophical terms, Badiou's project proceeds as if particular social arrangements existed independently of the subjects to whom they appear. Now, these subjects, psychoanalysis teaches us, are always shot through with particular libidinal interests and specific unconscious desires. Yet "the laws of appearance are intrinsic," Badiou argues, "and they suppose no subject."[3] Badiou's reading of Kant, for example, is emblematic of his desire to rid phenomenology, the study of appearances, of any trace of subjectivity as it has generally been defined through categories designating either a priori psychological forms of consciousness or the experiential contents of sense perception.

The gesture by which Badiou moves to isolate his "worlds" from subjectivity is certainly a politically strategic one in that he wants to tie his own concept of the subject not to the world of appearances, to the status quo of specific situations, but rather to a causatively prior ontological register of pure inconsistent multiplicity. In this way the category of the subject becomes inseparable for Badiou from his notion of truth. For this reason it remains by definition militantly at odds with the state of things as they appear to be. Because it emerges from the void of a given situation, a "place" defined by its minimal degree of phenomenological existence, Badiou's subject remains unmarked by the far-reaching discursive determinations that limit its agency in the representationalist (deconstructionist) and postrepresentationalist (Foucauldian and Deleuzian) versions of poststructuralism. Badiou's event, and the subject who remains faithful to it, are therefore beyond the realm of discourse and power as contemporary theory understands these terms.

Unlike hegemonic theory's variously configured post-subjects, then, Badiou's subject is a subject of radical innovation, one who always emerges in opposition to "the social" as it is defined in any given world-situation. Badiou offers, to my mind, an invigorating alternative to the attacks on the concept of the subject of the last few decades because his construal of this subject is posthumanist: nonintentional, antipsychological, transpersonal; but also unfashionably *autonomous* in relation to the status quo—capable, that is, of bearing witness to occurrences that fail to appear as phenomena in predefined political, artistic, scientific, and amorous situations. In this light, Badiou's notion of the subject as subject-to-truth is comparable to the Freudian subject as Lacan refined its concept, for the psychoanalytic subject of unconscious desire is also defined by its nonappearance in language and the social. Indeed, the Freudian subject is strictly correlative to a *violation* of social law.

There are further, less commonly acknowledged points of comparison between Badiou's formalization of what he calls pure multiplicity's transcendental indexation—the configuration of being-as-being (*être-en-tant-qu'être*) within the existential logic of a specific world—and Lacan's concept of the Other, his term for the fragile and contingent signifying structure that mediates the social relation. As is well known to readers of his later work, Lacan's account of what he terms the logic of the signifier became increasingly dependent on the formal languages of mathematics and logic. By severing transcendental indexation from the psychoanalytic account of a subject split by its insertion into language, however, Badiou's framework cannot properly take account of our libidinal investment in the social as appearance, in other words, why so many of us fail to bear witness to the fragile truths his philosophy aims to think. This means that Badiou's system cannot adequately acknowledge the unconscious resistance that dissuades inquiry into the multiples that fail to appear in a given world. For psychoanalysis, in contrast, the subject always has a *symptom*: the sign of its failure to accommodate itself, in Badiou's terms, to being as pure indifferent multiplicity; being, that is, "before" its appearance has been shaped by normative logics of existence or value—discourses, if you prefer.

Further, Lacan's idea that the subject is marked by a fundamental *manque-à-être* (lack-in-being) reminds us that the world of appearances cannot decisively be extricated from the defenses that the ego insistently puts up. For Lacan, we come to be as subjects of the unconscious in consequence of a resistance to being: a piece of being-jouissance is cast off into the unconscious to be replaced by desire's empty, virtual essence—a quantity, that is to say, of *nonbeing*. Transference is the concept through which psychoanalysis sets itself the task of explaining our resistance as subjects to the truths that Badiou so justifiably wants to valorize and bring to the power of thought. In its admirable intention to cast off the fearful and self-pitying modesty of so much contemporary discourse, Badiou's framework simply grants too much to the subject when it assumes a clean break with a status quo whose seductive powers are therefore counterstrategically underestimated. As subjects of the unconscious, we never cease definitively to resist. Our capacity to become Badiouian subjects-to-truth depends absolutely on our acknowledgment of this difficult fact.

Having said this, however, I want to stress that I do not wish my argument to participate in a skeptical reaction to what must be considered in today's philosophical and political climates Badiou's heroic reclaiming of the category of truth for thought. Indeed, Badiou's thesis concerning the identity of what he calls being-as-being with the history of mathematical formalization is in intimate dialogue with the later Lacan. It is not for nothing that Badiou calls Lacan one of his masters, though to my mind Badiou overstates his debt to the great psychoanalyst. The truth of psychoanalysis forces us to recognize that there is no once-and-for-all exit from the transference, no unproblematic or post-ambivalent access to being. Neither can there be any absolute reduction of the psyche, definitive overcoming of resistance, or realized, successful encounter with desire's traumatic real.

For Lacan, our capacity to function as social beings, even and especially in radical opposition to dominant traditions of thought, rests on the precarious illusion of the Other's consistency. We must believe (or act as if we believe: same thing, for the Pascalian Lacan) in the coherence and binding purchase of the logics that legislate collective life in the particular social world in which we live. The consequence of this for Badiou's project is that mathematical formalization can only be, as it was for Lacan, an *ideal*. Yes, desire is an illusion premised on misrecognition; an empty, baseless surplus over being. And yes, as Badiou maintains, the real—being—is no doubt best conceived in thought as a pure, inaccessibly and inconsistently infinite multiplicity from which nothing is missing, in which nothing lacks. Yet for all the evidence of its duplicity and unreliability, the greatest illusion of all is the one that upholds the possibility of the psyche's absolute dissipation. Though psychoanalysis certainly does not deny the possibility of the *experience* of being, for the speaking subject being in language, in consciousness, is always barred, unattainable, unsatisfying, elsewhere. *Les non dupes errent*, says Lacan, riffing on his name-of-the-father idea: those who are not duped (by the Other) err.[4]

Though Lacan in his later teaching fully embraces the project of formalizing psychoanalytic theory via the languages of mathematics and logic, his stance vis-à-vis the historical disciplines was identical to his position on the philosophical tradition. "The mathematical field is characterized by a hopeless effort to have the field of the Other as such hold together," he claimed, adding that this is "the best way to demonstrate that it doesn't, that it isn't consistent."[5] Mathematical formalization may be the only available means of transmitting knowledge outside the transferential dynamic, as Lacan believed, but the discipline itself is haunted by the same irreducible demand for consistency that defines what Freud calls transference love.

Even mathematicians are required to (attempt to) communicate with one another and the world in so-called ordinary language. For Lacan, this is sufficient proof that their formalized articulations will necessarily betray signs of the same unconscious demand for consistency to which their everyday utterances bear witness. Even when we grant that mathematics, at least since Cantor and Gödel, has learned to live with inconsistency as an inescapable feature of the multiple, it remains the case that no subject will ever be capable of living entirely within the mathematical world without risking a radical psychotic break that would effectively exile that subject from human sociality. For psychoanalysis, the final word is simply that there is no possible escape from the social relation and its necessary traversal by language, by the Other.

The irreducibility of our unconscious libidinal investment in the Other—the ineradicable nature of the symptom, in other words—is precisely what Lacan indicates with the symbol for signification $s(O)$ that occupies the bottom lefthand corner of his mature graph of desire (Fig. 1.1). Though the next section of this chapter turns to Freud's engagement with the problem of transference in his technical writings, it will be helpful here to frame this engagement through an anticipatory reading of Lacan. This framing will aim not only to unearth the foundation of Lacanian formalization in the Freudian texts, but also to contextualize the reproaches I will later make against the ambivalences that detract from the cogency of Freud's formulation of his transference idea.

Confronted by the Other's inconsistency, by its inability to decipher what the Other wants $d(O)$, the subject issues in the transference its demand for identity, for meaning $S\Diamond D$ (as opposed to unconscious signification; see below), which the subject experiences as a demand *from the Other* with which it might potentially comply. Our humanity for Lacan is defined by a radical uncertainty about what society expects from us, what role it wants us to play, what identity it expects us to assume. We respond unconsciously to this uncertainty with a demand for a path to follow, an ideal to uphold. This is the "convergent" side of the graph, the one representing the subject's wish that the Other hold together in such a way that its desire might be properly interpreted or read. Inevitably, however, the Other has to respond with a failure/refusal (Freud's *Versagung*) S(Θ), simply because its inherent inconsistency prevents it from doing otherwise. The social resists all our demands that it provide an unambiguous and just law to which our desire might unconditionally submit. We are never fully satisfied that we have succeeded in conforming to society's opaque expectations, that we have met the elusive criteria for the Other's love. The Freudian thematic of castration describes the unconscious event corresponding to the Other's nonresponse. In Lacanian terms, there is a fundamental and insurmountable disjunction between what the subject in the transference expresses as demand and what the Other in response is capable of signifying.

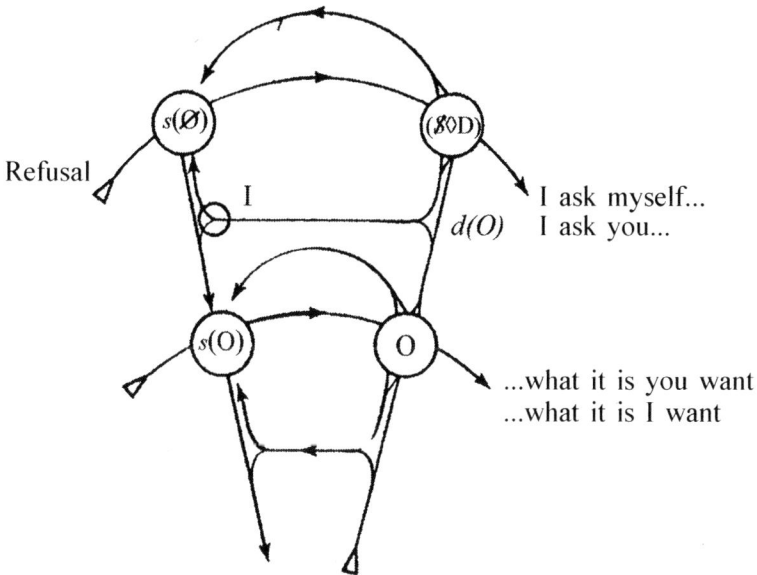

Convergent and divergent vectorization

Figure 1.1. Graph of desire; translated and adapted from Jacques Lacan, *Le séminaire, livre XVI. D'un autre à l'autre*, ed. Jacques-Alain Miller (Paris: Seuil, 2006), 87.

From this results the "divergence" of vectors on the lefthand side of the graph. Here the subject suffers the effect of desire's separation from what can be gleaned on the level of meaning from the social world. This in turn causes the subject to repress a representation of the trauma that this separation occasions. Because we fail to deal straightforwardly with the ambiguous contingency of the world, the psyche compensates by *constructing* a fragile consistency by excluding a representation that thwarts its establishment. If the world fails to tell me what I'm supposed to do with my life, well that's fine; I'll conjure a fantasy that makes up for the absence of meaning. This signification $s(O)$ is excluded from consciousness and comes to define the subject in its status as subject of the unconscious. This is precisely the signification that, by threatening to reemerge into consciousness, becomes the somatic symptom, otherwise known as the irrational, meaningless stuff of enjoyment or jouissance that can never be reconciled with our conception of ourselves. Though Lacan, like Freud, came to reject the notion that the symptom, like the transference, can ever be decisively dissolved, the unmasking of the enjoyment that it dissimulates precipitates the cure, opening up to the subject unforeseen possibilities for thought and action. In Freudian terms, this is the "terminable" aspect of analysis, the gateway to love in what I call its second, non- or post-transferential aspect.

Though he was not beyond manufacturing the odd topological representation, Freud, of course, did not display the same propensity for formalization as did Lacan, or at least the kind of logical formalization for which Lacan developed a predilection. Yet Lacan did not pull the algebra for his unconscious subject from out of thin air. For this reason it will prove highly instructive to take a detailed look at Freud's technical writings on the transference as a means of extracting from them what I will argue is their latent coherence. Though they do indeed betray on occasion signs of his own transferential symptoms, these writings in characteristic fashion furnish the tools required to rescue their author from his own ill-advised rationalizations. My wager is that we can discern through the haze of the ambiguities and contradictions statements which, when properly articulated, rectify the weaknesses of Freud's theorization of what Lacan with greater rigor would later designate with his concept of the analyst's desire.

In influential readings of the Dora case history, for example, feminist and other critics have justifiably decried Freud's need to play in analysis the role of the proper bourgeois father who succeeds in securing for his daughter-hysterics a respectable sexual future within the confines of conventional heterosexual marriage.[6] This unfortunate but (in historical context) hardly unusual bias is quite conspicuously on view in the technical writings I will shortly set myself the task of analyzing. The familiar complaint against Freud's shortcomings, though hardly inaccurate, nonetheless fails to tell the whole story, for it is clearly the case that the very availability of this critical reading is made possible by the wider theoretical and case-historical contexts that Freud himself so problematically but ethically lays out in his writing. Rather than dwell on these weaknesses that ensuing social change has made thoroughly patent, my aim in the next section will be to bring some conceptual clarity to Freud's fuzzy distinction between, first, what he calls the state of being in love, a passive aim which he associates with the narcissistic ambitions of the ego and, second, the satisfaction delivered by what he calls normal love, which he defines with reference to the libido's active targeting of what Freud calls reality. I will be especially concerned with exploring the role the transference plays in the transition from the former to the latter.

The Technique of Love

Written in the immediate prewar period between 1911 and 1914, the set of Freud's writings known as the papers on technique offers a wealth of material bearing witness to the underlying ambiguities that have muddled the formulation of the transference concept in psychoanalytic theory ever since their original publication. Indeed, this ambiguity gave birth to Freudianism's American bastard child—ego psychology, that is—the deeply ideological and liberalist tradition that so justifiably drew Lacan's ire in his early teaching. In this section I will explore how the transference informs Freud's evolving technical theory as well as the role this evolution plays in the radicalization of the Freudian project beyond its original liberal and humanist premises. Freud wavers between two incompatible views of the analyst's role in the transference. Should she aim to interpret away the hostile feelings of negative transference with the aim of maximizing her therapeutic powers of suggestion? Or should he rather base his interpretation on the assumption that the transference in all its manifestations is a form of resistance, which makes of his therapeutic task one of tracing this resistance back to its origins in the unconscious?

The second formulation is the correct one, to be sure. And Lacan makes exactly the right move when he abandons the misleading distinction between positive and negative transferences, together with the dangerous technique of suggestion that it enables. Regardless of its positive or negative content, the transference remains always and necessarily a form of resistance against unconscious desire, no matter whether it is viewed to emerge from the depths of either the analyst's or the patient's psyche. For these reasons Lacan was also correct to dismiss the legitimacy of the neo-Freudian notion of countertransference. The analyst's transference is no different in nature from the patient's; its interference in clinical work can only ever be an error for which the analyst must be held to account.[7] Despite the evident faults of his development of the concept, however, the core definition of transference as resistance against unconscious desire remains Freud's own. The originality and centrality of Freud's pioneering formulation of the concept are therefore not to be underestimated.

"The Dynamics of Transference" (1912), the second in his series of prewar technical papers, sees Freud explore the roots of resistance, the force that works to protect us from desires that threaten to bring our self-concept to ruin. Freud posits that it is in the nature of the transference to impose select criteria on those persons and social structures with whom and with which we become entangled, criteria that always eventually fail to be met. This is the same dynamic that Lacan would later discuss under the rubric of demand. As Freud puts it, early childhood "influences" set down for us what he calls "preconditions for falling in love."[8] Coining a typographical metaphor, he asserts that these conditions collectively make up a "stereotype plate" which is "constantly reprinted afresh in the course of a person's life" (100). Early childhood for Freud is first and foremost a time of amorous disappointment: faced with their incompatibility with what Freud calls reality, the incestuous desires of infancy succumb to repression, and representations of these desires' objects go on to form the templates to which all future loves of this variety are obliged to conform.

The "impulses" that give expression to the libido are divided in this way into two separate quantities occupying different regions of psychical space: one portion belongs to the "conscious personality," while the other is relegated to the unconscious (100). The consequence of this libidinal splitting is that the social interactions of adulthood are cast under the imposing shadow of "anticipatory libidinal ideas" (99): expectations, both conscious and unconscious, as to the dividend in pleasure that interaction with a given party will yield. Freud phrases his formulations conditionally, stating that only those subjects whom reality has failed to satisfy will fall victim to the insistent and irrational powers of love.

Yet Freud's statement at the very outset of the essay that his goal is "to explain how it is that transference is necessarily brought about during a psychoanalytic treatment" clearly implies that no subject escapes from childhood unscathed by frustrated love (99). This means that everyone suffers in everyday life from the effects of the stringent conditions they unknowingly lay down as prerequisites for engagement with a social world that, as a result, becomes prone to yielding mainly disappointment and frustration. Unconsciously, we abdicate the power to recognize and legitimize our being to certain others—individuals, certainly, but also institutions, brands, associations, identities—which then begin to act as magnets for libidinal investment. Freud's startling contention here is that infancy's inevitable emotional frustrations program us in our maturity to seek out particular social agencies blessed with the traits necessary to qualify as worthy alter egos cast off into the space of the Other.

On my reading, the most consequential aspect of Freud's description of these prerequisites for love is his qualification of the amorous passivity to which they give rise—the state of being in love, as he puts it—as *abnormal*. For Freud, our insistence that the world live up to select standards embedded in the unconscious is unambiguously pathogenetic. This thesis, I want to argue, is integral to the psychoanalytic argument: no effort to normalize love as it is here understood or to redeem it from neurosis is compatible with the Freudian ethos. The demand for love that fuels the fires of transference is a function of our desire not to desire—desire and the desire not to desire are, Lacan says somewhere, the same thing—and therefore steers us away from the "reality" with which we must grapple if we are to become normal: love-free, that is, as Freud understands the term in this context.

Moreover, this desirably normative aspect of Freud's technical papers is especially crucial for my purposes because it is intimately tied to the social Freud for which I want to argue, the one who deconstructs the binary, so to speak, between the private clinical practice of analysis and its public outside. Indeed, Freud squarely asserts that love's abnormality holds as firmly outside the analytic chamber as it does inside, where the derivative, surrogate quality of amorous passion helpfully makes itself plain. "If [being in love] seems so lacking in normality [in analysis]," Freud writes in a later technical essay, then "this is sufficiently explained by the fact that being in love in ordinary life is also more similar to abnormal than to normal mental phenomena."[9] No poststructuralist paranoia about normative regimes of discursive power should persuade us to discard this fundamental psychoanalytic truth. As I will explore in a variety of ways throughout this book, it is precisely this normative element of Freud's theory, its insistence on affirming the possibility of living a life beyond the limitations of neurosis, that signals how we can wrest ourselves, if not once and for all, from our dependence on the dictates of social norms.

In addition to being abnormal, the desire to be loved animating amorous passion is always a regressive function for Freud, since "there is no such state [of being in love] which does not reproduce infantile prototypes" (168). Two fundamental assumptions here inform Freud's understanding of transference love. First, love's demand sinks me into a quagmire of determinism: I can derive the fleeting satisfaction of self-regard that love can deliver only via select others who conform to my "prototype"; further, the agency through which my unconscious continually reissues its requirements can be neither cognized nor escaped. This means that the exercise of will remains in constant tension with the unconscious desire to identify appropriate social others to whom it can be abandoned. But second, precisely because Freud brands it a neurotic abnormality, this insistent determinism, instead of condemning us absolutely to a life of idiotic automatism, becomes rather a *propensity,* a tendency of the libido that may well be universal and ineradicable, but whose effects of determination are not utterly beyond our conscious control. For Freud, simply put, there has to be an alternative, more normal way to love.

Not without reason, decades of poststructuralist hyper-skepticism have programmed us to see only ominously coercive tentacles of power in dichotomies of normality and pathology. This overwhelmingly influential tendency can be traced back at least as far as Georges Canguilhem, whose book *The Normal and the Pathological* had a tremendous impact on the work of Michel Foucault. Yet I must insist that in this instance Freud's commitment to the normal has radically different implications.

The distinction between the normal and the abnormal, between a neu-rotic and a non-neurotic expression of the libido, is what enables us to think our capacity to moderate the tyranny of the unconscious. Freud-ian normality, understood as the relative rather than absolute beyond of transference neurosis, allows us to achieve a degree of autonomy with respect to infantile patterns that would otherwise condemn us to the blind, unthinking repetitions that deprive us of our capacity to love genuinely—motivated, that is to say, by something other than unknowing compulsion.

Thus far I have tried to show how a basic understanding of the transference inheres in Freud's technical writings, where it designates the mechanism through which an unconscious demand to be loved is made available to analytic thought in the clinical context. But how exactly does the transference emerge there? Freud argues that in analysis we cannot help but address our "anticipatory libidinal ideas" to the analyst, who gets added to the "series" of investments that form the history of our ego identifications, what Freud calls our "infantile imagos" ("Dynam-ics" 102). But Freud also makes clear that the analyst's addition to our history of love attachments helps keep the imago series beneath the threshold of consciousness, thereby prolonging a psychical status quo characterized for Freud by the libido's inwardly turned avoidance of reality. As long as the patient's unconscious is able to use the figure of the analyst as a means of propping up its infantile object attachments, in other words, it will succeed in keeping the libido on its introverted course, on the well-worn path of its secret archaic fantasies.

In its more technical usage in Freud's prewar papers, the term *transference* refers to the linguistic material produced through free association—the "transference idea," as Freud more precisely calls it (103)—that allows evidence of repressed desires to escape into con-sciousness in disguised form when the unconscious finds an opportu-nity to attach this evidence to the analyst's person. Not coincidentally, this phenomenon tends to occur at the precise moment when the patient's associations threaten to expose him to dangerous "complex-ive material," in Strachey's awkward rendering. The transference offers a distraction, a line of flight, an alibi: "No," it effectively persuades us, "you don't need to bring in from outside all those traumatically arousing fantasies since it's the analyst who is both the source of your libidinal conundrum and a prospective means of redress." Whenever a trace of one of these fantasies threatens to emerge into consciousness, an occurrence which Freud tells us happens "on countless occasions in the course of an analysis," a fragment of its representation amenable to recontextualization in the analytic here-and-how rises up to defend the ego from the more substantial part. By this time, Freud concludes, "the transference-idea has penetrated into consciousness in front of any other possible associations *because* it satisfies the resistance" (103–104).

This background material helps to explain the transference's paradoxical nature from the point of view of technique. Though Freud assures us that the transference is indeed the "most powerful resistance to the treatment" (101), its manifestation is a signal that the unconscious is on the brink of disclosing itself, indeed that it already has in its peculiarly dissimulated way. If the Lacan of *The Four Fundamental Concepts of Psycho-Analysis* defines the transference as a closing of the unconscious, then it is a closing that has the merit of revealing where the door can be found. More precisely, Lacan describes the transference as a positive sign that reliably indicates an absence, a presence that signals that something has been closed off. It is "both an obstacle to remembering," he says, "and a making present of the closure of the unconscious."[10]

Now, Freud's exposition of his transference idea in the technical papers is especially significant in the context of his work as a whole because it marks a significant shift away from a humanist view of the treatment as a reconstruction of psychical experience through acts of remembering. In these papers Freud begins to move toward a very different antihumanist way of thinking, which rests on the idea that an unbridgeable gap separates the unconscious complex from its possible means of representation in consciousness. This development is made increasingly tangible as Freud's concern for analytic recollection is supplanted by a stronger emphasis on repetition as the manifestation of memory's inevitable failure.

In "Remembering, Repeating and Working-Through" (1914), the second of his three "Further Recommendations on the Technique of Psycho-Analysis," Freud reminds his reader that this technique had already in its short history undergone two important modifications. A brief examination of these will develop my view of the nature and importance of the shift in Freud's thought. First, what had begun as an attempt to retrieve through hypnosis what the subject experienced at the moment of symptom formation is transformed into a more general project to reconstitute through free association the memorial representation of childhood from its defensive distortion by the unconscious. While it retains this new technique of free association, the second shift redirects its aim from a concern for memory and chronology to an examination of the mechanism of resistance properly speaking. With this crucial second shift, Freud abandons the hope that past experience can ever be integrally recovered; correctly rearticulated, that is, through narrative reconstruction. Freud's mature view of analytic technique no longer holds that the unconscious repetition indexed by transference mounts an obstacle that prevents a full reconstitution of experience in speech, be this experience construed as "merely" psychical or concretely lived. Though some ambiguity concerning this distinction remains consistent throughout his work, Freud more or less consistently shifts away from the more optimistic view. Indeed, Freud becomes increasingly convinced that the content of what is repeated in the transference provides the clue that indicates precisely to the analyst what the patient cannot remember; or *cognize*, we should rather say, since the true nature of the relation between the stuff of infantile fantasy and actual lived experience can never reliably be plumbed through analysis or indeed any other means.

A precise formulation of the link between transference and repetition is crucial for my purposes because it provides further evidence that for Freud the implications of his theory extend well beyond the confines of the clinic. Later in this chapter I will explore in further detail Freud's ambivalence with respect to these implications. For the time being, however, I wish to establish how integral to Freud's transference theory the reference to this social outside really is. In the "Remembering" essay, Freud defines the transference as a particular species of repetition, one that occurs in the specific context of analysis. "The transference is itself only a piece of repetition," he writes, and "repetition is the transference of the forgotten past not only on to the doctor but also on to all the other aspects of the current situation."[11] Freud's statement is curious because in logical terms it contradicts itself: transference cannot at once be a subset of repetition (first clause) and the set that includes it (the second). This point would remain marginal were it not for the fact that the sentence is emblematic of Freud's undisciplined and befuddling management of his key term. Nevertheless, a generous reading suggests that the word is used in the sentence in two different ways. In the first clause, transference specifically refers to the clinical context, whereas in the second it generically designates the shifting of infantile prototypes onto situations in the patient's life outside analysis. The point I wish to make here is that Freud links the more general of the two concepts—repetition—to "every other activity and relationship which may occupy [the patient's] life at the time." In illustration he gives some hypothetical examples: "if, for instance, he falls in love or undertakes a task or starts an enterprise during the treatment" (151). Clearly, whatever boundary might exist for Freud between the cozy confines of the analyst's office and the wilds of the outside world is eminently permeable; the patient's unconscious demand as expressed in the transference does not magically cease upon exiting the session. Though Freud overtly states that the repetition compulsion uncovered by analysis will persist in the patient's daily life, he does not, however, make clear that someone who is not undergoing analysis will also betray the effects of transference's "failure to remember." One possible skeptical-Foucaultian critique takes shape: there is nothing in Freud's technical papers that refutes the contention that repetition is merely a creation of analysis; that the patient only suffers its effects outside the clinic because the clinic has already, by some insidious black magic, installed it at the heart of the patient's psyche.

At this juncture, the more faithful Freud reader can take advantage of his useful distinction between repetition (generic) and transference (specific) to make a helpful suggestion, central to my claim concerning Freud's transference theory. Though transference in its precise technical sense is indeed a creation of analysis (since a reference to the analyst inheres in its very concept), repetition for its part most certainly is not. In other words, transference is simply *the kind of repetition that takes place in analysis.* Its occurrence there happily renders it more accessible to interpretation than are the generic repetitions that wreak havoc on ordinary life. This clarification of Freud's argument—it is already there, I am saying, as an unformulated, half-acknowledged assumption—is what allows me to assert that no distinction of significance can be drawn between the dynamic that regulates our relation to the analyst in the transference and the one that overdetermines the general orientation of our desire with respect to the social world. The psychical agency of the unconscious pays no heed to the frontier that our cherished liberalism interposes between the scene of analysis and its social or political "outside."

In Lacanian terms we can say that there can be no legitimate differentiation between a psychical and a social "real," since the real is precisely the register—structural in its status, neither "subjective" nor "objective"—that prevents us from drawing the distinction in the first place. The corollary of this is that the concept of the subject in psychoanalysis is neither "individual" nor "collective" in the familiar liberal-political senses of these terms. It is not individual because it is not defined psychologically: linked with notions of selfhood, character, or personality. But neither is it collective, since, resistant to language, it cannot be communicated or shared, cannot become the stuff of an articulated, socially symbolized group identity. For these reasons the psychoanalytic hypothesis of the subject—though we cannot know the subject in its content we know with certainty that there has to be one—flies in the face of, first, empiricist and cognitivist psychologisms, which want to isolate, however relatively, the matter of consciousness from its unconscious and sociosymbolic determinations; and second, sociological reductionisms, which evacuate the social of both its distortion by desire's real—jouissance—as well as the possibility of the reshaping of the social through the exercise of a nonintentional will: through genuine amorous, scientific, artistic, and political acts, for example, to refer to the four conditions of Badiou's philosophy.

Resisting the Transference

In the next section I will draw on these last points to argue for the tremendous theoretical significance of a marginal comment that Freud makes about his own early-twentieth-century Viennese social environment. The comment betrays the extent of Freud's long-recognized investment in his bourgeois class status and helps bring forward, between the lines as it were, the properly political ramifications of the transference idea. It will first be necessary, however, to accomplish the more workaday but still engaging task of exploring the ambivalences of Freud's technical theory. These ambivalences agglutinate around both the specious distinction between positive and negative transferences and the set of contradictory comments on the role of suggestion in analytic technique.

   In "The Dynamics of Transference" (1912), Freud introduces his infelicitous distinction in response to the difficulty he encounters as he tries to explain the transference's complicity with resistance, the most common clinical manifestation of which is a sudden stoppage in the patient's associations. Freud describes the transference in this context as "a relation of affectionate and devoted dependence" on the analyst which has the effect of facilitating the flow of the analysand's discourse. He points out that it is not at all obvious why such sentiments should fail to inhibit the patient's sense of shame, since shame, Freud here assumes, tends to emerge automatically alongside the disclosure of censored thoughts. For Freud, this conundrum forces the analyst to separate out "the transference of affectionate feelings from negative ones, and to treat the two sorts of transference to the doctor separately" ("Dynamics" 105).

Freud's next move in the paper is to subdivide the category of positive transferences according to whether their emotional contents are "admissible to consciousness" or rather "prolongations of [these] feelings into the unconscious" (105). This gesture allows Freud to do two things. First, he can assert categorically that the underlying essence of human affect is erotic. The virtuous appearance of the seemingly unsensual emotions—"sympathy, friendship, trust, and the like" (105)—dissimulates their origin in patently sexual interests. The roots of every laudable feeling on the surface of consciousness, in other words, penetrate deeply into the censored libidinal soil of the unconscious. Second and more importantly, however, Freud can also safeguard the conscious, "unobjectionable" part of positive transference as "the vehicle of success in psychoanalysis" (105), a function that it also had, he claims, in the other techniques for curing neurosis in practice at the time. "We readily admit," Freud is now able to conclude, "that the results of psychoanalysis rest upon suggestion," bearing in mind, he adds, that we are to understand this last term in his colleague Sandor Ferenczi's sense, that is to say as "the influencing of a person by means of the transference phenomena which are possible in his case" (106).

Now, the idea of suggestion that Freud here advances presupposes that it is both possible and desirable for the analyst to know what is best for her patient. Embedded in the very notion of analytic influence, more specifically, is an idea of the end to which such influence is exercised. Freud's assertion claims for the analyst determinate ethical knowledge, which it is his duty to communicate to the patient during treatment. It also betrays the workings of an analytic ideal, or more precisely an ideal of the analyst, which imbues the analyst with moral authority of the kind that brings to mind such "oriental" figures as the guru or the sage. Through his claim that for the analyst any notion of the patient's good can only function as a deceptive and clinically disastrous distraction, Lacan decisively rejects this tendency in Freud's technical theory, in my view with excellent reason. Yet I also want to suggest that it would be unwise to reduce Freud's motivation here to a self-serving desire to legitimize the profession of analysis by idealizing the analyst's function (though this undoubtedly plays an important role). In the main, Freud's suspect statements about the analyst's part in the transference arise rather from his concern that the analytic bond be sustained, that the analyst succeed in preventing the analysand from breaking off the treatment in a decisive gesture of resistance which would bring the cure to a premature and unsuccessful end.

It is likely this very worry that causes Freud, in a clear instance of theoretical regression, to backtrack from his original definition of the transference when he develops his restrictive category of transference-resistances. Like the more general distinction between positive and negative transferences on which it is based, the idea of transference resistance allows Freud to maintain by opposition that the transference can indicate a patient's voluntary immersion in the analytic process and therefore that it is not always and necessarily an outcome of the ego's defensive ambition to resist it.

Freud in this vein writes in "On Beginning the Treatment" (1913) that the analyst's first communication to the patient, which risks being unwelcome, "should be withheld until a strong transference has been established."[12] Having learned from experience that the analysand will not always be well disposed to her interpretations, Freud advises the aspiring analyst to wait for positive indication that the patient is invested in her clinical function. This strategy ensures that resistance to the process is removed before the first clinical intervention is risked. Remarkably, this last unfortunate formulation has the effect of entirely separating analytic interpretation out from resistance, blatantly contradicting what Freud otherwise assumes to be an explicit premise: that analysis consists first and foremost in the interpretation of the forms of resistance to unconscious desire as made manifest in disguised form in the transference. Resistance, in other words, is precisely what fuels the process, what enables interpretation; without it there can be neither method nor practice.

Freud's patent concern to remain in the patient's good graces and to protect him from his own destructive impulses in fact leads the founder of analysis to claim that positive transference can even work to put the reins on compulsive repetition. The patient's faith in the analyst's technique, so it would seem, can even grant him immunity from the virulent powers of the unconscious. As is the case in so many aspects of his writing on transference, a curious but illuminating double-mindedness colors this most egregious feature of Freud's discussion. Illogically, he broaches the topic of repetition by subtly undermining the very point he seems to want to make. Alluding to the shift from memorial reconstruction to free association as the preferred modus operandi of analysis, Freud states in "Remembering, Repeating and Working-Through" that "remembering in the old manner is the aim to which [the analyst] adheres, even though he knows that such an aim cannot be achieved in the new technique" (153). Apparently under the assumption that positive transference can fill in the breach, Freud goes on to suggest that "if the attachment [to the analyst] has grown into something at all serviceable, the treatment is able to prevent the patient from executing any of the more important repetitive actions and to utilize his intention to do so *in statu nascendi* as material for the therapeutic work" (153). Freud's logic here is informed by the theoretical principle that what the patient cannot remember must be repeated, acted out in the form of an uncontrollable compulsion which the analyst in the clinic is capable of reining in.

This is Freud in his alternative and lesser-known persona of optimistic humanist, the Freud whose contentions still contain remnants of the belief that the "abreaction" effected by the talking cure can fully flush out unconscious material from the psyche. At this stage, Freud has only partially come to terms with the consequences of that assumption's abandonment. If the adoption of free association implicitly acknowledges the impossibility of past experience's full narrative recovery, thereby exposing the patient to the disorienting agency of the unconscious, then a positive attachment to the analyst can step in to restore the sovereignty of consciousness over irrational compulsion. Freud's move unsoundly buttresses his original but increasingly besieged liberal-humanist vision. If analysis must acknowledge that there is no decisive escape from the unconscious overdetermination of will, then perhaps a generous inflation of the analyst's technical skill, consolidated for the patient in the transference, can safeguard the subject from his compulsive drive to self-destruction.

Felicitously, however, there are also characteristic indications that Freud is not entirely persuaded by this idealized picture of the analyst's power. Freud's views on technique are under pressure at both ends:

though acutely aware that the patient must harbor some attachment to the analyst to prevent her from bolting after the first unflattering interpretation, he is also increasingly worried by the ethical dangers posed by suggestion. The modesty qualifying Freud's advice on analytic intervention nicely conveys this dilemma. Though the analyst "best protects the patient from injuries brought about through carrying out one of his impulses by making him promise not to take any important decisions affecting his life during the time of his treatment," he must nevertheless take care to "leave untouched as much of the patient's personal freedom as is compatible with these restrictions" (153). Freud's anxieties are suggestively conveyed: paternalistic concern, the specter of guilt, a vulnerable liberalism and the ideal of neutrality all vie for supremacy in this ambivalent statement, a compromise formation if there ever was one. From the comparatively "heartless" perspective of Lacanian technique, Freud's residual concern for the patient's good leaves him unprepared to acknowledge that the analyst must ultimately, though not without careful prior preparation, allow the patient to encounter the self-expropriating force of the unconscious without a crutch; to leave him *hilflos*: deprived of all means of resistance, helpless and undone before the real of desire.

Freud's need to defend a version of the analytic relation premised on sympathy clearly gives rise to considerable theoretical fuzziness. On my reading, there is one thought in particular that Freud proves incapable of admitting into his discussion. If we accept the basic Freudian premise that transference generically defined is the strongest form of resistance in analysis, then it follows that the nature or content of the affect it contains, positive or negative, is a properly indifferent consideration. In other words, the enthusiasms of positive transference—the array of agreeable thoughts and emotions that a subject will have toward his analyst—are as much a form of resistance as is the hostility of the negative one. The very idea of positive transference must therefore be a form of resistance to the implications of Freud's own technical thought.

This means that the patient's very faith in the analyst's proficiency will function, however counterintuitively, as an obstacle to the cure. The only non-transferential relation of patient to analyst is the indifferent one, the one that simply sees the patient accept interpretations with complete neutrality. The fact that such an antiseptic relation of patient to analyst is never clinically experienced only lends weight to the Freudian thesis concerning the transference's necessary universality.

Every affect that the patient exhibits toward the analyst must be viewed as integral to the transference in the precise sense that this affect can always potentially be shown to link up with signifying material giving expression to unconscious desire. Lacan's well-known definition of the analyst as *sujet supposé savoir* (subject supposed to know) nicely conveys this point: I am in the transference both when I gamely *suppose* that the analyst knows the elusive contents of my desire (Freud's "positive" transference), and when I complain hysterically that the analyst *is supposed* to know but does not, that both her technique and the knowledge on which it rests are fraudulent or even insidious ("negative"). That both logically incompatible ideas often prove to be co-present in the transference is merely one among myriad manifestations of the basic Freudian thesis about the underlying splitting of consciousness, the fetishistic cohabitation in different regions of the psyche of contradictory representations.

Now, surely the very legitimacy of the psychoanalytic project would be questionable were there not to be found in Freud's technical writings indications that, unlike most of those considered thus far, support the claim that Freud finally manages not only to revoke the premise of a link between the patient's affection for the analyst and the prospect of therapeutic success, but also to veto its clinical application through the technique of suggestion. Thankfully, then, in "Observations on Transference-Love" (1915), third and last of his prewar technical essays, Freud takes a more decisive view of what he had previously called positive transference. Indeed, a change in terminology from "positive" to "erotic" signals Freud's abandonment of the assumption that the patient's attachment to the analyst is by definition conducive to the cure.

This crucial shift is made apparent when Freud scolds those ill-advised analysts who "prepare their patients for the emergence of the erotic transference or even urge them to 'go ahead and fall in love with the doctor so that the treatment may make progress'" ("Observations," 161). At long last Freud acknowledges that this transference, which now explicitly lies at the root of the patient's "docility, her acceptance of the analytic explanations, her remarkable comprehension and high degree of intelligence," is the same transference that produces resistance: the "complete change of scene" that sees the patient "lose all understanding of the treatment and interest in it." The formerly cooperative patient suddenly changes her tune, deigning to speak or hear of nothing but "her love" which, naturally enough, "she demands to have returned" (162).

By the time "transference-resistance" emerges, Freud decides, the patient has already "been in love for a long time." The resistance begins to "make use of her love in order to hinder the continuation of the treatment, to deflect all her interest from the work and to put the analyst in an awkward position" (162–63). The patient's docile dependence and aggressive reproaches are therefore rooted in the same underlying love. An important general rule emerges from Freud's reconsiderations: the analysand will happily accept the analyst's interpretations as long as they miss the mark, as long as they fail in their professed task of forcing the expression of associations linked with repressed desire. As soon as a clinical intervention does violence to his ego structures, the patient will instantly issue his demand for love, insisting on hearing alternative interpretations that buttress his threatened self-esteem, perpetuating thereby his underlying self-deception.

Despite his prevarications, then, Freud does finally muster the courage to advise the analyst to resist the temptation to reassure the patient, to satisfy his demand for love. The price to be paid, of course, is that the analyst is forced to abandon *her own* ego commitments, to observe unaffected the tarnishing of the ideal image of the therapist as charismatic font of ethical knowledge, precisely the image that the patient is anyway prone to tear asunder with the taunts and accusations of so-called negative transference. This is the Freud that is to be retained, I want now to argue, the one upon which Lacan will elaborate his doctrine of the analyst's desire.

For Freud, analytic "neutrality"—I will argue later on against the appropriateness of the term—finally demands that the clinician renounce the full continuum of responses to transference love spanning the edifying acknowledgment of the patient's passion in word or deed to the enactment of this passion's repression through the imposition of moral or technical norms. Singling out *truthfulness* as the foundation of both the "educative effect" and "ethical value" of analysis, Freud offers as a fundamental principle "that the patient's need and longing should be allowed to persist in her, in order that they may serve as forces impelling her to do work and make changes" (164–65).

Freud's seemingly outmoded commitment to truth is not anachronistic, nor should we allow its value to be tarnished by the various theoretical skepticisms of the day. I would even suggest that Freud constructs a tremendously instructive "metaphysical" binary between, on the one hand, an idea of truth linked to the overcoming of resistance and the disclosure of unconscious desire and, on the other, a notion of inauthenticity—falsity, error—defined by the patient's satisfaction of the analysand's demand for love. "What we could offer" the patient in this latter mode, Freud concludes, "would never be anything else than a surrogate, for the patient's condition is such that, until her repressions are removed, she is incapable of getting real satisfaction" (165). Freud's epistemologically classical, indeed Platonic distinction between truth and illusion extends even to the idea of pleasure: next to the authentic satisfactions that Freud here insists are accessible through the cure, receiving a response to one's demand for love will yield mere ersatz versions of the real thing which ultimately can only disappoint.

At the outset of treatment the respective aims of analyst and analysand are always at cross-purposes. While the analyst must be intent on the disclosure of unconscious desire no matter the cost, the patient and his ego unswervingly defend the serial repressions that prop it up. It follows that a battle must take place and, as on reality television, there can only be one winner. Freud tells an "amusing anecdote" about an insurance agent on his deathbed to illustrate this agonistic, indeed dialectical, dynamic at the root of analytic practice:

> The insurance agent, a free-thinker, lay at the point of death and his relatives insisted on bringing in a man of God to convert him before he died. The interview lasted so long that those who were waiting outside began to have hopes. At last the door of the sick-chamber opened. The free-thinker had not been converted; but the pastor went away insured. (165)

The story discloses Freud's acknowledgment that the analyst's temptation to succumb to the patient's stratagems for affection and reassurance are motivated by a desire for power and influence. The kind of intervention to which this succumbing leads is rationalized with the assumption that the patient can be guided through suggestion toward a positive clinical outcome. Though, to be sure, this is a road he not infrequently traveled, Freud would eventually and decisively take another route. Like the pastor whose project to convert the unbeliever requires merely an outward sign of consent—how can he know what the insurance agent, or anyone else, really believes?—the analyst's duty is merely to impose the law of free association without being distracted by the patient's degree of faith in her as a representative of the practice whose legitimacy she is meant to embody. As it tends to do in the various psychological therapies, analysis degenerates, when this duty is not observed, into a war between mutually contradictory strategies of seduction: the patient insists on receiving evidence that he is worthy of love; the clinician gets caught in the trap of desiring to be helpful and to receive in return the patient's gratitude and acknowledgment of professional competence. Despite the many unfortunate lapses in Freud's thought, then, a fundamental rule of analytic technique emerges nonetheless: the analyst's key duty is to keep clinical work on the track of unconscious desire, unheeding of all distractions, especially those confabulations of the ego designed to safeguard both his own and his patient's good.

It is in this precise sense that the analyst's role is certainly not neutral. Indeed, Freud's commitment to the term is no doubt symptomatic, for his work offers ample evidence that he was often far from neutral—and not in the good way that I will develop in this chapter's final section—in his attitude toward the outcome of his analyses. Yet I do not want this acknowledgment to imply that Freud's inconsistency renders his overall technical theory suspect. This is the mode of argument, for example, that would have seen me cast dark aspersions on the implicit comparison in Freud's anecdote of the analyst with the pastor. Does this comparison not prove, so the story might go, that analysis installs a nefarious power relation, a quasi-religious ideology that demands of the patient the unthinking submission of belief? I have just claimed, after all, that the concept of analytic neutrality is misleading, which prevents me from chastising Freud for failing to live up to a false ideal.

What I want to suggest instead is more nuanced than the very contemporary skepticism that informs such charges. This chapter's basic premise has been that though its coherence is marred by contradiction and ambivalence, the proper theory of the transference, as well as its optimal clinical handling, are available to the careful reader of Freud's texts. Freud's attachment to the ideal of neutrality, I wish now to add, stems from his own transferential resistance to the consequences of the rigorous, "impossible" ethical task he assigns to the analyst. Neutrality, in other words, is the manifest representation of Freud's own latent amorous demand for social and professional respectability. It functions as a kind of alibi, as a disavowal of that demand. To conclude my reading of Freud, I now want to explore two specific expressions of this demand, which I intend—somewhat paradoxically, no doubt—to support my argument in favor of the strong Freudian thesis on the transference that they would appear at first glance to put in doubt.

Woman and the Riff-Raff

The first symptomatic instance that I wish to discuss relates to how Freud figures sexual difference into the analyst-patient relation. The term *androcentrism* instantly comes to mind: the list of critics who have issued this charge against Freud is long, their arguments oft, and usually predictably, rehearsed. I will argue in contrast that Freud's technical discussion of the transference is not androcentric. Though it is certainly undeniable that Freud with remarkable consistency assumes that the analyst is a man and his patient a woman, it becomes abundantly clear that what haunts his theorization is a decidedly feminine entity of a quite particular sort. This means that *gynocentrism* more accurately describes the way in which sexual difference leaves its mark on Freud's technical theory. At the center of Freud's discourse on the transference, plainly put, there is Woman. This is Lacan's *La femme*, the one that doesn't exist, as he notoriously argued, hence its alternative rendering as ~~La~~ femme or ~~Woman~~. The view for which I wish to argue is that Freud's sexual differentiation of the analytic relation bears consequences, though not disastrous ones, for his theory of the transference. These consequences bespeak a tendency toward theoretical regression in his writing which, I have tried consistently to show, nevertheless fails to sully its contents irremediably.

The emergence in Freud's work of a prototype figure for what Lacan would later call Woman is significant not because it proves that Freudian technical theory is androcentric or heterosexist, but rather because it functions as a symptom of Freud's resistance to the subjective destitution that, in the Lacanian view, is integral to the proper handling of the transference. At the conclusion of his final prewar technical essay, Freud adopts an uncharacteristically impersonal register to evoke the gritty self-discipline that the (male, heterosexual) analyst must exercise in order to maintain proper technique in the presence of his (attractive, intelligent, female) patients. His first gesture is to stress the importance of self-control with another telling analogical anecdote. The analyst who indulges the appetite to romance his patient just as she is beginning to benefit from the cure is like the "humorist" who throws a single sausage onto the track at a dog race, the winner of which will claim the prize of an entire "garland" of them (169). Naturally, the mischief maker's action causes the dogs to get distracted and fail to finish the race.

The challenge here is to refuse to become similarly distracted by dwelling unhelpfully on Freud's implicit comparison of his women patients with a pack of racing dogs. We must hold off on the obvious, though surely not irrelevant, charge of sexism because an even more curious and revealing passage directly follows. Confidently asserting that only "science" and "a few queer fanatics" (note the association, provocative in the contemporary context, of queerness with a lack of interest in sex) deny that "the union of mental and bodily satisfaction in the enjoyment of love is one of [life's] culminating peaks," Freud confesses in this safely anonymous mode that "to reject and refuse" a woman when she "sues for love" is "a distressing part for a man to play." Especially distressing, he goes on to claim, when the woman concerned is "of high principles," since it is perhaps "a woman's subtler and aim-inhibited wishes which bring with them the danger of making a man forget his technique and his medical task for the sake of a fine experience" (70).

The interpretive move to be avoided here is the one that would reproach Freud puritanically for the weakness his comments betray through their thin veneer of scientific detachment. This reproach assumes that his confessional indulgences detract from the coherence or legitimacy of his theoretical endeavors rather than furnish them, as I rather wish to claim, with the means to correct their unfortunate deviations. Some critics might wish at this juncture to argue in a sympathetic but revisionist feminist mode that Freud's depiction of the woman who causes him to "forget his technique" latently stresses her dignity, her power, the potential energy stocked inside her coyly dissimulated eroticism. Readers more skeptical of Freud might protest that this passage subverts the entire psychoanalytic project, alleging that it brings to light its disavowed dependence on the exercise of patriarchal power. For my own part, I want instead to argue that a widely read and characteristically "sexist" anecdote of Lacan's—one that, incidentally, sits comfortably alongside the Freudian vignettes on which we have been focusing—sets us on the proper course.

Near the end of *Four Fundamental Concepts,* Lacan compares the patient in the transference to the inexperienced diner (male and heterosexual, if you need to ask) at a Chinese restaurant who, uncertain of what to order, asks the establishment's *patronne* to recommend something. In Lacanian terms, the scenario illustrates the transference because the patron's request assumes that the woman restaurant owner—whose prestige is enhanced, we are meant to understand, by her exotic foreignness—knows what the diner should want from amongst the menu's offerings. *"You should know what I desire in all this,"* the customer effectively says, according to Lacan, who goes on to pose this question to his befuddled protagonist:

> At this point, when you abdicate your choice to some divination of the *patronne*, whose importance you have exaggerated out of all proportion, would it not be more appropriate, if you felt like it, and if the opportunity presented itself, to tickle her tits [*titiller ses seins*]?"[13]

The serious theoretical point that Lacan's provocative and no doubt deliberately politically incorrect mini-narrative is meant to convey is that there is an inversely proportional relation between the extent of the diner's deferential supposition of knowledge in the owner and the degree to which he sexually objectifies her, or more precisely one of her parts. Simply put, he exoticizes her desire to the extent that he fails to eroticize her bosom. I am tempted parenthetically to suggest here that an entire theory of colonialism could be built upon Lacan's "tasteless" story. To return to Freud's scenario, the analyst's countertransference toward his "woman of high principles" results directly from his failure to identify within her the libido's partial object, to admit that for the libido such an eminently respectable lady can only figure as an impersonal, dehumanized container for the object of the drive. We begin to see how Freud's example betrays the signs of that quintessential fantasy that combines within the single image of a principled lady overcome with sexual passion for her analyst those two most resilient figures of masculine psychic life: the virgin and the whore. More precisely, Freud's transported *bourgeoise* fuses two stereotypical fantasy-images into one: the ideal, noble Woman embodying everything in femininity worthy of esteem, and the slutty down-market temptress, whose body parts function as mere pornographic vessels for the ecstatic satisfaction of the drive.

As I will argue in chapter 2, the fantasy buttressing Freud's discussion accomplishes precisely the same task that Alcibiades' attempted seduction of Socrates sets itself in Plato's *Symposium*. The unconscious aim of transferential passion is to knock the idealized Other off its pedestal, to show that it is unable to live up to the standard that we ourselves have ascribed to it. What lends to Freud's figuration of the analytic relation its sexist dimension is therefore not its putative androcentrism, but rather the truth that Freud needs to "respect" his female analysands, that he must demonstrate in the name of a flattering notion of analytic professionalism his capacity to embody an ideal of gentlemanly restraint by resisting the impulse to return the passion of a worthy woman. In essence, Freud's self-deceiving confessional discourse allows him to have his cake and eat it too: he can indulge, however unwittingly, his titillating fantasy of clinical seduction while at the same time congratulating himself for resisting the temptation it proffers, unheeding of his own insight that "the patient's falling in love is induced by the analytic situation, and is not to be attributed to the charms of [the analyst's] own person" ("Observations," 160–61). Freud proves incapable in this instance of deflecting the desire to be acknowledged as an object worthy of his distinguished lady analysand's love and thereby of identifying the source of his own transferential passion.

I have premised this chapter on the argument that no conceptually significant distinction can be drawn between what is social and what is subjective in the transference. It follows that we should be able to detect socially inflected slippages in Freud's "psychology," marginal extraclinical comments that can be shown to bespeak the same structure that conditions his passionate fascination with intelligent and dignified ladies. It will come as no surprise, then, to learn that there are examples of precisely this in Freud's technical papers. The sociopolitical correlative of the Freudian Woman is the bourgeois class identification that determines yet another Freudian analogy, this one intended to illustrate the importance of the law of free association. The comment in question occurs in a long footnote of "On Beginning the Treatment" (1913), in which Freud outlines his experience of the wide diversity of patient reactions to this law's imposition. Free association requires that the patient be prohibited from withholding any thought whatsoever, regardless of its content. "It is very remarkable," Freud notes in this connection, "how the whole task [of analysis] becomes impossible if a reservation is allowed at any single place." In fact, to appreciate the disastrous consequences of even a single unchecked instance of such reticence, "we have only to reflect what would happen if the right of asylum existed at any one point in a town. How long would it be," Freud asks rhetorically, "before all the riff-raff of the town had collected there?"[14]

The analogy evidently rests on a comparison between the psychical material that the analyst fails to exhume from a patient's unconscious and a city's most unsavory social characters. These, perhaps by some gesture of municipal or philanthropic largesse, are granted reprieve from the severity of the law. Just as a single association withheld from interpretation can grant the unconscious ultimate victory in the great battle of analysis, so can a one-time extension of judicial generosity to the wretched of the town cause the perversion of the entire bourgeois social order; to its defeat, one could say by extension, in that other battle once known as the class struggle.

Neither should we be surprised to discover in *Inhibitions, Symptoms and Anxiety* (1926) a similar social analogy, which implicitly places Freud on the class struggle's opposite side. By way of illustrating the function of anxiety, Freud offers a comparison from the arena of politics. We can compare the ego, confronted by the "instinct" and giving in response the *"signal of unpleasure,"* to a "certain small faction" that "obtains command of the press" and manipulates public opinion in an attempt to prevent the passing of a measure that has the "support of the masses."[15] In this striking simile the censorious ego operates as an instrument of bourgeois ideology to curtail the political will of the social majority. The clear analogy between ego and bourgeoisie, id and "masses" or "riff-raff," sanctions the conclusion that Freud was on one level fully aware of the social implications of his metapsychology even though he exhibits contradictory perspectives on them. It is perhaps not insignificant that with respect to my chosen examples the "left" Freud postdates the "right" one of the prewar transference papers by some ten or eleven years.

I chose the preceding examples to support the claim that a precise structural homology can be drawn between the various strikingly bivalent motifs that animate them: the Asian *patronne* reduced to an erotic bosom in Lacan's anecdote, the dignified lady "fallen" into untoward passion in Freud's apologia, and the harmoniously twee town ruined by the smelly riff-raff from the first of Freud's papers on technique. In each image a *recherché* ideal is cut down to size by a base agency that effectively knocks it off its pedestal. In Lacanian terms, this agency is correlative to the raw object of the drive, which frustrates the ambitions of narcissism by making sure that our demand for love will be left unsatisfied.

It is no mere coincidence, therefore, that the ideal figures of Freud's and Lacan's examples—principled lady, exotic hostess, law-abiding town— give off that familiar whiff of arid bourgeois respectability, coupled in the second instance with clichéd colonialist orientalism. Each of these ideals is jeopardized by the uncanny power of alternative figures that are decidedly less respectable: the lady, shedding all pretence, indulging in a frank, "whorish" come-on; the Asiatic patroness giving her pinched and proper customers a full-on flash of her winsome breasts; the riff-raff escaping from their municipal shelter, spreading their obnoxious odors to even the most high-rent neighborhoods in town. As I will go on now to explore, each of these figures can be mapped precisely onto Lacan's algebra for the transferential relation. I have tried to show how this relation is conditioned by a dialectic between the convergent demand for love ($S\Diamond D$ in Fig. 1.1) and the divergent manifestation of the Other's failure to satisfy this demand. The Other in the transference must finally prove incapable of responding to our demand with a sign that meets my libidinal needs $S(\Theta)$; it can never furnish sustained and convincing evidence that I have the stuff required to make me worthy of its impenetrable desire.

The Fall of the Other

"Love as such hinges on the question asked of the Other as to what it can give us and what it has that can meet our expectations [ce qu'il a à nous répondre]," Lacan says in the transference seminar. It is therefore a question in analysis of "perceiving the relation that ties the Other to whom the demand for love is addressed to the advent of desire."[16] Desire for Lacan amounts to the inadequacy or failure of the Other's response to our demand; the negative excess over demand, in other words, to which the Other cannot answer. Now, Lacan qualifies his concept of the partial object with tropes and figures that connote abjection: the subject proves incapable of either recognizing this object as part of the self or eliminating it from its psychical economy. Crucially, however, Lacan qualifies this object fragment as a mode of the Other. "The Other [qua object] is not at all our equal, the Other to whom we aspire, the Other of love," he says, "but something that represents its degradation" (207). In the transference the Other's representation is divided into two very different appearances for the unconscious: an edifying but troublingly inaccessible ideal and a degraded partial object that must remain outside at all costs.

These two very distinct modalities of the Other in this phase of Lacan's teaching correspond to two equally distinct ideas of love. The first sees love as an exaggerated overvaluation (Freud's term) of the Other. Here the Other is the "subject supposed to know" O, the one who can reflect us back to ourselves in a flattering light. This particular Other—let's use Lacan's phrase "the Other of love"—"makes us not the subject of speech," who is subjected to the supremacy of the slippery signifier over reliable meaning, but rather "that special something which is invaluable, irreplaceable, the point where we can discern the subject's dignity." This Other corresponds to Freud's notion of the ego ideal. In contrast, the "other" Other Θ, that is to say the Other that yields way to the partial object, gives voice to what Lacan memorably calls "the terrible commandment of the god of love." This commandment enjoins us, Lacan says, "to make of the object that which designates for us something which is, first, an object, and second, an object before which we fail/faint [*devant quoi nous défaillons*], vacillate, disappear in our capacity as subject" (207). My argument in the remaining portions of this chapter will be that, contrary to what one might imagine, Lacan *wants* us to obey this "terrible" commandment that would have us "disappear" from our own self-consciousness. In fact, I will go as far as to claim that the love god's commandment articulates the fundamental ethic of Freudian psychoanalysis as Lacan sees it. It indicates as well Lacan's prescription for the outcome of the transference event.

In order to illuminate the collusion of ideality and resistance in the structure of narcissism, the destabilization of which occasions the event of transference, it will be helpful first to take a short technical detour through Lacan's reconfiguration of the inverted vase experiment in classical physics. This detour will not only provide a more precisely argued foundation for Lacan's exposition of his transference concept, a foundation that has the added benefit of elucidating the context needed to understand his symbolic notation for the psyche's component structures. The detour will also tie my definition of the transference more precisely to the field of vision, the object of concern of this book's final two chapters.

Lacan began to develop his modification of the experiment in the early 1950s. Its centrality to his life of teaching is highlighted by its survival of the radicalization of his thought which took place in his 1963–64 seminar. Though Lacan's contribution has been to a degree deftly, though far from exhaustively, handled elsewhere,[17] a look at his redeployment of the experiment through the lens of transference will give us a firmer grasp of the respective functions of what Freud called the *Idealich* (ideal ego) and *Ichideal* (ego ideal) in the structure of identification. This structure is especially important because it is precisely its vacillation, coupled with the anxiety that this vacillation sets off, which lies at the root of the subject's transferential passion.

The experiment is designed to produce the optical illusion of a bouquet of flowers. The first thing to note is that, though derived from the classical experiment (Fig. 1.2), Lacan's apparatus (Fig. 1.3) is considerably more complex than the original. Lacan adds a second mirror, a plane one, which has the effect of adding a virtual dimension to the experiment that did not exist in its classical version. Lacan calls his innovation metaphorical, perhaps because its actual experimental mounting presents logistical difficulties, but more significantly because the structures that it serves to represent do not depend on the literal presence of the mirror apparatus. Our relation as subjects to the "real world," we are meant to understand, is mediated by the same virtual identificatory dimension on which the experiment, quite literally, is meant to shed light.

In the original experiment, a classic of the physical subdiscipline of optics, a bouquet of artificial flowers is suspended upside-down inside a box, which is open on one side to a concave mirror. This mirror's center of curvature is positioned on a plane slightly higher than the one on which the flowers are located. An empty vase (or pot) is placed on top of the box. An observer is then positioned on the side of the box opposite the mirror at a minimum of three meters from the mirror such that the inverted bouquet is hidden from the observer's sight behind the box's closed side. On the condition that the apparatus is illuminated in conformity with certain optical laws, an upright image of the bouquet appears, looking as if placed in the vase on top of the box. This image is "real" in the sense that it appears in real space as opposed to the virtual space that one would see "inside" a plane mirror, for example. Though the image of the flowers appears clear and

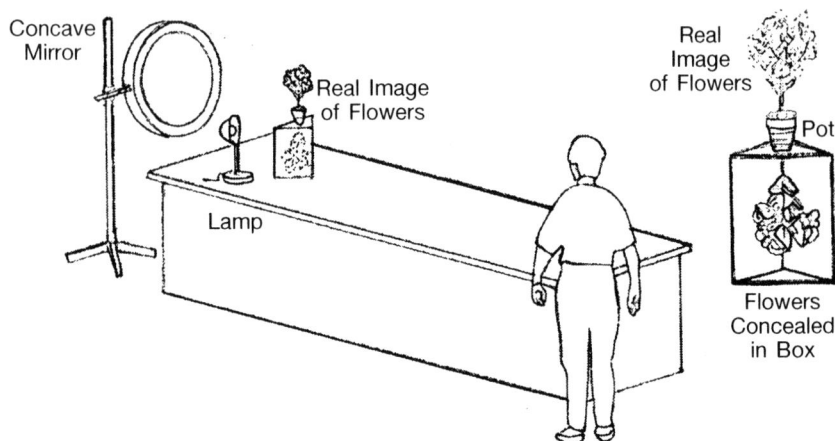

Figure 1.2. Classical inverted vase experiment.

convincing, the observer could nevertheless witness someone's hand, for example, pass through them. For centuries illusionists and prestidigitators have capitalized on the sense of wonder that this optical effect inspires.

Now, Lacan's reconfiguration of the experiment makes three main additions. First, as already mentioned, he adds a plane mirror, positioned on the side of the box opposite the concave mirror. Second, the observer is moved to the opposite side of the box, directly above and in front of the upper extremity of the concave mirror. Though the next alteration is more incidental, Lacan also reverses the positions of the vase and bouquet for reasons of "presentation and metaphorical utilization," as he puts it (*Le transfert*, 407). The result of Lacan's experiment is the same as the original's in that what appears to the observer is an image of a bouquet inside the vase. The difference, however, is that the image in Lacan's experiment is virtual rather than real. More precisely, it is a virtual image of the real image that appears between the two mirrors. In other words, not only is the image itself illusory, in the sense that it does not objectively exist, but the space "inside" the plane mirror in which the image occurs is illusory as well.

Two important points should be noted. First, in order to see the virtual image of vase and flowers, the observer must be positioned within a specific spatial field. Second, unlike in the first experiment, the observer in this field will not see the image of vase and flowers without

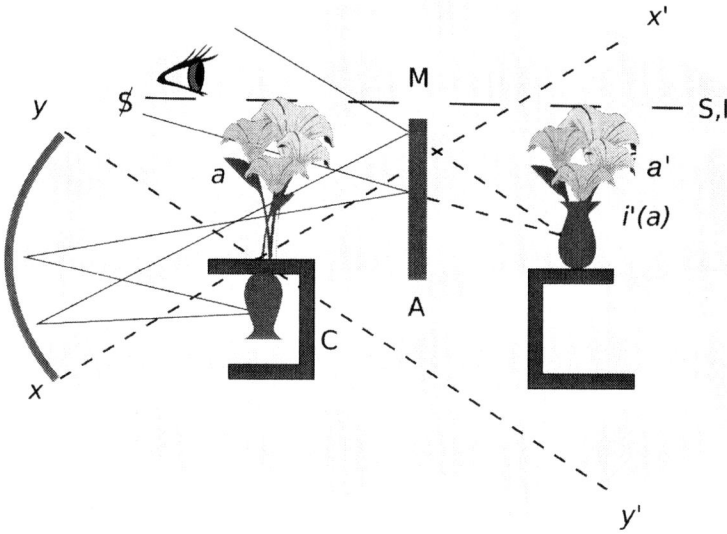

Figure 1.3. Lacan's apparatus; Guillaume Paumier, Madeleine Price Ball, and Mariana Ruiz Villareal (Wikimedia, free licence).

the intervention of the second, plane mirror, since she is placed on the wrong side of the apparatus. The success of the experiment depends on the presence of the plane mirror. But a further, crucial remark must be made. There is in Lacan's experiment the suggestion of subjective immobilization or stasis: to prevent the illusion of the bouquet from dissipating, the observer has to remain within a clearly circumscribed zone. The implication is that the apparatus would cease to function in the intended way were the observer to step outside it.

The more essential reason why Lacan calls his apparatus metaphorical is surely because within its logic the plane mirror "is" the Other, the structure he says is "involved in those elaborations of narcissism connoted respectively by ego ideal and ideal ego" (413). Lacan retreads the old mirror stage ground, noting the permanence and indestructible centrality of the human *Urbild* (image) in psychic life, as well as the insoluble dilemma that the infant faces before this alienated, foreign image of his own perfection: he must either suffer the pain of the discrepancy between the image's power of coherence and his own discombobulated prematurity, or else rage against the image in a fit of "aggressivity," tearing to pieces his only means of perceiving himself as a discrete self. The altered inverted bouquet experiment for Lacan is therefore a development of the prior mirror stage thesis. But here he makes more explicit the tertiary, properly symbolic aspect (the Other) of what had heretofore been meant primarily as an abstract illustration—"abstract" because never experienced in isolation—of the imaginary dyad between the infant subject and his first alienated ego structure.

As creatures of language our self-concept is necessarily mediated by an agency other than our own, the representation of which we are required to "introject" in order to recognize and be satisfied with ourselves; in order, quite literally, to (mis)conceive of ourselves as independent subjects. Lacan illustrates this second relation of dependency with an observation from early childhood, one that happens also to reveal how the symbolic function was presupposed, though not emphasized, even in the earlier mirror stage concept. "We must acknowledge," Lacan says, "the importance of the gesture in which the child turns his head to the adult holding him" in front of the mirror, but "we can't say exactly what he expects, if it's something of the order of consent [accord] or testimonial." Nonetheless, Lacan concludes, "the reference to the Other plays an essential role" (415). To some extent the infant can temper the frustrating threat posed by the image of her own never-experienced wholeness by turning to the Other for confirmation or reassurance, for a sign that the image "out there" indeed represents her and that it passes muster with this Other's desire. Thus, desire—the Other's desire, that is, for desire is always and only of the Other—liberates the subject from the intimidating spectacle of its comparative helplessness, but only at the cost of an acute dependency on the Other's continual reassurance—always mediated by the cultural world of signs and meanings—that it acknowledges, recognizes, and approves.

To return now to Lacan's modified experiment, we can say that the plane mirror represents the Other O and the virtual image of the vase is the *image de a*—not the partial object, note, but rather its image or analogue in the ego structure. This is the ideal ego (*Idealich*) in Freud's terminology. Lacan marks the actual bouquet of flowers in the apparatus with his symbol for the partial object *a*. He then draws a line connecting his notation for the subject's "fading" $, which he places in real space in front of the bouquet between the two mirrors, to two other symbols, S and I, situated in virtual space alongside the reflected mirror image on the righthand side of the diagram. S represents the "full" or "unbarred" subject of knowledge, the subject supposed to know in the transference, and I denotes the ego ideal, the point of identification that serves as its support.

Now, for the purposes of my argument we should observe that Lacan associates the ego ideal with the function in the transference of the Other, represented in the optical context by the plane mirror. Lacan explicitly qualifies the ideal ego as virtual and places it under the Other's dependence. Note, moreover, that the virtual image is produced as two separate functions come together: the virtual image of the bouquet (a becomes a') and the vase (C) changes to $i'(a)$; the virtual reflections are italicized and the real objects on the plane mirror's left are kept in Roman script. Whereas the real vase is entirely hidden from the subject's view under the box, the actual flowers are partially visible within the subject's real-space field of vision. The uppermost blossoms, to be precise, are within the perceiving subject's visual "cone."

Each of these details is shot through with significance. The ideal ego structure develops from the envelopment of the partial object—its idealization, if you will, in unconscious fantasy—through the mediation of the "unbarred" Other in its solicitation of identification in transference love. In other words, when I issue my demand for love to the Other, what I am asking for is the "sublimation" of my partial object, its integration within my economy of narcissism. Plainly put, I want the Other to tell me that my desire is not caused by something unworthy of me, that the innermost essence of my self is fully respectable, that it gives body to the being that I intend to be. This function of envelopment is therefore the form of resistance by which the self-expropriating partial object is made palatable to desire and integrated within the structure of self-love. Incidentally, it is also what Lacan wishes to signal through his reversal of the respective positions of vase and flowers through the experiment's modification.

In the present context, however, the most essential observation to make is this: whereas the source of the object's fantasy-container (C) is entirely inaccessible to consciousness (it is hidden from the observer under the box), an aspect of the real object (i.e., the real bouquet) protrudes into the subject's field of vision, potentially jeopardizing the impression of reality created by the virtual image. This intrusion of the real object into the field of vision implies that the dynamic Lacan represents in his apparatus is not a fully stable one. In other words, though I may from time to time succeed in establishing an empathetic relationship with my Other—rest assured, that is to say, that I am acknowledged as the self I aspire to be—doubt will eventually set in, and I will be faced anew with the same old nagging doubt about what I am from the perspective of the Other. This insight allows me to formulate the most precise definition of our concept thus far: transference consists of our resistance to the threat of *a*'s protrusion into our ego structure, *a* being the partial object undomesticated by the edifying ambitions of the ego in its never-ending and often provocative enlistment of the Other's elusive sanction.

From Partial Love to Anxiety

Before broaching Lacan's discussion of the implications of this threat for analytic technique, it will be helpful to revisit the function, crucial to the transference dynamic, that he designates by I in more concrete clinical terms. In the preceding analysis, I corresponded to the function of the plane mirror in its capacity to produce the convincingly real image of vase and flowers. A consideration of the role played by the ego ideal in exemplary clinical cases has the benefit of shedding light on its workings in what we call ordinary life. With some consistency Lacan has been criticized for offering an abstract, formalized psychoanalytic theory far removed from clinical experience. Indeed, for many Lacan's enlistment of the inverted vase experiment no doubt contributes to this impression. The conceptual jump that Lacan makes from the Freudian concept of the ego ideal to his own notion of the *trait unaire*[18]—the signifier that the subject unconsciously selects in an attempt to totalize or close off the ego system—may not be self-evident. Neither perhaps is the crucial role played by de-sexualization in the dynamic of narcissism. A prime opportunity therefore presents itself here to explore an instance of the importance of clinical experience in Lacan's teaching.

In the exposition of his unique trait concept, Lacan draws significantly on the work of first-generation Freudian Karl Abraham, specifically his key 1924 essay "A Short Study of the Development of the Libido." This essay is chock full of evidence showing how the "introjection" through which the subject selects her ego ideal is always partial with respect to the field from which the selection is made. It also illuminates how the phallic aspect of this introjection works to cleanse the object from the indignity of unconscious desire.

Already in this most summary of introductions there is a hint of the central thematic of ambivalence in Abraham's discourse on introjection: the object-part selected from the Other as a sign of its love can only imperfectly camouflage its origins in a lowly "bad" object, one that must be excluded from our psychical economy if we are to establish a sense of subjective autonomy. From this contention Abraham develops the properly post-Freudian (I use the term pejoratively) notion of a post-ambivalent stage of the libido, a stage of normality (Abraham's term) at which the subject proves capable of loving its object wholeheartedly, unconditionally, in this way perfectly "adapting itself to the external world."[19] This is the aspect of Abraham's discourse from which Lacan with good reason takes his distance. "It does not suffice to qualify as post-ambivalent the entry to the genital stage," Lacan says. "No one has ever entered it" (*Le transfert*, 449). For Lacan there is no possible middle ground between I and *a*; between, that is, the ego structure that undergirds the subject's perception of its dignity and the real object that obliterates that dignity, subverting the pretension of consciousness to take itself as a worthy object of knowledge.

Abraham is on solid ground, by contrast, where he describes the function of this object fragment, which is to establish an ego-self deserving of the Other's love and to repress, however imperfectly, its derivation from "prior"[20]—anal and oral—stages of libidinal organization. In helpful illustration Abraham recounts select details from the case history of a depressive patient who admits himself into a nursing home during one of his bouts of illness. Relatives arrive for a visit one day and, wishing to elevate his spirits, they lead him on a walk through the town's public gardens. On the way back the patient suddenly stops in front of a bakery, impulsively buying a loaf of a local specialty called Johannes bread.

In the course of a session the patient unearths a buried memory while narrating this episode to Abraham. Opposite his childhood home there stood a small shop owned by a widow who would give him pieces of this special bread when he came over to play with her son. "At that time," Abraham explains, the patient had already had "the fateful experience which was the origin of his later illness—a profound disappointment in his love-relations with his mother." Quite logically, Abraham surmises that the widow functioned for his patient as a mother-substitute, and he identifies the Johannes bread as the "symbol" of his patient's "desire for maternal love and care." Yet Abraham also proffers the suggestion that this symbol of love is marked with ambivalence because, he explains, "its long shape and brown colour reminded [his patient] of faeces." The patient's association lends support in Abraham's view to the striking idea that "the impulse to eat excrement" is effectively "an expression of the desire for a lost love-object" (15).

In the paper's wider context these details are given in illustration of Abraham's theory of melancholia. In a thoroughly Freudian vein, Abraham argues that in general terms depression stems from a primitive fixation of the libido on a love object which has been incorporated into the ego to compensate for its prior loss. For Lacan, in contrast, these same details serve to show how the introjected "object"—Freud's *Ichideal*—is best understood in the Saussurean idiom as a signifier. In contrast to the enveloping or containing function of the *Idealich*—recall the image of the vase enclosing the bouquet in the experiment—the ego ideal features a properly synecdochic function: it is a part of the object that represents, or rather signifies, the "whole" object isolated or abstracted through the agency of the unconscious from its original and unwholesome fantasy context.

Whereas Abraham unhelpfully intends his essay to chart out what he views to be the stages of normal libidinal development, for Lacan its true subject matter is instead "the function of the partial in identification," as he puts it. In Lacan's view, more precisely, the subject's identification with the ego ideal is "an identification through isolated traits, traits which are all unique and have the structure of the signifier" (444). Through the signifying work it does in the patient's unconscious, the Johannes bread functions as his ego ideal I—the point of identification, disjoined from its link with the figure of the widow (his "primitive" Other), that allows him to perceive himself as a complete being: as an image-object *i(a)*, that is to say, which meets the criteria for the Other's love.

For Lacan the story does not end there, however. As the analysand's further associations reveal, the object of identification never quite succeeds in repressing its abject flip side, in this instance its derivation from the fecal object of the anal drive. Abraham is to be commended for the insistence with which he stresses that in the patient's fantasies the phallic loaf of bread is never far removed from its libidinal connection with excrement. As I have already suggested, the context from which the ego ideal is abstracted is indeed the libido, the drive, insofar as *its* object—*objet petit a*, the real of desire—cannot partake of the signifying function, cannot even appear to consciousness in the form of a discrete image. In consequence, this partial object remains embedded in the psyche as the ego ideal's obscene, and therefore repressed, residue.

This is the train of thought that leads Lacan to claim that Abraham's work illuminates "the relations between *i(a)* and *a*" (444): between, to translate, the object-image as it appears from the perspective of the ego ideal in the finished form of the ideal ego and, on the other, the object properly speaking in its necessarily partial aspect, as the "bad object" that cannot be assimilated into the ego and that ruins the pleasing view from the ego ideal. To anticipate this point's importance for the problem of transference, we can say here that the analyst's work of interpretation aims precisely to enable the analysand to separate these two functions. The outcome of this work, as I will explore in more detail at this chapter's conclusion, largely depends on the analyst and the "position" she adopts with respect to her patient's desire.

Before broaching the question of transference directly, however, we can shed more light on the significance of this distinction between the partial object and its idealization in narcissism by considering Lacan's comments on Abraham's discussion of another remarkably illustrative case history, this one involving a hysteric. This hysteric, Abraham writes in "Development of the Libido," presents three main symptoms: "a marked pseudologia phantastica"—pathological lying—"dating back to her sixth year," "severe impulses of kleptomania," and "attacks of despair" causing "uncontrollable fits of weeping of many hours' duration" (132). Abraham traces the appearance of these symptoms to the patient's castration complex, compounded in this particular case not only by "envy of her more favoured younger brother," but also what Abraham calls the "psychological" loss of her father. The patient as a young girl developed "an especially strong transference-love" for him, a love that then "suffered a sudden check" at age six when, convalescing from an illness in their bedroom, she witnessed her parents having intercourse. At this time, Abraham explains, the patient "lost all emotional contact with her father," specifying that she grew unable "to form any kind of mental image of him" (132).

On the basis of further clinical revelations, Abraham concludes that the patient's emotional indifference sits alongside "a quite specialized compulsive interest in one particular part of [her father's] body, namely, his penis." By this time the father "had ceased to exist as a whole person" for the patient, who begins unconsciously to identify herself "now with him, now with his genitals, which had become for her his representative" (133). Abraham adds that the objects of his patient's kleptomania—money, pens, pencils, "and other male symbols"—suggest a desire symbolically to castrate her father. More precisely, the hysteric's "dreams and day-dreams contained ever-recurring images of castration by means of biting," which leads Abraham to conclude that "the aim of her phantasies was not to incorporate her love-object as a whole but to bite off and swallow a part of it and then to identify herself with the part" (134). For Abraham, such a partial incorporation is the psychical sleight of hand that enables us to keep a part of the love object as our "own property for ever" (136). This incorporation has the comforting effect of anaesthetizing the psyche as much as is possible to the wrenching pain of loss.

Now, Lacan makes use of Abraham's discussion to elaborate on his notion of the *trait unaire*, or unique trait. He seizes in particular on the reciprocal implication of the patient's melancholic identification with her father and her fantasies of castration. Supplanted by both her brother and her mother as the privileged object of her father's love, Abraham's hysteric tarries with her loss by unconsciously incorporating a part of his body, a gesture that numbs the wound's pain by withdrawing her conscious investment in his image. At a later point of the analysis when she begins to improve, the patient has a dream in which she "sees her father's body and notices the absence of pubic hair" (143). Informing his reader that pubic hair had always represented her father's genitals "in a number of earlier dreams," Abraham notes the logic of mutual exclusion that governs the relation between the two fantasies. Whereas "before, when she had had a compulsion to stare at her father's genitals, her love-interest had been turned away from all the rest of him," now "she was repressing what had then exercised a compulsive power in her consciousness" (143). Her father's psychical representation is literally split in two: it appears in the form of either his penis separated off from the rest of his body, or else that body minus any evidence of the genital presence. Never do the two fantasy images appear at the same time. This clinical insight leads Lacan to the crucial observation that what Abraham puts forth in his essay is the idea that "it's to the extent that the genitals are invested by the subject that in the object they are not" (446).

Important to note here is how Lacan connects a certain representation of the male genitals—the phallus, to be precise—to the *subject* and phallic lack to the *object* of love. Abraham's idea of partial love designates "in the most formal way," according to Lacan, "a love of the object from which a part is excluded." Lacan's reading makes the assumption that a proper appreciation of Abraham's work requires one to know the nature of the relation between "the object of desire" and its "libidinal correspondent" (453). To refer back to the Lacanian algebra, this is the relation between the partial object of the libido a and its imaginary correlative $i(a)$ as it appears from the desiring perspective of the ego ideal. The split in the father's representation effectively functions to deceive the subject as to what form of the object is invested with libido. "It's to the extent that the real phallus remains, unknown to the subject, that around which maximum investment is conserved," Lacan concludes, "that the partial object is elided, removed from the image of the other as invested" (453). For the hysteric, in short, the father is only loveable if the body part that signifies his sexuality, and therefore his lack, disappears from view.

This insight concerning the centrality of de-sexualization allows Lacan to claim that the place "where we symbolically see the phallus is precisely where it is not" (454). With this Lacan means to say that the image of the father *sans* genitalia—he is not castrated, note, but rather purified of all marks of sex; innocent of even the prospect of loss or incompletion, of desire—is the ultimate imaginary representation of the phallus precisely because all evidence of the real organ is missing from it. Compare Abraham's earlier clinical narrative: whereas the Johannes bread functions for the melancholic as the phallic signifier I, in other words as the point in the Other where he can see himself as an object of maternal love $i(a)$, the real phallus a, the true source of his libidinal investment, takes the fantasmatic form of the turd. The patient's compulsion to buy Johannes bread therefore does the work of any symptom worthy of the name: it acts as a precarious compromise formation which allows the subject to maintain his comforting ego structure without having to renounce drive satisfaction, which remains, at least for a time, safely buried beneath the threshold of consciousness.

The preceding clinical material is key to my argument because Lacan goes on to argue that the aim of the transference's interpretation is to effect the separation of the two functions $i(a)$ and a. The subject in analysis must bring to his awareness some evidence of the true object of the drive, even if this awareness can only take the form of self-absence or self-ruination. The patient is required to separate this object out from its narcissistic idealization, and then to withstand the subjective destitution—this is what Lacan means by the "fading" of the subject—that results when the ego comes crumbling down. The main theoretical conclusion to be drawn from this is that the experience of the partial object and the enjoyment that it provides—jouissance, that is to say—is structurally incompatible with the egoic, self-relating subject of love who succeeds, though only for a time, in soliciting the sign from his Other that he meets with its approval. Jouissance can never become an object of consciousness; we can never, as it were, directly witness ourselves enjoy.

But how are we to relate Lacan's clinical insights to transference theory, more specifically to the question of what this theory might suggest with respect to the study of art, culture, or politics? As I have already intimated, my answer takes its points of reference from the function of the analyst in the transference. Lacan's greatest contribution to the Freudian discourse on transference lies in how he relates his formalization of the fragile structure of love to the old Freudian problem of the analyst's technique. Lacan brings welcome clarity to Freud's ambivalent insight that the analyst has an indispensable role to play in the separation of desire's object from its compensatory and defensive idealization. In short, the analyst must ensure that her desire indexes to the analysand the partial object a, and she does this by "embodying" the barred subject S, the degraded subject who has been shown to lack in knowledge and who has fallen as a result from her pedestal. The analyst's task is to move from being the reassuring Other of transference love—subject supposed to know, potential guarantor of the patient's worthiness for love—to acting as a conduit for unconscious desire by disrupting the circuit of narcissism that the patient's amorous demand aims to set up. This is how Lacan rectifies the Freudian and post-Freudian pseudo-concept of countertransference: the analyst's role is simply to sustain (his) desire, to prevent this desire from issuing a sign of legitimization with which the patient could reassure himself, secure in the knowledge that the Other has recognized and sanctioned his innermost being.

As the term itself suggests, countertransference is simply the clinical manifestation of the analyst's own transference, and Lacan dismisses the idea's legitimacy for two reasons. The emergence of countertransference in the form of a demand for recognition is not only unethical and clinically disastrous, since it inevitably leads to the complacent, Oprah-brand "I'm okay, you're okay" ethos of New Age therapeutic discourses. Additionally, the idea rests on a false and unnecessary theoretical distinction, which assumes that the analyst's transference must in some significant way be different from the patient's. Lacan's lesson is that it is precisely the analyst's own *resistance to the demand of transference-love* that *causes* the patient's transference to occur. The analyst's refusal to give the patient's ego the sign of approbation it so craves has the effect of forcing the patient onto the path of the unsettling real of desire.

This last point is one way of making sense in the clinical context of what Lacan means when he cryptically defines ethical love as "giving what you don't have." The analyst gives to her patient the gift of a nothing, the gift of renouncing any claim to know the ultimate content of desire. Epistemologically speaking, the analyst responds to the analysand's supposition of knowledge with an open display of the non-knowledge of jouissance that indexes knowledge's limit; the truth, that is to say, that the unconscious prevents knowledge from being amenable to grounding or completion. The analyst's reticence dislodges the patient's entrenched ego ideal, which precipitates the patient into the no-man's-land between this ideal and its repressed libidinal support, the reserve of jouissance that it works to dissimulate. The transference is thus the patient's last stand, her last desperate plea to the analyst to protect her from the traumatic emergence of enjoyment, which promises to bring her most cherished idea of herself to ruin.

I have tried to show how Freud's anxieties regarding his developing insights into analytic technique create unhelpful ambivalences in his theory. How à propos, then, that for Lacan the problem of anxiety plays a key role in his formulation of the analyst's function. Lacan's discussion of anxiety spells out in straightforward terms how the patient comes to experience the transference as well as what it means precisely for the analyst to sustain (his) desire as the transference takes place. Lacan brings to the level of the concept Freud's intuition that anxiety is central to the dynamic of transference. The crux of Lacan's argument is that in order to precipitate the transference and facilitate its interpretation, the analyst must abstain from acknowledging anxiety, both the patient's and her own. I claimed above that the event of transference coaxes the patient to issue his final demand to be spared the expropriating force of jouissance. As Freud already observed, this demand is habitually accompanied by the issuing of an anxious sign of discomfort. The analysand issues this demand in the hope of being granted a reprieve from the anxiety accruing from the encounter with the mystery of the Other's desire.

In his transference seminar Lacan cites a crucial passage from *Inhibitions, Symptoms and Anxiety* (1926) in which Freud develops a characteristic neurological analogy to compare the organism's evasion of dangerous external stimuli through perceptual withdrawal and motor discharge—think of a gazelle, for example, taking off at the first sign of a leopard's proximity—with the ego's evasion of dangerous internal stimuli through the mechanism of repression. "The ego withdraws its (preconscious) cathexis from the instinctual representative that is to be repressed," Freud writes, "and uses this cathexis for the purpose of producing unpleasure (anxiety)."[21] Bear in mind that Lacan relates the Freudian drive-representation in the unconscious ("instinctual representative," Strachey's term for *Triebrepräsentanz*) to his idea of the partial object, and the production of the sign of anxiety to the "fading" subject S in its encounter with the "fallen" Other Θ. "What does the withdrawal of cathexis from the *Triebrepräsentanz* mean," Lacan asks his audience, "if we apply it to our own formulation? It means that anxiety is produced when the cathexis of small *a* is transferred to [*est reporté sur*] the S" (424). Translation: when the analysand engaged in free association is confronted with an internal "stimulation"—a psychical representation, that is—that threatens to dredge up repressed, what Freud calls "complexive," material, the release of psychical energy that results from the ensuing withdrawal of unconscious investment in that material manifests itself as anxiety. In short, the mental work that the psyche would have undertaken to bring the traumatic representation to consciousness, in the process flooding the bodily ego with disruptive symptomatic intensities, is instead left free to circulate in the form of a vague and apparently objectless but intensely stressful feeling of discomfort.

Lacan's instructive formalization of Freud's theory of anxiety allows me to establish a crucial connection with the transference. When the Other Θ fails in its "duty" to reflect back to me an agreeable image of myself, thereby threatening me with an encounter with the unwholesome partial object *a*, I call on the Other to provide a sign of warning, to give me time to build up resistance to the anxiety that, however unpleasant, will keep me safe from the traumatic self-ruination of enjoyment. By provoking the Other into issuing this sign, the subject aims to sustain a relation with desire while at the same time keeping the amorous structure of narcissism precariously intact.

Recall that in Lacan's modified optical experiment the dual mirror mechanism functions to project an image of the vase around the flower stems. The patient in the transference calls on the analyst to perform an analogous enveloping function, as it were to "wrap" the partial object *a* with an image *i,* seen from the perspective of a privileged signifier I—Abraham's "partial love," Freud's *Ichideal*—which allows this object to appear to the patient's consciousness in a flattering light. However, given the restrictions of the experimental apparatus (recall that the observer must be placed in the specified "cone"), as well as the limited viability of such empathetic, call-and-response communication between patient and doctor, it happens that this enveloping function must inevitably fail, leaving for the subject only a disquietingly palpable absence, which is haunted nonetheless by the fleeting, shadowy presence of the partial object that threatens to tear self-consciousness asunder.

The analyst's duty to embody the barred Other Θ works to precipitate the eclipse of the subject-as-ego, to wrench the subject from the defensively passionate attachment to its self-image as reflected through the Other. "If S is the place," Lacan says, "that from time to time can find itself empty, meaning that nothing satisfying happens there with respect to the appearance [*surgissement*] of the image, then we can conceive that it's to its call that the production of the signal of anxiety responds" (425).[22] Made anxious by the prospect of losing sight of its intensely invested self-image, the subject in the transference beseeches the Other to give a sign of warning that would allow the partial object to be wrapped anew in the comforting cloak of idealization.

This last observation explains why Lacan qualifies anxiety as a means of *sustaining* desire. Since an unmediated encounter with the partial object requires the traumatic eclipse of consciousness, the unconscious produces anxiety as a sort of compromise. This compromise perpetuates the subject's relation to desire, gives this subject a reason for living, without having to succumb to "fading," without effectively disappearing as an object of (its own) consciousness. Anxiety also works to circumvent the subject's complete collapse into its seductive but alienating alter ego. Marked by taboo, the ideal ego provides the subject with a self-concept sufficiently distanced and menacing as to render a perfectly accomplished alienation both impossible and undesired. The perseverance of the analyst in her desire—her "fecund *Versagung* [refusal/failure]," to quote Lacan's suggestive Freudian phrase—can succeed in putting the patient's phobic construction in abeyance. "The analyst refuses to offer his anxiety to the subject," Lacan says, "and leaves exposed the place where he is called upon as other to give the signal of anxiety" (432).

In the transference seminar Lacan provides a golden opportunity to return to the question of the transference's social implications, the ones we first saw emerge in the form of Freud's symptomatic ambivalences. As he was wont on occasion to do at this stage of his teaching, Lacan uses an ethological analogy to illustrate his contention. The analyst who panics and responds to the transference by giving the signal of anxiety behaves like the animal responsible for communicating to the herd the presence of a dangerous predator. Once the signal of danger is given, the entire herd sets off in the same direction as if all its members belonged to a single body. For centuries the indigenous peoples of the North American plains took advantage of this behavior to coax herds of bison to plunge to their deaths at the bottom of rocky precipices. For Lacan this herd mentality is imaginary: it rests on a logic of collective identification comparable to the one Freud spoke of under the heading "group psychology," and therefore its vestiges are clearly distinguishable in the behavior of human collectivities. What sets us apart from our fellow mammals, however, is our dependence on the symbolic function, which makes of us something more than mere "social animals" (431). This symbolic function empties out a lack in being, a space of desire, which indexes an objective dimension of freedom—the possibility to act, that is to say, against the herd.

The prospect of successful clinical practice depends for Lacan on the analyst's capacity to resist the temptation to respond to the patient's transference by producing the signal of danger. It follows that the patient in this view is *not* destined to dart off with the herd, to seek refuge in the same old neurotic symptoms. There exists the horizon of the act, the creation of the new and unforeseen. It is hardly a coincidence that Lacan associates human creative potential with the sense of danger, both individual and collective, as I suppose we are still required to say. In sum, *anxiety is an objective indication of the possibility of freedom*, of our capacity to act in novel, seemingly impossible ways.

Our volitional power to remain indifferent to anxiety, to pursue desire beyond the limit that the sign of danger is meant to impose, is the exciting, authentically subversive challenge that the transference event issues to us, both within analytic practice and "outside." Lacan's intervention enables us to identify the limits that Freud's phobic object—the bourgeois lady—imposes on his nonetheless pathbreaking papers on technique. It also allows us to discern a surprising catalyst for Freud's psychoanalytic desire: the obscene, déclassé underside of the Viennese bourgeoisie. An uncanny partial object—the social riff-raff—is symptomatically excluded from, yet integral to, Freud's enterprise; indeed, it is a veritable unconscious incarnation of the object-cause of psychoanalysis as such. Freud's heroism therefore consists in the fact that despite the contradictions and ambivalences, he left his faithful reader—Lacan, to my mind, is the key example here—the tools required to articulate the authentic kernel of his theory.

Not unlike Freud, then, the singular artist is the one who dares to pursue desire beyond the limit of anxiety. Our task as cultural theorists and critics is simply to follow them in the same way that Lacan "follows" Freud, refusing to see signs of anxiety where there are none, and dismissing them in instances—hardly uncommon—where they betray the presence of ambivalence, hesitation, compromise, or even treachery. Each of the chapters that follow is an act of fidelity to the work of its central figure or figures, an attempt to think through the consequences of the work in its authentically innovative audacity as it dares to move beyond the phobic and conservative forces of a formidable but hardly invincible transference love.

II

Socrates, Analyst

An Original Transference

Lacan bases his reading of Plato's *Symposium* dialogue on the premise that the text pivots around what he calls "the first analytic transference" on record.[1] This chapter's relation to the preceding one is primarily illustrative: for the most part it treads the same theoretical ground, but through the lens of a radically different, decidedly pre-Freudian context. This context has the tremendous benefit of illuminating a striking but imperfect ethical kinship between psychoanalysis and the Greek, and by extension Western, philosophical project, at least to the extent that this project has been indelibly marked by Plato's account of Socratic teaching. More specifically, my reading of the *Symposium* through Lacan aims to show how an embryonic formulation of the ethical realm beyond the transference, never properly spotted before Lacan, inheres in Plato's illustrious dialogue.

Since not every reader will be familiar with the text, I will provide to begin the briefest of overviews. Still, readers with a fresh recollection will likely follow my argument more easily. Opening with an elaborate framing device that separates us from the event it depicts by both time and two intermediary narrators, the *Symposium* recounts the proceedings of a philosophical dinner party in honor of Agathon's victory the previous day at the Athenian festival of tragedy. One by one, each of the six attendees offers a speech in praise of love, obeying with varying degrees of strictness acknowledged rhetorical conventions for discourses of this kind in such circumstances. Before Socrates, the final speaker, is able to conclude his presentation of the famous mysteries of his teacher Diotima, however, the banquet is interrupted by the entrance of the drunken Alcibiades. The famous notable and warrior, known as a longtime enthusiast of Socratic teaching, proceeds to offer a scandalous account of the vain attempt he made in his youth to get his mentor Socrates "to fuck him," as Lacan plainly puts it (34). The reported narrative then abruptly ends as more drunken revelers enter the room and the original witness to the occasion falls asleep, no doubt feeling the effects of the large quantities of wine consumed.

The novel premise of Lacan's interpretation of this already thoroughly dissected text is that Alcibiades' complaint against Socrates manifests what Freud called transference love. Lacan adds that Socrates' response to Alcibiades' complaint can be fruitfully compared to the act of analytic interpretation as the psychoanalyst defines it. This chapter examines some highlights of Lacan's reading of the *Symposium* in the view of contrasting the principles that animate it with those that animate competing readings. It will also further elucidate the theoretical discussion of the transference concept I undertook in the first chapter. I aim not only to show in precise terms how Socrates' response to Alcibiades' outburst anticipates the development of analytic technique, but also to explain why for Lacan it falls short of being an exemplary manifestation of what he calls the analyst's desire.

We saw in chapter 1 how Freud, however unwittingly, compares the analyst's position with that of the social "riff-raff." Similarly, Lacan ties the effectiveness of the Socratic intervention to the fact that the philosopher "is nowhere to be found" within "the order of the city" (19). The other symposiasts, by contrast, can be located with certainty within that order. Representing a cross-section of the Athenian cultural and political elite, their eulogies display the conventional opinions that Socratic teaching aims so subversively to displace. No doubt it is only retrospectively from the moment of Alcibiades' boozy arrival, however, that we are meant as readers to appreciate the extent of the banality of what the five initial speeches have to offer, at least on the surface. As twenty-first century readers of Plato we are at an intimidating remove from the social and cultural contexts of both the event and its literary representation. For this reason we cannot avoid relying on the scholarly debates and specialist writings that precede us when we ask ourselves how we are meant to understand the various encomia.

Lacan's approach to Plato heeds noted classicist Leo Strauss's warning that the convictions of a philosopher who wrote only dialogues and whose main character is a man notorious for both his irony and self-professed lack of knowledge of all subjects except love cannot be gleaned from the texts with any degree of confidence.[2] Yet Lacan goes one step farther than Strauss, as one might expect from the reader of a discourse—Freud's—that, perhaps more than any other in the history of thought, casts a suspicious glance on what we might call the ideal of the idea, questioning its claim to be a form of knowledge that transcends human embodiment and its traversal by the laws of unconscious desire. Lacan premises his reading on the assumption that the *Symposium*'s rhetorical mode is comic, indeed that it inserts cutting shards of playfully subversive irony even in those places that seem irreproachably sincere. Thus the Socratic interrogation of love unfailingly reveals the presumption, the hubris, of "that incorruptible, material, super-essential, purely ideal, participatory, eternal and uncreated order" that Plato has us discover, as Lacan puts it, "ironically perhaps" (97).

As he goes about framing his reading of the *Symposium* in the transference seminar, Lacan makes two key points, which will prove helpful to retain as I develop my own argument about its significance for transference theory. First, Lacan abides by the Greek terms for the partners of love because they bring to the fore the nonreciprocity and asymmetry of the love relation, which in truth is not a relation in the proper logical sense of the term. Lacan takes on the Greek assumption that one must be either an active or passive partner in love: *erastēs* or *erōmenos*. The lover is characterized by the lack that drives him to seek completion in his partner; Lacan adds only that the lover lacks knowledge of what he lacks. Similarly, the beloved remains ignorant of the quality within him that attracts the lover's desire. In his appropriation of these Greek ideas for psychoanalysis, Lacan stresses that "what the one lacks is not what is hidden in the other" (53), whence the well-known Lacanian aphorism "there is no sexual relation."

Second, Lacan subtends that love is a metaphor or signification that sees the active lover, or rather his function, substitute itself for the function of the beloved. In Lacan's early teaching, metaphor designates the realm of signification, that is to say in semiotic terms, the relation between the signifier and the signified. In contrast, metonymy names meaning's endless deferral from one signifier to the next. I take Lacan's association of love with metaphor to imply that there is a transformation from a passive state of being loved or lovable, of being capable of apprehending in oneself that quality or object that attracts the lover's desire, to an (active) *act* of loving. Though this act is addressed to, performed on behalf of, the beloved, it can be motivated only by lack, since it is the beloved, not the lover, who "contains" the object that is meant to fulfill desire. Here we gain additional insight into what Lacan meant by his other great aphorism for love, "giving what you don't have," which similarly puts forth the idea of a gesture or offering that remains somehow devoid of content. This is Lacan's idea of authentic love, the love beyond the transference as I began to define it in the previous chapter, as opposed to Freud's transference love, which works as a form of resistance against the real of desire, against the traumatic lack in the Other. Before giving more substance to this still rather murky formulation, however, I will turn to a consideration of how the *Symposium*'s first speeches develop ideas of love which, Lacan contends, it was Plato's intention to subvert.

Of Love Spheres and Stranded Vessels

Collectively, the *Symposium*'s first three discourses—those of Phaedrus, Pausanias, and Eryximachus—offer a lofty idealization of love in its putative function as a catalyst for aesthetic, political, and moral virtue. These forms of love qualify as instances of resistance in the Freudian framework, and Lacan argues that Plato's presentation of them is designed to invite ridicule. It comes as no surprise, then, that there are cracks on the surface of this first happy construct of love through which can be glimpsed the unsettling message that Alcibiades will introduce at the moment of his inebriated entrance. Yet this message only becomes apparent from the perspective of Lacan's premise of a thoroughgoing Platonic irony at work in a variety of complex ways throughout the *Symposium*. Indeed, by the end of Eryximachus's eulogy—last of the dialogue's three initial "minor" speeches—the attentive reader will have been forced to rethink whatever sunny thoughts he might harbor on love's powers of moral edification.

But it is only with the seminal narrative of mortal hubris and divine retribution recounted by the comedian Aristophanes, Socrates' declared enemy and satirist foil, that we are given a less optimistic, indeed tragic—actually *tragicomic*, to be perfectly precise—discourse on love, one that explicitly attributes pain and loss to *erōs*, in fact depicting *erōs* as something suffered as punishment from the gods. Aristophanes' discussion refutes the prior speeches' contention that the desires of love are signs of the gods' approval of our wisdom and right action. For

Aristophanes, love results rather from our having acted *against* divine will. In the context of Greek antiquity this implies that love can be decidedly incommodious, indeed, that it can be a pain in the neck—or the side, as it were, bearing in mind the punishment Zeus metes out to his rotund and jubilating creatures.

For those in need of initiation or reminding, here is a brief summary of the origin of love as Aristophanes tells it. In the beginning, so the story goes, human beings were spherical in shape with two pairs of arms and legs, two heads turned outward, and two sets of circumferential genitals positioned so as to enable copulation with the earth. These creatures came in three varieties, the first composed of two male halves, the second of two female, the third of one of each, and they bounced around and rolled about with such gleeful abandon that the gods were no longer able to control their behavior. For this reason Zeus decides one day to punish them by splitting them in half, stretching their skins to cover their wounds and turning their heads around so as to place the scars left by their violent division in full shameful view. Unfortunately for Zeus, however, his plan fails to come off, for as soon as the partners rediscover one another they reunite in wanton bliss, foregoing the necessities of life in order to prolong their passionate but nonsexual union—"nonsexual" because they reunite on the "wounded" side on which separation was effected and not on their circumference where the genitals are located. Fearing a stoppage in the sacrifices that humans normally perform in his honor, Zeus engages in a second surgical intervention, this time transferring the half-spheres' genitals from their former outside to their former inside, thereby inaugurating, so we are told, a regime of sexual reproduction, or more properly sexuality, since only one of the three possible kinds of union is quite evidently capable of producing reproduction as its outcome.

Offering his strange little story as an explanation for how "the innate desire of human beings for each other started," Aristophanes adds that this desire "tries to make one out of two," aiming in this way to "heal the wound in human nature."[3] This wound's kinship with the psychical wound of castration forming the bedrock of Freudian theory is made quite evident in the gloss on the myth that Aristophanes himself provides. But the myth becomes even more interesting from the psychoanalytic perspective when Aristophanes specifies that the intense emotion unleashed when a male "lover of boys" rediscovers his long-lost other half—by this time the poet has cast aside his impressive appreciation for the diversity of what today we call object choice in favor of an altogether more Greek pederastic androcentrism—goes well beyond mere sexual feeling. The intensity of these new desires in fact transcends the capacities of human understanding, causing the men who experience them to act in ways they can only fail to fathom. "It's clear that each of them has some wish in his mind that he can't articulate," Aristophanes says. "Instead, like an oracle, he [only] half-grasps what he wants and obscurely hints at it" (192d).

Lacan adds to these precocious intimations of a desire beyond the limits of human consciousness the argument that the violation of spherical perfection, a form lauded, again perhaps ironically, for its haughty self-sufficiency in Plato's *Timaeus*, but also in Empedocles and Greek geometry more generally, is a conceptual condition for the advancement of *epistēmē*—science, Lacan translates—which he associates with the particularities of Socratic teaching in its formal, analytical emphasis on what today we would call signifying oppositions or binaries. When Zeus splits the gleefully bouncing human balls, and the halves proceed to struggle with the symbolization of their newfound desires, in Lacanian terms he puts into effect a transition from imaginary completion and self-sufficiency to a symbolic law premised on loss and division. To illustrate his contention Lacan offers an example from the history of astronomy. Kepler corrected the Copernican "historical fantasy" (113) of spherical perfection by demonstrating that the planets' orbits are elliptical rather than circular, illustrating in this way how the astronomical real tends to violate the geometrical ideality with which our intuition seems so enamored.

Unfortunately, however, this intuitive contemplation of the cosmos can only impede the advancement of thought. More precisely, the fascination exercised by the spherical form effectively lures human desire in a way that halts, on the concrete level of the history of science, the progress of astronomical knowledge. It does this according to Lacan by positing a simple, geometrically idealized cosmos that can be contemplated in its perfection on the condition that the observer is positioned on the outside. Aristophanes' peculiar myth effects for Lacan a tragicomically derisive deflation of the sphere in its function as a figure through which the powers of human consciousness, and by extension its apprehension of the cosmos that surrounds it, are granted foundational pride of place in thought. The sphere is the shape into which human subjectivity projects an image of a perfectly self-sufficient consciousness devoid of lack and desire. Indeed, in Lacan's view this projection proved so intellectually inhibiting that it forestalled for centuries the advent of the decidedly anti-intuitionist linguistic-semiotic, logical and mathematical forms of thought that together make up the wagon to which Lacan chose to hitch the destiny of both the Freudian tradition and his life of teaching.

In more general terms, Aristophanes' mythical anticipation of the Freudian castration complex leads for Lacan to an insightful and bitingly ironic assessment of the amorous ideals expounded in the previous speeches. Doubtless aware of the impression created by his literary notoriety, for instance, Aristophanes warns Eryximachus that he does not intend his contribution to be taken as "just a comedy directed at Pausanias and Agathon" (193b), known then as now to have been a romantic couple after a modified form of the pederastic ideal. (Agathon was around thirty years of age at the time of his victory at the Athenian tragedy festival and therefore long past his best before date as ideal boyfriend material.) Moreover, though he is the symposiast meant to follow Pausanias according to the order established at the outset of proceedings, Aristophanes is forced to postpone his intervention due to an "attack of hiccups" caused, Lacan suggests in agreement with the mainstream of interpretation, by a wild fit of laughter during Pausanias's speech (185c).

With these clues in mind, it is difficult not to discern the thick and also very contemporary sarcasm that imbues the comedian's ode to the bold and masculine young men who actively seek to gratify their lovers and who, "when grown up, end up as politicians"(192a). True to form, this aspect of Aristophanes' speech mounts a devastating satirical attack against the corruption, both moral and political, of the pederastic ideology to which not only Pausanias, but also a significant portion of the Athenian elite, subscribed. I would only add that the charge of homophobia here would simply be anachronistic, since though love in the elite fifth-century Athenian context of the *Symposium* was in no manner associated with heterosexuality, Aristophanes' irony targets a specific theory and practice of pederasty, the only discursively extant form of what we now call homosexuality in existence at the time.

I have shown how Aristophanes' myth of love's origin succeeds in correcting the delusion that man occupies a privileged position as observer of nature's complete and perfect form. Yet the comedian also introduces a properly romantic—and familiarly proto-modern—element to his discourse on love which clashes strangely with the acerbic tone of what precedes it. Pleading now to be taken in all seriousness, he enjoins us to be "well ordered in our behaviour towards the gods" lest "we be split up further, and [forced to] go around like figures in bas-relief on gravestones, sawn in half down the nose, like half-dice" (193a). Grown accustomed to his discourse's comedic register, we read the Aristophanic myth paying full attention to its ridiculous images of bouncing rounds of flesh and surgically relocated genitalia. Here, in sharp contrast, the reader is earnestly called upon to heed what can only be called the story's moral. Though he admits that it is only "the ideal," Aristophanes submits that the "human race can only achieve happiness if love reaches its conclusion, and each of us finds his loved one and restores his original nature" (193c).

The tragicomic tale gives way to a sincere, indeed melodramatic afterword, which forces a specific interpretation of the myth celebrating restoration, reconciliation, and wholeness. Indeed, "perfect happiness" (193d) can be achieved if we obey the gods and remain constant and monogamous in love. In the end, Aristophanes returns to his true conservative and comic—in the literal sense that things turn out all right—mode. If the gods forcibly separate us from a part of ourselves, then this is only to intensify the experience of the blissful return to our original nature, steeped in divine favor and moral virtue. This is not the idea of love in favor of which Lacan wants to argue, nor the one he sees implied by Socrates' response to Alcibiades. Aristophanes was on the right track in Lacan's view with his mythological anticipation of the Freudian castration complex. But then he falters badly, revert-ing back to a naively ingenuous—from Aristophanes' own perspective, though perhaps not Plato's—celebration of a sexual relation embodying a sovereign moral good.

We are therefore obliged to look elsewhere for Plato's idea of love as Lacan wants to construe it. This idea begins to emerge, though not without ambiguity, in the penultimate eulogy, the one voiced by the gathering's freshly decorated young raison d'être. At first glance, Agathon seems only to extend the *Symposium*'s apparent regression toward a more or less idiotic celebration of romantic love and con-ventional moral piety. His association of love with youth and beauty, coupled with his praise of love's power to nurture virtue, justice, and even poetic inspiration, comes off as hopelessly clichéd even to the casual contemporary reader. Taking the cue from Socrates' seemingly scornful dismissal, many commentators have considered Agathon's eulogy to articulate Plato's derisive view of the superficial and antiphilosophical nature of the Sophists' discourse, conventionally taken to have been a major influence on tragedy's smooth new superstar. Indeed, Plato portrays Agathon as a young man motivated not by a dialectical concern for truth, but rather by a desire to be recognized as an intellect to be reckoned with by all the right people, the crème de la crème of Athenian society. This society of the wise, incidentally, is precisely the crowd from which Socrates excludes himself as well as his students as he ironically lauds Agathon for his dramaturgical success.

Yet intriguingly, in spite of the tragedian's famous good looks and intimacy with all things superficially beautiful, Lacan insists on giving Agathon more credit, granting that his discourse is chock full of "ineptitude and nullity" (138), but adding that we are meant to view the smarmy upstart as in on the joke, at least to some degree, as "he doesn't really know himself what he's doing"(132). We are presented in Agathon's discourse in Lacan's view with yet another eulogy of love that cannot be taken at face value. Whether its declaimer is aware of it or not, this discourse singles out attributes of love that turn out to feature less than felicitous connotations.

That there might be more going on than meets the eye where Agathon is concerned is signaled right from the beginning of his speech. In support of his claim in favor of the god's youth and sensitivity, Agathon compares Eros to the goddess Delusion (*Atè*) as Homer's Agamemnon evokes her in *The Iliad*. Readers familiar with Lacan's extensive discussion of Sophocles' reference to *atè* in *Antigone* will know that this comparison does not bode well for love.[4]

According to Agamemnon, whom Agathon quotes in his speech, Delusion's feet are far too sensitive to tread on the ground, so she walks instead on the heads of men, causing significant discomfort, as one might well imagine. While for Homer the heads of mortals provide a perfectly suitable surface for Delusion's precious extremities, Agathon disagrees, countering that human skulls "are not at all soft" (195d-e) Eros seeks the requisite softness "in the characters and minds of gods and humans" instead, carefully stepping aside when his feet are presented with someone "with a tough character" (195e). Already there is an ironic edge at the most manifest level: the comparison of love to a divinity associated with disaster and catastrophe contrasts glaringly with the sweetness that Agathon explicitly attributes to Eros.

Additionally, however, the absurdist Homeric example, coupled with Agathon's literalist objection, is clearly designed to signal that we are far from the grave ethos of high tragedy. Whether we are meant to be laughing *at* Agathon as a representative of Athenian tragic discourse (there is of course much derision of tragedy in Plato) or rather *with* Agathon and his ambiguously ironic eulogy of Eros, it is clear that what we are witnessing is something far more consequential than the puerile celebration of amorous virtue that we encounter at first glance.

From the psychoanalytic perspective, for instance, Agathon goes on to evoke a number of themes which Lacan associates with love in its alienating and transferential dimension of demand. Indeed, Lacan argues that this is so to the extent that it becomes possible to read the tragedian's eulogy as a sustained ironic critique of the very ideology of love that it appears to support. The association of love with delusion and softness is already in synchrony with the themes of misrecognition and lure with which Lacan evokes the imaginary ego. In this sense, love is for those who are too "soft" to overcome an illusory but comforting ego's formidable powers of resistance to unconscious desire.

Additionally, Agathon ascribes grace of form to love's god, adding that his "beauty of complexion" sees him gravitate toward flowers; not just any flowers, mind you, but rather those that are "full of bloom and fragrance" (196a-b). Doubtless it is merely coincidental that, as we saw in chapter 1, Lacan chooses to illustrate the imaginary and symbolic mechanisms of the ego's psychical construction through a modification of the classic inverted vase experiment in physics, an experiment that produces the optical illusion of a bouquet of flowers in a vase. Yet it remains the case that the image of flowers in bloom evokes precisely the kind of eyecatching, pleasurable, and immobilizing contemplation of beauty that characterizes both Agathon's depiction of love's virtues and Lacan's thematic of the human ego as an illusory, virtual lure.

To put ourselves on less speculative ground, let's note that Agathon's premise that love nurtures the four so-called cardinal virtues more directly conveys the psychoanalytic notion of the ego as an object of misrecognition and instigator of resistance. In the realm of justice, love fosters respect for political convention according to Agathon; it elicits obedience to "whatever is agreed by mutual consent" as well as acceptance without complaint of what the laws of the polis "define as just" (196c). In accordance with the libidinal constancy that the Freudian pleasure principle works unsuccessfully to legislate, love also facilitates the second cardinal virtue—moderation—through its accomplishment of a "mastery of pleasures and desires" (196c). This mastery is also reflected in the third virtue of courage, which enables Eros to capture and dominate one of the most formidable of divine objects: Ares, god of war. Lastly, love's sympathy with wisdom provides artistic inspiration, turning everyone it touches into a poet. This proves to Agathon that the love-god is himself a master of the arts, literary and otherwise, since, as Agathon puts it—in striking opposition, be sure to note, to the Lacanian aphorism for authentic love beyond the transference—"you can't give someone else what you don't have" (196e). For Lacan, as we have seen, authentic love is indeed a gift, though one not of poetic inspiration, but rather of (a) nothing. The logical extension of Lacan's saying is that whoever views himself as having something worthy or lovable to give will eventually find himself impotent, unable to love. In sum, none of these elements of his speech would seem to furnish evidence that Agathon is anything but perfectly sincere as he offers his platitudinous outline of the virtuous effects of love.

The detail giving Lacan the clue that love on the contrary can be most calamitous lies in another quotation, the sole quotation in a eulogy overflowing with them whose source, it turns out, even the most assiduous classicists have failed to trace. In fact it is entirely possible that there is no such source, no tragedy lost in the dusts of time from which, as some have conjectured, Agathon quotes himself. It may not be too fanciful even to think that by inserting a quote recognizable as a fabrication by his contemporaries, Plato may have wished to index his irony here in an especially obvious way. At any rate Lacan sensibly points out that Agathon's metaphor for the peaceful rest that love is supposed to furnish—"windless calm at sea" (197c)—cannot have been a particularly reassuring one for the seafaring Athenians, for whom calm seas could signify only "that nothing is working, [that] the vessels are stranded at Aulis." To emphasize the incommodiousness of such a state of affairs, Lacan notes that "when this happens to you at sea, it's extremely annoying, as annoying as when it happens in bed" (132). The sections of Agathon's speech that precede these lines now appear in a quite different light.

Lacan's allusion to erectile dysfunction, as it is called in the age of Viagra and its proliferating pharmaceutical brethren, is far from gratuitous, for it signals precisely the kind of abatement of desire or return to libidinal equilibrium that Freud himself associates with the pleasure principle's particular and precarious brand of oceanic love. This love is precarious because it depends on the satisfaction delivered by a lost object recovered by means of hallucination and therefore not really, physically, there. Despite its relentless cheeriness, Agathon's encomium is for Lacan the first example in the *Symposium* of a fully derisory discourse. Its final rhetorical flourish, usually taken as a mockery of the sophistical excesses of the school of Gorgias to which Agathon is believed to have belonged, proffers for Lacan an onslaught of key terms which connote in their cultural context the hubristic and disorienting aspects of love, the ones that demonstrate how love is "never in its place" and "always out of season" (134). The irony here is especially thick: love is not the salubrious organizing principle of beauty and the four cardinal virtues, but rather the harbinger of chaos, what makes everything seem to go to hell. This is more or less what happens not only when Alcibiades arrives on the scene, but also in the analytic chamber when the transference rears its passionate head.

A Pregnant Beauty

As Agathon's eulogy concludes, the narrative voice of our reporter Apollodorus intervenes to spell out, perhaps for those disillusioned souls who have seen through the cracks of Agathon's precious speech, how love can be a source of edification. He opines that Agathon "had spoken in a way that reflected well on himself and on the god" (198a), leaving all symposiasts, seemingly oblivious to Agathon's possibly unintentional irony (we are given in any case no evidence to the contrary), feeling rather pleased with themselves. All except for Socrates, of course, who demonstrates that he is quite aware that Agathon, whose beauty has effects from which even he cannot claim immunity, is not in control of his own message. No doubt Socrates' response to Agathon's encomium is cutting: its method, the philosopher claims, proceeds as if "it doesn't matter very much" if "what you say isn't true"; as if what really matters is merely giving "the appearance of praising love" (198e). Adding insult to injury, Socrates asks Phaedrus for permission to question Agathon, leading the young tragedian in classic Socratic fashion to admit that if the god Love desires beauty and goodness, it follows that Love itself can be neither beautiful nor good. Despite the sternness of his rebuke, however, Socrates admits to feelings of shame at the prospect of following Agathon's apparently wildly successful speech with his own, confessing that he is tempted to run away, aware that he "couldn't even get close" to the "degree of beauty" in Agathon's speech (198b). It would be too easy here to assume that Socrates' modest confession is merely another aspect of his ironic appraisal of Agathon's speech. According to this interpretation, we are meant to understand that Socrates' assessment of Agathon's contribution as a tough act to follow is a clue that it is in fact anything but. One even occasionally finds appended to this argument the idea that Socrates offers Diotima's teaching as a concession to Agathon in compensation for the humiliation of the earlier cutting assessment. Yet I also want to argue that it would be a much bigger mistake to think the opposite: that Socrates' shame is caused by an unfeigned sense of inferiority, by the voice of an internal critic telling him that he could not possibly live up to the standard set by the young literary star. We know that this cannot be the case because of the ample evidence Plato provides showing that Socrates, despite his evident attraction, has sized Agathon up to be a pretentious and social-climbing intellectual pretty-boy, all glitzy sophistical bluster and no truthful dialectical substance.

As we saw in chapter 1, the affect of shame for Lacan is not caused by the kind of melancholic and inhibitory self-beratement that arises when you compare yourself to a perceived better. Rather, shame occurs in consequence of our painful acknowledgment that the Other inevitably fails to live up to the expectations that we unconsciously place upon it. Shame is a sort of objective correlative of jouissance, an involuntary sign made manifest in the body indicating that the idealized Other upon whom we rely for our self-concept has collapsed, paving the way for the eruption of obscene, asocial drive satisfaction. Socrates' shame, that is to say, results from the disjunction that separates his investment in the tragedian's illustrious good looks and newfound cultural prestige from his awareness of the embarrassing irony of Agathon's discourse, an irony that for Plato as for Socrates comes at least partly at the tragic poet's own expense. As we will shortly see, it is no coincidence that it is this same affect of shame that most patently marks Alcibiades' testimonial of his futile attempt to provoke Socrates into behaving as the *erastēs* that he desires him to be. Shame is thus the consequence of the incompatibility of enjoyment and sociality, of the impossibility of accessing jouissance in a purely private place at a remove from the constraints on sexual freedom imposed by the social relation.

We are therefore forced to the conclusion that Socrates' appraisal of Agathon's eulogy is indeed cutting. This harshness, much discussed in the classicists' commentaries, cannot be unrelated to the fact that Socrates, as Alcibiades' impassioned speech will make abundantly clear, remains far from indifferent to Agathon's powers of attraction. As we have already seen, Socrates reproaches Agathon for giving merely the appearance of praising Love. Noting the homonymy between the names of the mythical Gorgon figure and Gorgias, bright light of the Sophist school to whose tradition the style of Agathon's discourse is held to belong, Socrates naughtily implies that this discourse, in its impressive but diversionary flourishes, has the effect of turning its audience to stone (198c). Agathon's idea of love for Socrates is at bottom concerned with giving off the right appearance, about saying whatever is necessary to ensure that one can see oneself flatteringly through the Other's approving look. By making the god called Love "look as fine and good as possible" (199a), as Socrates puts it, you can bask in his reflected glow. As one might by now expect, however, there is a price to be paid. Philosophically speaking, the effort to construct in language a flattering self-image can only bring the work of the Socratic science of the signifier to a grinding halt.

Socrates' critical assessment of Agathon's eulogy argues outright what has only up to this point in the *Symposium* been hinted at between the lines: love is necessarily premised on lack. Whereas the previous eulogists' offerings were concerned with establishing the provenance of Love in accordance with generic convention—"whether Love is the child *of* a particular mother or father," to be precise—Socrates chooses instead to redirect attention toward what, "something or nothing," it is "Love's nature to be love *of*" (199d). Having led Agathon to acknowledge that love is surely love of something, Socrates goes on to demonstrate that, like the rich man who wants to remain rich, the general rule that "desire and love are directed at what you don't have" (200e) holds true even for those who are presently in possession of their object. That is to say, what is desired in such cases is this object's "continued presence in the future" (200d).

This aspect of Socrates' argument is crucial from our psychoanalytic perspective because it establishes that human desire features a timeless dimension, one which corresponds precisely to the property that Lacan attributes to his object of desire, namely that it is always something more, something other, than whatever temporal object in the physical world we choose to embody it. Psychoanalysis agrees with Socrates that desire is correlative to dissatisfaction, since the object's presence can only be made manifest through its nonmaterialization in every possible object of experience. As Socrates shows, this truism also holds for the very notion of time, since the future by definition has yet to be experienced. In this sense, love as Socrates formulates it reveals its kinship with the illustrious Platonic idea, which similarly remains irreducible to any of its incarnations as they appear to human sense perception. The idea, too, resonates with desire as psychoanalysis conceptualizes it in its transcendence of all phenomena on the level of their availability to consciousness as data for the senses.

Yet it is not until Socrates ceases to speak in his own voice, effacing his grave philosophical persona to relate his teacher Diotima's quasi-mystical vision, that we are provided with the *Symposium*'s ultimate formulation of love's complicity with the ambition of the idea in its most idealized, and therefore transferential, form. In effect, Diotima provides a kind of how-to manual for those who seek after love in its absolute form: the contemplation, as she figures it, of beauty in itself. Considering that his professions of knowledge are famously restricted to love's relatively modest purview, the fact that this vision issues forth from Socrates in this strange transsexual ventriloquist mode might seem to present a conundrum. Why should the philosopher cede the floor to a singular but obscure goddess absent from all extant fragments of classical Greek culture precisely when the time comes for the most complete formulation of the only subject he claims to know?

Lacan's answer to this question advances the view that this peculiar move serves as confirmation *avant la lettre* of the psychoanalytic premise of an underlying disjunction between love and knowledge. As subject of the unconscious I am incapable of knowing whence I love; of directly—for such knowledge can be gained indirectly through an analyst's interpretations—bringing to consciousness the psychic structures that make up my *Idealich* and *Ichideal*. In this sense Diotima speaks through Socrates as if from his unconscious, from a methodological location cleanly severed from philosophical dialectic. This no doubt explains why Lacan does not dismiss the notion that Diotima represents in effect "the woman in [Socrates]" (147).

More rigorously, Lacan connects the text's shift in enunciation from the austere dialectician to the enigmatic priestess to a change of register from *epistēmē* to *mythos*, that is, from a formal or logical emphasis on the negative relation between signifiers to an altogether different, substantive concern for the signified, for presence and meaning. This distinction between registers, incidentally, may equally be applied to the terms *metonymy* and *metaphor* as Lacan appropriates them from structuralist linguistics, the former referring to the endless substitution of signifiers that articulate desire, the latter to what Lacan calls the signification of love. For Lacan, therefore, the transition from *epistēmē* to *mythos* is precisely equivalent to a transition from metonymy (desire) to metaphor (demand-side—transferential, that is—love) as he defines these nonparenthesized terms. In this sense the transition can only be viewed psychoanalytically as an instance of regression, as an example of what is to be avoided as one confronts the transference event.

We have seen how love as Diotima conceives it consists in the apprehension of beauty in itself. Crucially, this beauty for her remains absolutely independent of—unrelated to and unmediated by—anything outside itself. In Diotima's own words, beauty appears to the subject of ultimate love not "in the form of a face or hands or any part of the body," nor "as a specific account or piece of knowledge," nor yet as "being anywhere in something else," but rather "in itself and by itself, always single in form" (211a-b). Diotima's love, unlike Lacan's, is therefore nothing like a signifier. For this reason, Lacan argues, her teaching requires presentation through means other than Socratic method. Whereas, as we will shortly see, Alcibiades' transference-love makes him desperate to provoke Socrates into issuing a sign of love, an action that would unveil this love's dependence on, indeed causation by, uncertainty about what the Other wants, Diotima's vision of pure beauty-love, in all its presentist and self-sufficient certainty, requires no such reassuring symbolic proof. Lacan generalizes that "we see myths appear" in Plato "when they are needed to make up for the deficiency in what can be ascertained dialectically," that is to say by following the strict logic of the signifier to the exclusion of everything else (147). We can conclude that for Lacan's Plato love lies beyond the limits of possible knowledge; it aims at a certainty that simply cannot be established within the signifying system in its operation at the level of consciousness.

We are now in a position to examine the pivotal elements of Diotima's teaching. Before she gets to revealing the "mysteries" (210a) with which we now associate her name, the priestess begins her discourse in the conventional way adopted by Agathon: by establishing the love-god's parentage, in this instance through the story of his birth from the union of Poverty and Resource. The details of this narrative are worth considering more closely because they offer crucial insights into Lacan's understanding of the problematic of love, insights that Diotima will to all appearances forget immediately thereafter, as if through Freudian secondary revision. Appropriately enough, the occasion for the fateful meeting of Love's progenitors is a feast of the gods in celebration of the birth of Aphrodite. Evidently suffering from the consequences of her name, Poverty has approached the venue's gate to beg "as people do at feasts." Resource catches her eye in the garden of Zeus, where he has retreated and fallen asleep after drinking too much nectar, as people evidently also do at feasts. The conception of Eros then takes place. Diotima depicts Poverty's action as a deliberately devised plan to "relieve her lack of resources," and the offspring of this union of opportunism and inebriation comes to feature attributes of both his parents. Like his mother, Love is "always poor" and therefore "always lives in a state of need," says Diotima. And though no evidence is provided to show that Resource was even awake either before or during his conception, we are told that like his father Love "schemes to get hold of beautiful and good things." Some further qualities and aptitudes of Love should also be retained: "neither mortal nor immortal," Love "desires knowledge and is resourceful in getting it," being "a lifelong lover of wisdom" and "clever at using magic, drugs and sophistry" (203b-e).

Numerous observations can be made concerning this richly suggestive passage. First, the myth associates love with the coming together of conscious intent and obliviousness, suggesting a phenomenon composed of both (active) conscious and (passive) unconscious parts, and linking the former with the qualities of lack and need. Second, love targets knowledge or wisdom but is itself devoid of them. It is remarkably skilled at acquiring these virtues, and crucially, its skills include deception and the capacity to access states of altered consciousness. Further, Love's status is an intermediate one between mortal and divine. As such, he is classified as one of the spirits, whose function it is, according to Diotima, to "carry messages from humans to gods and from gods to humans." These gods "do not make direct contact" with mortals, she continues, but rather "communicate and converse with [them] (whether awake or asleep) entirely through the medium of spirits" (202d-203a).

If we recall that one of Lacan's central theses about classical Greek culture is that the gods operate on the level of what he calls the real, then the affinity between the activity of these Diotimean spirits and the psychoanalyst's "unconscious structured like a language" thesis becomes quite startling. Though Diotima's final vision will effectively run amok through these insights, it remains the case that the first portion of her discourse suggests in a truly proto-Freudian vein that love—in its transferential mode; as the failure that triggers the desperate reissuing of demand—emerges in the form of a message from the real. Further, this message is communicated through "spirits" which begin in this light to show an uncanny resemblance to the signifiers of unconscious desire, the ones that haphazardly surface in our everyday utterances from some "divine" region beyond our conscious control.

With all of this in mind, it comes as no surprise that Lacan shows tremendous interest in these details of Diotima's discourse. To be sure, the love-god's issuance from both his mother's self-interested machinations and his father's drunkenness evokes the Freudian theme of the subject's division between the ego ideal and the repressed *Vorstellungsrepräsentanz*; in ordinary language, the fact that we pay for our capacity to develop a positive idea of ourselves through the censorship of (the representation of) a fantasy satisfying taboo desires. Further, Love's love of wisdom recalls the transference as expressed in Lacan's properly epistemological formulation, according to which we are tied to the Other through the mechanism of a supposition of knowledge— the *sujet supposé savoir*—whose power over us paradoxically increases as we become more skeptical that this Other in fact knows anything we do not already know. Finally, Diotima's myth of the birth of Eros conveys the time-honored theme of love's connection with illusion: the quest for love and the virtue of wisdom are both premised on a mistake, a misrecognition. The famous Socratic exhortation to "know thyself" acquires in this light a pleasingly anti-contemporary, paradoxical twist: true knowledge rests on the acknowledgment of the illusion of self-knowledge, of knowledge that would pertain to the self in its cherished particularity. The road to truth, in other words, can only be blocked by today's ambient neo-Stoic concern for the self and its cultivation, for the buttressing of the self against all that which threatens to erode its foundations.

While this first portion of Diotima's teaching is rich in provocative implication, sketching out as it does a pre-Freudian mythology of a subject divided by the effects of signifiers in the unconscious, for Lacan it only goes downhill from here. This unfortunate regression is enabled in Diotima's teaching by the transition from a negative idea of love linked to an absence of virtue to a positive idea premised on the capture and eternal possession of pure, absolute, and undivided being. Diotima's discourse begins its downhill slide when she claims that all beings are "pregnant in body and in mind." Love's object is not merely the passive contemplation of beauty, but rather an active "giving birth in beauty." In this light we can understand why "when a pregnant creature comes close to something beautiful it becomes gentle and joyfully relaxed, and gives birth and reproduces" (206b-e). Here we are reminded of the release or absence of libidinal tension associated with the death drive in psychoanalysis. In Diotima's discourse as in psychoanalysis, this drive is linked with a decidedly nonsexual or nonbiological reproduction, one whose aim is not to propagate the species but rather, *contra* psychoanalysis, to foster ideals of virtue and deliver the sanction of the gods. In Lacanian terms, Diotima effects what we might call a domestication of the death drive: she constructs a fantasy according to which there is no unconscious real of desire, no jouissance beyond symbolization that forever separates the pure drive from all possible conscious representation. Jouissance, the concept that for Lacan cannot be divorced from the ruin or undoing of consciousness, is for Diotima a sign for the completion or perfectibility of consciousness and the triumphant extermination of desire. Psychoanalytically speaking, the Diotimean contemplation of beauty in itself offers a final suturing of the wound of castration, of the painful scars left by Zeus's punitive incisions in Aristophanes' altogether different myth of love.

Though she accurately illustrates the involvement of the beautiful in a dimension beyond the cycle of life and death, Diotima misidentifies this dimension as the seat of knowledge and virtue, one which it is our ethical duty to occupy. In Diotima's view, immortal beauty is not a sort of indexation of death-bearing jouissance as it is for Lacan, but rather a function of the ego that works to reconcile the self to itself. Beauty becomes an object that we can fully integrate into our self-concept, producing a happy, self-sufficient subjective perfection not unlike Aristophanes' bouncing bundles of joy. As Martha Nussbaum nicely puts it, the *erōs* that targets Diotimean beauty amounts to a "desire to be a being without any contingent occurrent desires." It is, in other words, a meta- or "second order desire that all desires should be cancelled."[5]

Whereas the beautiful for Lacan is "what guides the subject in his relation with death insofar as he is at once distanced and guided by the immortal," for Diotima it becomes the allegedly attainable "goal of the pilgrimage" on the "path towards being" (156–57). No doubt many readers will find these comments irritatingly cryptic. I suggest nonetheless that they offer a coherent speculative thesis concerning the Platonic view of beauty's function. This thesis not only reinforces what Lacan argues in his "Kant with Sade" essay, but also rigorously parallels the (partial) dispelling of illusion—fantasy traversal, in Lacanian terminology—that can accompany the experience and interpretation of the transference. For Lacan, the function of the beautiful in human psychic life is to shield us from death-bearing jouissance; it is what stops us from being consumed by the object of the drive, from succumbing to fantasies of annihilating, or being annihilated by, the Other. To the extent that, as Diotima prescribes, we become fascinated by beauty's lure, however, we remain blissfully but dangerously unaware of what beauty serves to conceal.

The danger lies in the inconvenient truth that we cannot help but suffer from the repeated frustration of our passionate attempts to climb to the top of love's ladder, to extend the corny Diotimean metaphor. The essence of beauty therefore corresponds to nothing like the brilliantly transcendent vision of knowledge and virtue that the priestess wants to see in it. Instead, the beautiful makes manifest the prospect of subjectivity's terminal collapse, the end of psychic life as such. Even more consequentially for the *Symposium*'s interpretation, however, Lacan wants to argue not only that Plato is fully aware of this danger that beauty presents, but also that Plato wants his reader to know that he knows. Evidence for this is offered in Socrates' *faux-naïf* responses to Diotima's view of love's ambition of immortality. These responses range from the subtle—"Well, Diotima, you're very wise, but are things really as you say?"—to the explicit, as in Socrates' choice of simile in the comment that immediately follows. Conveying the remarkable but suspect extent of Diotima's conviction, Socrates relates (as recalled by Apollodorus): "like a perfect sophist, [Diotima] said, 'you can be sure about this' " (208b-c). Declared enemies of Socratic dialectic, the Sophists first voiced the allegations that would eventually lead to Socrates' execution for corrupting the Athenian youth. For Lacan, in the final analysis, Diotima represents the unconscious on the level of wish fulfillment, of a willful blindness to the path toward the real that the event of transference serves to indicate, if only to those who know where to look.

The Part of Love

Now, surely it is not coincidental that it is precisely at the moment of Diotima's most *recherché* of formulations of her idea of the beautiful that we hear the bacchanalian flute music signaling the entrance of Alcibiades and his co-revelers. In Lacanian terms, we might say, the stage is set for the return of the real precisely at the moment of the most extreme imaginary alienation. Alcibiades' sudden disruption of proceedings suggests the "aggressivity" that results from egoic mis-recognition; it is a form of acting out which can only be a symptom of the operation of the transference. In Alcibiades' confession, according to Lacan, Plato provides the most arresting and illustrative testimonial to the transference's entrancing effects in the entirety of the Western cultural tradition.

Narratively speaking, we are immediately presented upon Alcibiades' entrance with a more or less classic triangle of (modern) love—the only idiosyncrasy, I suppose, is that it is composed entirely of men—involving the new arrival, the famous philosopher, and the freshly decorated tragedian in complex relations of admiration, passion, and jealousy. From here on in, Plato's narrative will demonstrate how, contrary to romantic convention's faith in the sexual relation, "there must be three for love," as Lacan suggests (162). As he takes a seat beside Agathon, adorning him with ribbons in honor of his victory, Alcibiades fails to notice Socrates on his opposite side. Made uncomfortably aware of his presence, Alcibiades proceeds to complain bitterly of Socrates' jealous objections to his mingling with other men, accusing the philosopher of playing his "usual trick of turning up suddenly" where he is least expected and, referring to Agathon, of having plotted to lie beside "the most attractive man in the room" (213c).

In the spirit of the disruption caused by Alcibiades' rude party crashing, Eryximachus, noting that the prestigious new symposiast has yet to offer a speech, proposes to switch things up, substituting for the eulogies of Eros in general a rather more provocative game. According to the new rules, each participant at the conclusion of his speech can order the person on his right to do whatever he wants. For Lacan, this shift from Diotima's emphasis on the vanishing duality of the aspiring initiate's identification with sovereign beauty to the tripartite quality of this new chain-like procession of demands (each symposiast receives an instruction from one neighbor and gives one to the next) signals a transition from the imaginary to the symbolic registers. Whereas the subject who ascends love's ladder proceeds "on the path of identification" (168) toward the achievement of a reflection back to himself of his virtuous self-image, the symposiast following Eryximachus's rules can only have the (verbal) message given to his neighbor relayed to someone else, and therefore taken beyond his purview, removed from his control.

For psychoanalysis, castration is the psychical mark of this transition from imaginary to symbolic orders, and its consequence is the "loss" of the object—we lose an object we never in fact had—that then serves to cause desire. With this in mind it makes abundant sense that Lacan would read Alcibiades' depiction of his passion for Socrates as a kind of précis of the object relation: the difficult psychical predicament, that is to say, under which the object places us as subjects. Speaking of this object, Alcibiades' effort to come to terms with his transference passion pivots around the central image—note how he tells us that it is by means of images that he will sing Socrates' praises, images that will not ridicule or deceive but rather "bring out the truth" (215a)—of the *agalmata* that he sees scintillating inside his mentor's deceptively unattractive body. Classicists don't seem to know with certainty exactly what this term referred to in classical Greek culture. In its general usage, in fact, the term's meaning seems to have been close to "image." Here, however, the sense appears to relate more specifically to a shining or jewel-like object. At any rate, Alcibiades refers to "statues of Silenus," leader of the satyrs—creatures, incidentally, tied in various ways to the figure of Socrates—which, when opened up, are shown to contain "statues of the gods inside" (215b).[6]

Socrates is like such statues, Alcibiades proceeds to explain, not only because of the hidden treasures of wisdom that he carries inside him, but also because he has powers of seduction comparable to those of Marsyas. Now Marsyas, we know, is a noteworthy satyr who by means of his flute music was known to "cast a spell over people" (215c). Only Socrates, of course, creates such effects of intoxication with his bewitching dialectical interrogations instead. Alcibiades' description of the almost mad passion that Socrates inspires in him stresses the properly causal function of the jewel-like objects dissimulated beneath his ugly appearance. Significantly, with the entrance of Alcibiades we haven't entirely moved on from Diotima's obsession with beauty: the secret figures of which he speaks are said to sparkle and shine in a way at least as alluring as was the case with the undivided object of Diotima's virtuous vision. But whereas Diotima's image is a purely reflective one—it occurs entirely within the realm of the visible, dissolving the distinction between what sees and what is seen—Socrates' *agalmata* are withdrawn from view, tucked away behind a surface seemingly designed to spoil the aesthetic appetites of vision. This is the paradox of Alcibiades' testimony: the truthfulness of the image of beauty is directly correlated to the fact that for most it remains invisible. To make a philosophical comparison, it fails to materialize in a way amenable to the universal communicability that serves as the criterion of the beautiful in Kantian aesthetics, for instance.

Alcibiades declares to everyone that he, and he alone, can see Socrates' hidden treasures perfectly well. Yet it is also clear that this availability to his perception in no way satisfies the desire to which the treasures give rise. The *Symposium*'s emphasis on the properly subjective aspect of amorous passion has generated what I now want to claim is the most ideologically significant discordance within the dialogue's reception. A comparison of Lacan's view of the Platonic *agalmata* as figures for the drive's partial object with Martha Nussbaum's rival interpretation of them as indications of desire's power to personalize or individuate the Other will allow me to define two starkly different views of love and, in so doing, bring further clarity to what I think Lacan wants to say about the transference. Lacan for his part wants to qualify Alcibiades' passion as a symptom of love's inevitable failure insofar as love functions as an assertive plea for the recognition of the self in its difference or specificity. In contrast, Nussbaum reads the expression of this passion as a philosophical rebuttal of "Platonism" (though clearly not the same Platonism as Lacan's, or Badiou's for that matter): the valorization of idea, mind, and generality over sense, body, and particularity. But whereas for Nussbaum this particularity relates to an idea of the individual as a uniquely whole person, desire's particularity for Lacan is inseparable from the partiality of the object that causes it. This partiality has the effect of attenuating desire's concern for the person, granting desire in this way its attribute of abstract generality, one which inherently can be universalized to all person-subjects in spite of their obvious and manifold empirical or phenomenological differences from one another.

Before getting to the specifics of Lacan's contention about the role of the partial object in the transference, however, it will be helpful first to spend some time acquainting ourselves with the details of Nussbaum's remarkably subtle interpretation of Alcibiades' entrance. For Nussbaum, Alcibiades' drunken interruption of the banquet signals a transition not from the imaginary or symbolic to the real, as Lacan's interpretation implies, but rather from the austerely permanent ideality of philosophical transcendence—the aforementioned Nussbaumian "Platonism"—to the sensuous fleshiness of a contingent and vulnerable human embodiment. In this vein she takes Alcibiades' wish to seat himself next to the smarmy Agathon as an ironic subversion of Diotima's ambition to attain the *agathon*, the "repeatable universal Good" (*Fragility*, 185). We have seen how Lacan relates the shift from abstract eulogies to speeches of praise respectively to the imaginary and symbolic registers. Nussbaum for her part chooses to interpret this textual turn not only as further indication of Alcibiades' concern for experiential specificity, but also as a sign of the properly poetic and rhetorical, as opposed to formal and logical, qualities of his discourse.

> Asked to speak about love, [Alcibiades] has chosen to speak of a particular love; no definitions or explanations of the nature of anything, but just a story of a particular passion for a particular contingent individual. Asked to make a speech, he gives us the story of his own life: the understanding of *erōs* he has achieved through his own experience. . . . And, what is more, this story conveys its truths using images or likenesses—a poetic practice much deplored by the Socrates of the *Republic*, since images lack the power to provide us with true general accounts or explanations of essences. (185)

Here one can certainly quibble with Nussbaum on a point of plot. As we have seen, Eryximachus is the one who formally chooses to change the rules of the game; therefore, Alcibiades' confession surfaces in response to the desire of another symposiast. In fact, almost immediately after declaring himself the new master of ceremonies, Alcibiades explicitly cedes command over proceedings to Eryximachus, as if further to underscore how his inebriation—not only by drink, but also by his wild passion for Socratic discourse—causes him to subsume his own volition under an alien will. This may seem like a piddling qualification; yet Nussbaum's formulation lends a degree of subjective sovereignty to Alcibiades' discourse that in my view it does not have.

On the contrary, all the evidence suggests that Alcibiades is compelled by an irrational passion to speak the way he does; his speech is as far removed as could be from the self-consciously materialist subversion of the pretensions of a putative Socratic idealism that Nussbaum wants to see in it. For my purposes, however, the true significance of the quote lies in its articulation of what I want to call Nussbaum's liberalist personalism, which blinds her to the truth that Alcibiades' outburst manifests the transferential failure of love. As I have indicated, this outburst for Nussbaum rather bespeaks desire's dependence on, and determination by, subjective experience. This view leads Nussbaum to cast love's essence as a concern for the integrity—sanctity, even—of the Other in its singular personhood, its psychological individuality. Viewed in this light, the comparison to the Silenus statue conveys through what in its own context was an object of everyday experience "something of the feeling of what it is like to want and to want to know [Socrates]" (185).

More precisely, Nussbaum wants to specify the *erōs* she wishes to define through reference to the person of both its subject and its object. This means that desire's particularity arises from two facts: it is experienced by Alcibiades and inspired by Socrates. Someone else's desire for Socrates will be different in the same way that Alcibiades' desire for someone else will be as well. Because it is not "repeatable," then, this desire fails the test of philosophical legitimacy as defined by Socratic method as Nussbaum construes it. In accordance with numerous love clichés, Alcibiades' all-consuming desire for Socrates is an immediate and once-in-a-lifetime event. Though it is clear that Alcibiades continues to suffer its effects years after its onset, both the occurrence and the qualities of this love are inherently unique. And, crucially for my purposes as I will shortly detail, this uniqueness pertains to Alcibiades and Socrates equally, such that Alcibiades' *erōs* becomes for Nussbaum the very guarantor of not only the difference of one from the other, but also of each from everyone else. This is precisely what explains for Nussbaum why Alcibiades

cannot describe [his] passion or its object in general terms, because his experience of love has happened to him this way only once, in connection with an individual who is seen by him to be like nobody else in the world. The entire speech

is an attempt to communicate that uniqueness. . . . He
mentions Socrates' virtues in the process of describing the
wholeness of a unique personality. (187)

I want to suggest in sharp contrast to this view that the uniqueness Nussbaum considers so integral to the *Symposium*'s alternative,
non-Diotimean concept of desire refuses to sit well with Plato's
choice of the *agalmata* image, which she weirdly insists on seeing as
emblematic of desire's concern for the integrity of the person. For if
Socrates contains or envelops these precious treasures, as Alcibiades
makes abundantly clear, then they can hardly stand as a figure for his
subjective wholeness. Here Lacan's view of *agalma* as a figure for the
object's partiality—its status as less than, as subtracted from, whatever
whole of which it might once have been part—makes considerably more
sense. The *agalmata* cannot be signs of personal essence because they
are removable from their container, and are therefore uncannily supple-
mentary, *alien* to their host. The precious object that my lover sees in
my person is "in me more than me," as Lacan says; it is a quality that
disturbingly exceeds and subverts my personhood.

Further, if Socrates' *agalmata* are hidden inside of him, if their
visibility requires that he be "opened up," then they are not clearly
visible, certainly not to anyone other than Alcibiades. The *Symposium*
repeatedly stresses in fact that Alcibiades' passion is inextricably linked
to the fact that only he, as far as we know, has ever seen them, and
only on one miraculous occasion: "I don't know if any of you have
seen the statues inside Socrates when he's serious and is opened up,"
he asks his fellow party people. "But I saw them once," he continues,
"and they seemed to me so divine, golden, so utterly beautiful and
amazing, that—to put it briefly—I had to do whatever Socrates told
me to" (216e–217a). These comments would imply a strange concept
of personhood intelligible to only one privileged other, and certainly
not to the self: Socrates squarely denies that he contains anything like
what Alcibiades says he sees in him.

In a moment we will need to address in more detail the peculiar
and important effects of this discovery on Alcibiades' will. For the
time being, however, note that Alcibiades' perception of the *agalmata*
gives rise to such an inebriating passion that he basically loses the
ability to act according to his own volition. To wit: "I've been struck
and bitten by the words of philosophy," he exclaims, "which cling on
more fiercely than a snake and make someone do and say all sorts of

things" (218a). If, as appears to be the case, Nussbaum is motivated by a properly humanistic desire to see in Alcibiades' love for Socrates a psychological concern for individuality—no doubt an inappropriately proto-modern one—then surely the *agalmata*, by virtue of both their excessive, detachable, even alien relation to their host, as well as their capacity to offer only fleeting appearances causing a loss of self-control in those whom they most selectively address, are at minimum a problematic choice for its textual figuration. Contradicting Nussbaum's interpretation of it, Alcibiades' confession teaches the lesson that despite my best efforts I can never quite rest assured that my partner loves me "for myself," nor can I definitively ascribe what attracts me in my partner to any describable quality of his personhood.

Love, Ménage à Trois

My sense in fact is that Nussbaum's liberal humanism causes her to interpret Alcibiades' discourse in a way that is both historically and philosophically unfounded. Yet she is much too skilled and sophisticated a reader of classical Greek culture not to offer remarkable insights. I want now to suggest that she is on much firmer ground in her appraisal of Alcibiades' reaction to Socrates' refusal to comply with his demands. This discussion will set the stage for my exposition of how Lacan's assessment of Socrates' response to Alcibiades' confession brings clarity to Lacan's conceptualization of the transference.

I propose to review the details of the new arrival's indiscreet reportage as a means of first contextualizing that discussion. Alcibiades pulls no punches as he relates the story of his encounter with Socrates. Back in the day when he first came under his philosophical mentor's spell—a time, he specifies, when he was "incredibly proud" of his "good looks"(217a)—Alcibiades undertook to seduce Socrates on the assumption that, if Socrates "gratified" him, he would be in a position—the double entendre is here both à propos and unavoidable—to absorb the full extent of the philosopher's teaching. Realizing that the success of his plan requires them to be alone, Alcibiades develops the habit of inviting Socrates to the gymnasium, where they "exercised and wrestled together on many occasions with no one around" (217c).

When the disciplined Socrates fails to make a sexual move on any of these occasions, however, Alcibiades decides to adopt a more direct tactic, proceeding to invite his would-be lover to an intimate dinner.

Finally, on the occasion of the second such dinner, Alcibiades succeeds in distracting Socrates through conversation well into the night, such that by the time their discourse comes to an end it is too late for the philosopher to return home. Getting right to the point, Alcibiades directly propositions his companion, only to have Socrates flatly reject him by comparing the proposed exchange to a trade of "gold for bronze" (219a): the gold of philosophical knowledge, that is, for the bronze of sexual gratification. And thus, on that fateful and traumatic occasion Socrates "completely triumphed over my good looks," Alcibiades complains, "and despised, scorned and insulted them." "When I got up the next morning," he concludes in unsubtle style, "I had no more *slept with* Socrates than if I'd been sleeping with my father or elder brother" (219c-d).

Alcibiades' main reproach against Socrates is that he tricks his students into thinking he is sexually interested in them only prudishly to withhold "gratification." Simply put, Socrates is for Alcibiades the consummate tease. Nussbaum's appraisal of the effects of this withholding of consummation insightfully identifies its importance for the love relation and accords with Lacan's view. "Alcibiades begins as the beautiful *erōmenos*," she writes, "but seems to end as the active *erastēs*, while Socrates, apparently the *erastēs*, becomes the *erōmenos*" (188). Indeed, Alcibiades says as much himself when he alludes to two fellow victims of the alleged Socratic trap: "[H]e deceives them into thinking he's their lover and then turns out to be the loved one instead of the lover" (222b).

To be perfectly precise, Nussbaum's assessment of the dynamic accords with Lacan's to the extent that it is taken to qualify Alcibiades' desire: Alcibiades begins as Socrates' beloved (everyone knows that Socrates was once a lover of Alcibiades in the "Platonic" sense, we are told on a number of occasions), but winds up as Socrates' active, desiring lover. The assessment remains incomplete if we consider it from Socrates' perspective, however, since Socrates dramatically denies in response to Alcibiades' praise that there is anything inside him remotely worthy of love. Further, if we are to follow Lacan in viewing Alcibiades' confession as an outline of the logic of transference, then we must also see in this reversal of function something more consequential than the mere "confusion about sexual roles" (188) that Nussbaum sees in it. Indeed, the frustration of Alcibiades' demand to be recognized by Socrates as his object of desire is both catalyst and symptom of the transference as Lacan wishes to conceptualize it.

Two conditions must be met in order for the event of transference to occur. First, an especially idealized Other—an ego ideal—must be present, one assumed to be uniquely qualified to recognize our being, to articulate the knowledge of which this being is held to be composed. "You're the only lover I've ever had who's good enough for me," Alcibiades tells Socrates (218c). In the Freudian terminology with which we acquainted ourselves in chapter 1, Socrates is a perfect candidate for Alcibiades' "stereotype plate." Second, this worthy Other must *withhold* the sign of its love. "But you seem to be too shy to talk about it to me," Alcibiades complains (218c). The Other's nonresponse then causes the anxiety-ridden subject to attempt to provoke the Other into issuing this sign. The shift in function from *erōmenos* to *erastēs* on the side of the *subject* in its relation to the Other is therefore a structurally necessary consequence of love in the dimension of demand. This is so because the Other is by definition incapable of providing a fully satisfactory response to love's insistent call.

Further, it is crucial to remark that this shift in function is in effect the reverse of the one that occurs in what Lacan calls the signification or metaphor of love. Here "the function of the *erastēs* takes the place of the function of the *erōmenos*" on the side of the *object* (53). In other words, in love as it is here defined the desiring subject becomes the love object of the former beloved, who is now transformed into a lover. In this precise sense, the transference, properly speaking, and love (in the sense of Freudian transference love) are phenomena which depend on logically opposite structures. We can conclude from this that the transference is the response of the unconscious to the unavoidable interruption of the love relation of narcissism, one that (potentially—the causality is not necessary) forces the subject into actively assuming (the Other's) desire. This means that in order to deal properly with the transference the subject must acknowledge that she does not have what the Other wants, indeed that the enigmatic object of the Other's desire will remain forever indiscernible, always out of reach.

Though she fails to appreciate how integral to the experience of love is this forcing of desire in the transference, Nussbaum nicely illuminates how the frustration of amorous demand has the effect of inserting the subject into the social world, even if this insertion, at least in its symptomatic aspect, tends to be accompanied by disorientation and violence. Like Lacan, Nussbaum reads Alcibiades' testimonial as evidence that he has been wrenched by his passion from the role of Socrates' beloved, his *erōmenos*. Citing Kenneth Dover's analysis of Greek erotic painting,[7] Nussbaum notes that two taboos govern the representation of the beloved in this tradition: "he will not allow any opening of his body to be penetrated," she summarizes, nor will he "allow the arousal of his own desire to penetrate the lover." Indeed, Dover's work underscores how the classical Greek pictorial tradition is rife with representations of lovers affectionately touching the faces and genitals of beautiful boys who nevertheless, quite implausibly, display no visible signs of sexual arousal. "Though the object of importunate solicitation," Nussbaum relates, the *erōmenos* "is himself not in need of anything beyond himself. He is unwilling to let himself be explored by the other's needy curiosity, and he has, himself, little curiosity about the other. He is something like a god," she concludes (provocatively in the present context), "or the statue of a god" (188).

Thus, Socrates has the effect of preventing Alcibiades from assuming a function that closely resembles that of the statues Alcibiades claims to see inside the philosopher. Socrates ignites an uncontrollable passion in Alcibiades which literally opens his body up to the Other, compelling him to insist that it is his transcendental duty to gratify Socrates both sexually and otherwise. Alcibiades is found out, revealed, made visible by his passion in a way that makes him feel uneasy and vulnerable. As mentioned previously, two key consequences ensue: Alcibiades feels shamed and humiliated, and he becomes "more completely enslaved" to Socrates "than anyone else has ever been to anyone" (219e). Psychoanalytically speaking, the affect that Alcibiades experiences—shame—is the direct result of his inability to coax from his chosen Other a confirmation of the being he wishes to see himself to be. Because as speaking subjects we are incapable of providing such confirmation for ourselves, we must rely on others to provide it for us. The feeling of shame is thus the objective correlative of the jouissance Alcibiades experiences in apprehending Socrates' *agalmata*. Alcibiades falls from the pedestal on which he formerly stood as Socrates' beloved down onto the earthly level of a disorienting enjoyment he can only fail psychically to map.

Alcibiades quite literally loses himself as a result of Socrates' inability or refusal to provide the amorous gratification he demands. The result is the emergence of two conflicting desires that together define the transferential dynamic. On the one hand, there is a renunciation of will: Alcibiades tells us in no uncertain terms that Socrates' wish is his command. The toppling of the ego of narcissism is such an unpleasant prospect that to prevent it Alcibiades is subjectively prepared to abandon his volition as such. This assertion remains true even if this abandonment manifests itself objectively as its opposite, namely as the ambition to subjugate, to dominate the Other. "There is a strong possibility that Alcibiades *wants* Socrates to be a statue," Nussbaum astutely notes (196).

On the other hand, however, Alcibiades' quintessentially subjective perception of the *agalmata* dissimulated behind Socrates' ugliness is already evidence from the Lacanian perspective that the partial object—and therefore the ego-shattering real of desire that is its effect—has already emerged. Alcibiades' predicament is that he wants to become the integral but passive object of Socrates' love but *at the same time* escape from the stultifying and incapacitating identification that lies at its root. The event of transference properly speaking signals our defensive unconscious response to a tipping of the psychical scales from the former to the latter. Indeed, this tipping is precisely what analytic interpretation, indeed the entire practico-theoretical edifice of Freudian analysis in its most advanced formulation, is designed to instigate, if not to force. In this precise sense, then, we can agree with Nussbaum's suggestion that the entrance of Alcibiades in the *Symposium* provides an authentic "expression of unregenerate *erōs*" (196), indeed, the most authentic one in the entire text.

Nussbaum provides fascinating cultural-historical evidence, in fact, the same body of evidence that Lacan refers to in his seminar, that illuminates the phenomenon inherent in the transference event of the substitution of a destructive disaggregation of the self for a respectful, ego-propping concern for the integrity of the Other. Note that this evidence supports Lacan's interpretation of Alcibiades' discourse rather than her own. The historical Alcibiades, about whom we know a great deal, thanks in particular to Plutarch, was an influential political and military leader of the democratic, anti-oligarchic persuasion, a man of great distinction known as much for his sensitivity to criticism and gossip as he was for his beauty and vanity. Like many readers (and writers) of self-help pop psychology, "he loved to be loved," as Nussbaum puts it, making "deep demands on the world, both emotional and intellectual" (165). Yet Alcibiades was also associated, at least according to urban legend, with iconoclasm, profanity, and transgression. Though an Athenian by birth, he allied himself with Sparta and then with the Persians at subsequent moments of his tumultuous and controversial career.

One fateful night, we learn, "he went for a walk through the streets of Athens and defaced the statues of the gods, smashing genitals and faces." To be sure, Alcibiades was generally notorious for "profaning the mysteries" of Athenian religious life (166). Lacan for his part draws attention to further illuminating details, including an episode during which Alcibiades is recalled to Athens at the height of the Peloponnesian War to account for the "mutilation of the Hermes," just one incident among many that paint the picture of a figure who harbors "contempt for form, traditions, laws, and no doubt even religion itself" (32). Alcibiades' life trajectory as a whole puts into relief the aims of the two contradictory transferential passions: to guarantee a pleasing reflection of oneself in the Other and to break free from the resulting prospect of a paralyzing dyadic fusion. These details of the life of the historical Alcibiades signal that one of the outcomes of extreme imaginary alienation is a perverse form of acting out through which castration, having failed to have its full and proper effect on the subject, is symbolically inflicted on the Other as a means of escaping from a suffocating identification; of carving out for oneself, however problematically, a space for desire.

All of this evidence unearths a somewhat surprising simpatico between aspects of Nussbaum's and Lacan's readings of the *Symposium*. The two readers finally part ways, however, in their respective assessments of its overarching significance. Nussbaum concludes her discussion with the contention that it offers a tragic vision of the fundamental incompatibility between the disciplined austerity of Socratic philosophical method and the unhinged Dionysiac abandon of Alcibidean *erōs*. One must choose one or the other, this view holds, and each option comes at a cost. Whereas Diotima's vision of beauty demands the sacrifice of sensuous embodiment, the path of "authentic" *erōs* in Nussbaum's view denies the possibility of rational consciousness as such.

Nussbaum reminds us that by the time of Apollodorus's fateful encounter with Aristodemus, the event serving as the occasion for the dialogue's narration, Alcibiades was already dead. She interprets Plutarch's story about the illustrious man's final dream the night before he was murdered, pierced by the arrows of his numerous enemies, as a kind of transvestite wish-fulfillment designed to rail angrily against the injustice of the impossible dilemma just outlined, a dilemma that, incidentally but importantly, suggests an analogy with what for psychoanalysis is the foundational conundrum of human existence, that of sexual difference.

The dream's central image depicts a courtesan cradling the head of Alcibiades, who is dressed in women's clothing, as she applies makeup to his face. "In the soul of this proudly aggressive man," interprets Nussbaum, this dream

> expresses the wish for unmixed passivity: the wish to lose the need for practical reason, to become a being who could live entirely in the flux of *erōs* and so avoid tragedy. But at the same time it is a wish to be no longer an erotic being; for what does not reach out to order the world does not love, and the self-sufficiency of the passive object is as unerotic as the self-sufficiency of the god. It is, we might way, a wish not to live in the world. (199)

This insightful analysis suggests in its nonpsychoanalytic idiom that Alcibiades' desire is finally to be released from desire's conditions and exigencies. Like a good hysteric, Alcibiades calls on Socrates to be his master and, after Socrates betrays him by choosing to praise Agathon instead, Alcibiades suddenly and inexplicably disappears from the narrative as if swallowed up by the returning revelers' wild flute music, would-be victim of a predicament from which there is no escape except wanton self-destruction.

To my mind there is little doubt that Nussbaum is correct when she says that Alcibiades' speech articulates a protest against desire. Yet her analysis simply ends on this "tragic" note, leaving her reader to think that for the likes of Alcibiades—but who has never suffered from a version of his dilemma?—there is in the *Symposium*'s world simply no way out, no "third way" alternative other than blind iconoclastic aggression to the forced choice between the endless frustration of impassioned demands and the joylessly disembodied rigors of dialectical asceticism. On Lacan's reading, however, Socrates' turn to Agathon at the dialogue's climax is a crucial detail, one which Nussbaum's analysis gives short shrift. The brouhaha erupting between confessor and mentor about who should sit next to whom is in fact the key to deciphering the structure of love that binds together the banquet's key participants. More precisely, Alcibiades concludes his exasperated discourse by asking Socrates to allow Agathon to sit between them, violating in this way the rule imposed by Eryximachus according to which it should now be up to Socrates to offer a speech in praise of Agathon.

Alcibiades' preferred seating order, from left to right, is Socrates—
Alcibiades—Agathon. As we have seen, Alcibiades argues for this arrangement by warning Agathon that Socrates' love is mere pretense; he should
therefore keep his distance from the disingenuous philosopher. Socrates
in turn accuses Alcibiades of trying to undermine with his outrageous
speech Socrates' relationship with Agathon. "You did this because you
think that I should love you and no one else," Socrates claims, "and
that Agathon should be loved by you and no one else" (222d). Though
he eventually qualifies Socrates' interpretation as unsatisfactory, Lacan
claims that it still correctly draws attention to the tripartite quality
of love's structure, unveiling in this way the disjunction between the
claims of the ego and the otherness of desire. In the Greek idiom of
love, Alcibiades wants to be both *erastēs* and *erōmenos*—exclusive lover
of Agathon, sole beloved of Socrates, conveniently positioned between
the two so as to form a complete amorous chain. In psychoanalytic
terms, Socrates is installed as Alcibiades' ego ideal I and Agathon as
his ideal ego *i(a)*. Socrates' dialectical wisdom, that is to say, furnishes
the idealized perspective from which Alcibiades desires to apprehend his
own person. This person is in turn vicariously figured by the equally
idealized person of Agathon, desirable for both his physical beauty and
his newfound cultural prestige.

In the final analysis, the content of Alcibiades' unconscious fantasy is *to see himself in the person of Agathon as Agathon is desired by
Socrates*. From the perspective of psychoanalysis this is the fundamental structure of love as resistance, the demand-side love that aims to
forestall the encounter with the real, with the partial object of the
drive. Yet the rather awkward syntax of my italicized rendering of the
relation is perhaps not unrelated to the fact that it is untenable. It is
untenable because it rests on the repression of the knowledge that it
is Agathon—not Alcibiades—who is the true object of Socrates' desire,
as the text makes clear on numerous occasions. This is the reason why
for Lacan Socrates' insistence on praising Agathon, of openly expressing
his desire for him, qualifies as an interpretation of Alcibiades' transference: it confronts Alcibiades with the fact that he does not qualify as
an object of his idealized Other's desire. This Other, imbued through
fantasy with special transcendental knowledge, can only prove incapable
of sanctioning the subject's being as worthy of love. For Lacan, there is
no getting around the fact that eventually the Other will let me down

by failing to conceal from me my own troubling ontological lack, my essential unworthiness for desire.

Though Socrates' intervention qualifies in this sense as an analytic interpretation, Lacan makes clear that it is not the best one. Here the question of Socrates' desire—or rather the desire of the analyst, to be precise—takes center stage, and it is no coincidence that this question forms the cornerstone of the transference seminar's underlying argument. But this should come as no surprise, for if desire is the desire of the Other, as Lacan never tires of reminding us, and if the Other of the subject in the transference is embodied by the analyst, then the analyst's interpretation can only be a function of her desire. Simply put, the analyst must have the right kind of desire in order to guide the patient towards the transference's elusive beyond. This is where Socrates fails, according to Lacan. Socrates fails because at the conclusion of the dialogue his desire remains captured by the lure of ideality. Though Socrates untiringly parries Alcibiades' advances and expresses skepticism concerning Diotima's mystical vision of the beautiful, it remains the case that the dialogue ends with Socrates on the verge of singing another symposiast's praises, of constructing yet another ideal ego in the person of Agathon, thereby returning the dynamic of the symposium to what it was prior to Alcibiades' unruly intervention.

Socrates' interpretation effectively says to Alcibiades: "no, I can't love you in the way you want me to love you because in truth what you love in me is my love for someone else—Agathon." This is surely the point that Lacan tries to make in the seminar when he links Socrates' claim to knowledge in love with the phenomenon of "deception" (*tromperie*) (198). Socrates deceives himself with respect to desire when he claims to know its object, when he persists in the liberalist Nussbaumian delusion that a person can succeed in embodying this object in its purportedly available completion. More technically, Socrates' desire for Agathon remains trapped within the illusory imaginary-symbolic apparatus of the ego, namely I and $i(a)$. By praising Agathon, in other words, Socrates in effect praises his own worthiness as concerns love, and in this sense his discourse fails to break with Diotima's beautiful image of a self-contemplating desire. In contrast, the Lacanian analyst can indulge in no such luxury. Unlike Socrates, the analyst is obliged to keep desire oriented toward its real—the partial object of the drive, a bereft of i, of its enticing image or figuration. This desire is by definition an unconscious desire; it is simply unavailable to the forms of possible knowledge. Socrates' desire goes astray where it suggests to Alcibiades a concrete, identifiable, *personified* object—this is the one whom you *really* love. "I do not contain the object you see inside me," Socrates effectively says, "but Agathon does, or at least he may." The correct interpretation in the Lacanian view would rather have been this: "what you love in truth is *objet petit a*, and it is always elsewhere, always beyond, and always causes the ruin, the putrefaction, of what you aspire to be."

What fascinates the subject in the Other at the moment of the transference is an object of which this Other necessarily remains unaware. As I indicated in chapter 1, Lacan's idea of the "subject supposed to know" must be read in two different ways. First, I suppose that the Other to whom I address myself can tell me something about my desire that I don't already know; this explains why I go into analysis or simply why I even bother to address my desire to the social world. In addition, however, this Other is supposed to—*should*—know my desire, which assumes of course the possibility that it in fact does not. The Other's desire is so fascinating, troubling, and enigmatic precisely because it betrays the lack of knowledge within the particular other who, for someone in a specific situation, is meant to contain it. Our relation to the Other in the transference is marked by a fundamental disjunction between the knowledge that the Other is able to communicate and a mysterious "something else" that exceeds this message, causing it to appear as an impenetrable enigma, as an opaque will that cannot be fathomed.

When the analyst's interpretation succeeds in suggesting that the patient does not quite have the goods when it comes desire, the disjunction between the supposition of knowledge and the intimation of its absence is made manifest, and transferential passion rears its resistant head. Whatever evidence exists of the nature of the Other's desire will cease abruptly to convince, and the Other will then take on the full patina of its contingency and banality, its inadequacy with respect to what we need it to be. The true end of analysis comes about not when knowledge and desire are sutured together in the form of a reassuring norm or standard, but rather when they are decisively separated, when the subject can confront the difficult truth that desire cannot be reconciled, that its object can never become an object of presentation, can never materialize in the phenomenal world. Despite its apparent difficulty, this truth also has the effect of a liberation, for it means that we are free to give love in the absence of the knowledge that we have anything desirable to give. For if we wait for evidence of such knowledge to appear, we condemn ourselves to reissue the same pattern of demands to the Other, demands which, as Alcibiades' testimony compellingly shows, will only sentence us to a term in the prison-house of frustration.

III

Like a Pack of Rats

Will the Real Frantz Fanon Please Stand up?

The editors of an important UK-published essay collection on Frantz Fanon, that paradigmatic theorist of colonial race relations and anticolonial struggle, identify five stages in the reception of his work over the half-century since its appearance.[1] There was first a period of direct and pragmatic application of his theories to the activities of revolutionary third world anticolonial movements in the 1960s. This stage can be emblematized by such figures as Fidel Castro, Ernesto "Che" Guevara, and Paulo Freire on the side of revolutionary anticolonialism, and Hannah Arendt on the side of liberal or pacifist ambivalence.[2]

A period of biographical work took center stage in the late '60s and early '70s. This current explored the impact of Fanon's lived experience on his textual production, highlighting from among the events of Fanon's life trajectory his enlistment in the French military during World War II; his medical and psychiatric training in Lyon under the tutorship of Edmond Tosquelles, theorist and practitioner of *social-thérapie*; his administration of the Blida-Joinville psychiatric hospital in the hills south of Algiers during the national liberation struggle's bloody late stages; and finally, his exile in Tunisia, hospitalization in Rome, and death from leukemia under the suspiciously cavalier watch of the CIA in Washington, D.C.[3] Next, the focus shifted to an evaluation of the political-theoretical aspect of Fanon's work. This current set itself the task of analyzing Fanon's adaptation of classical Marxist theory to fit the particular class dynamics and political antagonisms of colonial Africa at the decadent moment of its historical decline.[4]

The penultimate stage, refreshingly relativized when viewed in this wider context, is the one most familiar to Anglo-American academics of

the late twentieth and early twenty-first centuries, the period of Fanon
as "postcolonial theorist." Though the texts in this group are too heterogeneous to be succinctly summarized, it is still possible to say that
they collectively articulate the manifold ways in which Fanon's work
has met up with poststructuralist literary theory and the discourse of
cultural studies. These texts are distinguished by a number of trademark
concerns: the status and agency of the postcolonial subject; the difficult encounter of the revolutionary and liberationist aspects of Fanon's
theory with postmodernist political skepticism's concern for oppressive
universalisms and the "totalitarian" eclipse of freedom; the interrogation of allegedly troublesome passages dealing with feminine sexuality,
Antillean homosexuality, and the status of the woman in Muslim society; and finally, the depiction of an allegedly sexist black postcolonial
masculinity purged from the feminizing or castrating impact of the
history of colonial oppression.

As might be expected, the anthology's instructive summary of
Fanon's reception culminates in the fifth and final stage of Fanon studies.
This is where the editors locate their own collective intervention, which
they define in pragmatic, interdisciplinary, and explicitly political terms.
Against the Fanon of postcolonial theory, they admirably highlight not
only the anticolonial, but also the properly socialist, aspects of Fanon's
work, dramatically marginalized in the preceding stage. The anthology's
main aim is to substitute for the cultural studies or poststructuralist version of Fanon, which tends to foreground the earlier work antedating
its grounding in concrete social struggle, a contrasting approach bearing
faithful witness to Fanon's work as a whole. Readers are enjoined to
resist the forces of disciplinary particularization and professionalization
that in the editors' view have whitewashed the radicalism of Fanon's
theoretical intervention. In their summary the editors sketch with
admirable clarity the extreme fragmentation that has characterized the
field of Fanon studies virtually since its inception. This fragmentation
is surely not unrelated to the difficulty of accommodating a genuinely
radical anticolonial theory within the ideological and political-economic
conditions of academic publishing and university labor at the current
historical moment.

As one peruses the vast and multilingual field of secondary criticism on Fanon, one is struck by the coexistence of a wide variety of
traditions and approaches that function in almost complete ignorance
of one another. There is the Marxist Fanon, the Lacanian Fanon, the
homophobic Fanon, the existentialist Fanon, the postmodernist Fanon,

the essentialist Fanon, the anti-essentialist Fanon, not to mention the feminist and the androcentric Fanons. Indeed, as Henry Louis Gates Jr. puts it in a memorable if cynical phrase, for the fields of anticolonial criticism and postcolonial theory, Fanon is very much "a Rorschach blot with legs."[5]

Becoming quite discouragingly clear through the haze of the Fanon industry's prolific production during the past two decades is that what I want to risk calling the authentic Fanon disappears under the weight of his interpreters' and appropriators' discourses. In this light the antirelativist and anti-postmodernist stance of the anthology's introduction—its half-implicit contention, that is to say, that there is indeed a specificity, a truth, to be found in Fanon's body of work—is one that I want to valorize and put to work in this chapter.[6] Rereading Fanon through the lens of transference theory will allow me not only to reconnect Fanon scholarship with the political bite that has it sit uncomfortably alongside dominant trends in contemporary cultural studies and postcolonial theory. It will also assist in capturing the movement of his thought from the furious ambivalences laying bare the wounds of his alienating acculturation into a racist and dependent Martinican society, to his unconditional support for the anticolonial cause in not only the nascent Algerian nation, but also the global beyond.

Above all, Fanon's body of work bears witness to an exuberant and youthful brilliance. Indeed, it conveys in the most vivid terms the alternately anguished and ecstatic passions of a mind in revolt against its own conditions of historical possibility. As Fanon's readers, we are struck by the sense that the texts struggle to say something radically new, and that all the intellectual traditions appealed to—Marxism, existentialism, phenomenology, and psychoanalysis, to name the most important—do not suffice to capture the painful specificity of the radical colonized intellectual's situation. This situation is suspended in a precarious intermediary zone between native and metropolitan cultures and languages; between traditional, un- or partially assimilated rural peasant classes and the significantly Westernized indigenous bourgeoisie; and between the scattered activists of the emerging postcolonial nation and the depressed socialist constituencies of postwar Europe, themselves greatly enfeebled by unprecedented postwar economic growth and the increasingly unavoidable evidence of the crimes of Stalinism.

The Fanonian intellectual is neither bi- or multicultural nor hybridized, as the mainstream of postcolonial theory would have us believe. The space he inhabits is rather a kind of no-man's-land, an emptiness beneath the surface of appearances that we can best evoke through Alain Badiou's notion of the site. Especially illuminating in Fanon's context is the site's second property, which, as Badiou explains, pertains to "the instantaneous revelation of the void that haunts multiplicities through the transitory annulment that it performs on the gap between being and being-there."[7] The emergence of Fanon's voice is an event that issues forth in Badiou's terms between the being of pure inconsistent multiplicity and the organization of this multiplicity within the logic of a particular situation. In less technical terms, the truth of Fanon's work cannot be accounted for in the dominant idioms of postwar European thought; this truth extends far beyond the mere appropriation of progressive European ideas for anticolonial strategy. Instead, Fanon gives body to the absent and silent subject of European colonialism, making visible the barbarism on which empire is built. As Sartre influentially argued, Fanon's discourse cuts at the very heart of Europe's idea of itself, forcing it to see itself reflected back from the perspective of the colonized other.[8]

The publication of Fanon's work helped make retrospectively manifest the prior absence of a radical anticolonial voice speaking from the colonies, one capable of exposing the foundation of human suffering that had supported the colonial project, including the especially entrenched, century-long French one in Algeria. The sudden conspicuousness of such a voice, so conspicuous that *The Wretched of the Earth* was met with censorship in France, constitutes through its maximal "intensity of existence" (*Logiques*, 393) what Badiou calls a singularity. The utterances of the subject who dares to speak from this position will necessarily enact violence, as do all singularities worthy of the name, against not only colonial subjectivity and its sociosymbolic points of reference, but also the familiar modes of reception of the European theoretical languages that have engaged with the problem of colonialism. With Fanon the third world suddenly found its voice, and the prospect of a radically new global order—postimperial, postcapitalist, multinodal—appeared, however briefly, tantalizingly within reach.

The poststructuralist and cultural studies reception of Fanon's work has glossed over not only its ferocious singularity, but also its organic unity. Any consideration of Fanon that takes the view that his work offers a coherent anticolonial political theory must depart from the premise that the perceived tension between its psychological and political dimensions presents a false problem. Indeed, the crucial underlying antagonism left unidentified by the anthology's outline of Fanon's reception is indeed this split—characteristic not only of the fourth, cultural studies phase of Fanon scholarship, but of his reception as a whole—between the (nominally) psychoanalytic and avowedly poststructuralist approaches to his work that focus almost exclusively on *Black Skin, White Masks,* and the materialist, sociological, or at any rate self-consciously radical anticolonial perspectives that prioritize *The Wretched of the Earth* and sometimes also the collections *A Dying Colonialism* and *Toward the African Revolution.*[9]

This peculiar but widespread critical bifurcation has had a debilitating effect on our capacity to extract from the body of Fanon's texts a general theory of colonialism and the means of resisting it. As David Macey aptly puts it, "the 'post-colonial' Fanon is in many ways an inverted image of the 'revolutionary Fanon' of the 1960s, and one is hard pressed to find serious critical efforts to resolve this contradiction."[10] The liberal and humanist West has had a notoriously difficult time thinking through a tension it has tended to construe between the psychic and the social, the individual and the collective. This difficulty has prevented many of Fanon's readers from thinking both of his two major books in relation to one another as part of a unifiable whole.

Classically, critics who focus on *Black Skin* emphasize the cultural components of (post)colonial subjectivity, that is to say the manner in which the colonial "gaze" imprisons the black Antillean subject in a web of discourse and imaginary identifications which construct a troubled and divided subject beset by deep ambivalence and an acute sense of dispossession. Readings in this vein implicitly dismiss radical forms of political agency which would be less overwhelmingly conditioned by the strategies of cultural imperialism and assimilation that have determined in this view the construction of postcolonial subjectivity. Additionally, Fanon's central thesis, that the debilitating psychosocial effects of physical and symbolic colonial violence can in part be overcome through carefully organized armed resistance, is anxiously cast aside. No alternative means of psychological redress is offered by way of compensation.

Conversely, commentators drawn to Fanon's later texts reproach the poststructuralist critics of *Black Skin* for enacting a culturalist, depoliticizing reduction of the postcolonial condition to a suspect subjectivism which appears to have a place neither for Fanon's theory of anticolonial national consciousness nor for his notion of the role strategic violence plays in the creation of the new socialist humanity. Though I find it significantly truer to Fanon's desire, work from this perspective tends nonetheless to give *Black Skin* short shrift, virtually dismissing the text in its entirety as the immature work of a mind incapable of formulating its ultimate message prior to the decisive politicizing encounter with the Algerian struggle.

The underlying tension in Fanon's reception, split between rival focalizations on one or the other of his two major texts, is in my view the underlying principle shaping interpretations of Fanon's work in the Anglo-American field over the last few decades. Indeed, its powers of methodological determination appear to be so absolute that his more radical commentators take the view that the psychoanalytic aspect of Fanon must lead inexorably to the political skepticism and modest reformism of poststructuralist cultural studies. Critics who support the materialist version of Fanon can entirely dismiss his investment in psychiatric or psychoanalytic approaches to the interrogation of colonial subjectivity. Conversely, the influential theorists of postcolonial subjectivity ritualistically take their distance from the political Fanon, reiterating Hannah Arendt's reprimand of Sartre for his allegedly reckless or unethical, Fanon-inspired endorsement of violence.

This set of assumptions has the unfortunate consequence of obscuring the insight that what appears to the materialists as the subjectivist side of Fanon's concerns depends on the acknowledgment of the formative role that properly socioeconomic factors play in the negotiation of postcolonial consciousness. Conversely, what the poststructuralist cultural studies camp has (mistakenly) attacked as Fanon's politically dangerous accommodation of violence is firmly grounded in a view of the transformative subjective effects of the execution of strategically anticolonial *acts*. In other words, Fanon's work proceeds under the strong assumption that the psychological or subjective and the political or revolutionary aspects of the colonial condition are inseparable, indeed, that they form part of a unique psychosocial whole. My own reading of Fanon will therefore assume the argument I developed in chapter 1, namely, that Freudian psychoanalysis is decidedly postliberal in the precise sense that its conceptuality does not assume the distinction between individual and society. The present chapter similarly assumes that we cannot hear Fanon's message unless we move beyond this central liberalist tenet. Like Freud's unconscious desire, Fanon's anticolonial project disrupts the basic categories of liberal thought.

Fanon essentially reiterates the dialectical process involved in healing the wounds of colonial alienation, outlined in individual psychological terms in *Black Skin, White Masks*, in the collectively subjective framework of *The Wretched of the Earth* or *A Dying Colonialism*'s "This Is the Voice of Algeria," for example. That there is no articulation between the two approaches in Fanon's oeuvre, no available transitional writings that think through the sudden movement from one to the other register, only underscores the truth that the dialectic of subjectivation is *transpersonal*: it casts the distinction between individual and collective interest or will into methodological irrelevance. Simply put, it makes little difference whether Fanon is writing about the struggle to break out of the inhibiting identifications of his Martinican youth or the appropriation of radio technology by Algerian society as a whole in its struggle against French colonial occupation. The dialectical structures at work in both instances are fundamentally the same.

My approach to Fanon's work is based on the premise that the underlying object of his inquiry is the mode of the "native" subject's relation to his historical sociosymbolic reality, that is to say to the Other. Fanon's analysis dissects how the colonized subject's apprehension of this reality determines the extent of the revolutionary or complicit character of his stance with respect to the colonialist status quo. This is to say that Fanon's method, properly speaking, focuses neither on the subjective nor on the socioeconomic and historical aspects of the colonial situation. Rather, he scrutinizes the psychopolitical dynamic through which the colonized subject works through her amorous investment in the colonial apparatus—its exalted figures of authority and prestigious cultural monuments—finally bringing herself to tarry with the horrific real of colonialism's historical violence. The stifling effects of what Freud called transference love leave their mark on each of Fanon's two central and dialectically opposed figures of colonized subjectivity: the culturally alienated middle-class intellectual, more metropolitan than the European himself, and the illiterate or uneducated peasant, who viscerally rejects all aspects of colonial culture and technology to the point of losing sight of the means by which they might suggest valuable avenues of resistance.

Fanon's subject is a political subject who has always already decided—even if this choice is in no manner consciously assumed—to adopt an emancipatory or reactionary position with respect to colonial power. To put it in a way specific to Fanon's Algerian context, the decision to join the resistance is the only properly subjective choice, the alternative being the stultifying psychopathology that results from the passive internalization of colonial violence. With respect to the controversy about the politics implicit in Fanon's psychoanalytic reference, I concur with the more radically politicized interpreters of Fanon that he is at his weakest when he makes explicit his debt to the psychoanalytic tradition. However, I will argue against the view that the problem lies with Fanon's reliance on psychoanalysis as such. The difficulties arise instead with the particular kind of psychoanalytic theory that shapes Fanon's discussion of colonial subjectivity. Indeed, Fanon's work has very little directly to do with psychoanalysis properly speaking, or rather properly conceived. As I will explore in detail in the next section, his major influence in fact was not Freudianism, but rather the school of social psychiatry pioneered by Edmond Tosquelles. Simply put, Fanon's debt to psychoanalysis, and to Lacan in particular, has been massively overestimated in his cultural studies reception.

Though there can be no doubt about Fanon's belief at his specific historical juncture in the psychological and political necessity of violence—organized armed struggle, more exactly—in third world anticolonial action, the *cause* and *object* of this violence emerge with more ambivalence from the texts. This is where the psychoanalytic concept of transference will provide crucial interpretive guidance; indeed, it will allow for the recuperation of the authentically subversive kernel of Fanon's thought. In essence, this chapter will aim to offer a fresh psychoanalytic reading of Fanon which argues *against* the specific psychoanalytic and psychiatric ideas on which Fanon draws. My underlying suggestion is that Fanon's body of work effectively enacts an interpretation of the author's own transference with respect to French colonial culture. This interpretation enables him to articulate what remains the most inspirational and politically astute theory of anticolonial resistance on record, one whose lessons extend well beyond the horizon of Fanon's own mid-century, and now decidedly historical, cold war–defined period of decolonization.

A Gift of Quinine

It remains the case nonetheless that one of the reasons for which Fanon's texts have proven so valuable to colonial and postcolonial studies is that they do *not* center on the ultimate utopian moment when the subject of anticolonial struggle successfully escapes the imprisoning logic of the colonizer-colonized binary. It is for this reason that Jean-Paul Sartre's dialectic of colonialism, outlined in his key essay "Black Orpheus," is so useful to the interpretation of Fanon's work. Taken as a whole, the texts spend less time outlining the properties of the revolutionary anticolonial subject than they do evoking the dialectic of this subject's coming into being.[11] Indeed, there is much to be said for the claim that Fanon's work is a kind of Hegelian phenomenology of the effects of, and liberation from, the history of European colonization. One of the great strengths of Fanon's work is therefore its memorable evocation of the ways in which the colonized subject gets symptomatically waylaid, as it were, on the road to revolutionary desire.

More precisely, when Fanon explores the reasons for the difficulty of creating a national anticolonial culture, he discusses the relation of the colonized population to the colonial situation as a psychosocial whole. The psychoanalytic references that support this aspect of Fanon's work, particularly in *Black Skin* but also in *The Wretched of the Earth*, are to post-Freudian thinkers who were influenced by, among other traditions, ego psychology and existentialism, thinkers such as Alfred Adler, Anna Freud, Germaine Guex, and even Carl Jung. In spite of their manifold differences from one another, these authors collectively articulate a revisionist attitude toward the spirit of Freudianism, the same revisionism that would be aggressively attacked during Fanon's lifetime as conformist and ideological by Lacan in his early seminars. Though unquestionably productive for the field of postcolonial theory in its cultural studies and poststructuralist incarnations, in my view the Lacanian, proto-deconstructionist Fanon that has been developed by such figures as Homi Bhabha on the basis of the extended footnote on the mirror stage and a couple of summary references in *Black Skin* is very much a retrospective fantasy. As Neil Lazarus has persuasively argued, Homi Bhabha's approach rests on the unsound premise that Fanon's "preeminent claim to our attention is not as a theorist of decolonization or revolution, but of the 'subversive slippage of identity and authority.' "[12]

Indeed, despite its canny illumination of the interdependence of the psychic and the social realms, Bhabha's most recent discourse on Fanon's work in the introduction to the Philcox translation of *Wretched* makes numerous unfortunate errors. For example, Bhabha reiterates the standard-issue poststructuralist fear of a "universalist ontology" in Fanon as well as some discomfort with his valorization of violence, which, so Bhabha supposes, easily leads to "state terror and religious fanaticism."[13] Even more egregiously, Bhabha's appraisal of Fanon's concept of national consciousness mistakenly attributes to it the condition of "cultural homogeneity" (x), giving short shrift to Fanon's key premise that popular anticolonial praxis produces a noncultural and properly political brand of solidarity. Finally, contradicting his valuable problematization of the psychic-social binary, Bhabha's foreword exhibits the same latent liberalism that animates the Fanonian reference to ego psychology. Fanon's work in Bhabha's view ultimately concerns the "fragility of the individual," a fragility that can hinder "the ethical and imaginative act of reaching out towards rights and freedoms," testing in the process "the quality of our characters" (xl–xli). In short, Bhabha's Fanon could have been a speechwriter for the Barack Obama presidential campaign. Indeed, Bhabha's analysis leaves entirely unacknowledged and unexamined Fanon's thoughtful recontextualization of Marxist political theory to suit the socioeconomic specificity of the postcolony.

The putatively psychoanalytic element of *Black Skin, White Masks* that perhaps initially attracts a critic such as Bhabha is so problematic in Fanon's work because it imposes a liberalist ego-psychological rhetoric of personality and selfhood on a politically revolutionary doctrine that would be much better served not only by a rigorous appropriation of Lacan's critique of ego psychology, but also by the linkage I propose in this chapter between Lacan's transference theory and Fanon's ambivalent evocation of the object of anticolonial desire. Fanon's reliance on ego-psychological models of psychosexual development joins forces with the influence of the Tosquelles school of *social-thérapie* to persuade him to adopt an unhelpfully integrationist view of psychotherapeutic practice in his Algerian psychiatric writings.

As Patrick Taylor astutely suggests, the normative force of the social group in social therapy emerges from a banal cultural relativism which remains blind to the impact of the socioeconomic totality on group identity in the colonial-imperial regime. In short, the "social" in social therapy is an anthropological, rather than a socioeconomic, concept. "To attempt to integrate the patient [of *social-thérapie*] into colonial society would reinforce relations of domination," Taylor writes. "The patient learns to recognize him- or herself in relation to a particular group but not in relation to the social totality or to the assumption of his or her dignity in relation to that totality."[14] For this reason, Fanon's psychiatric writings sit uncomfortably alongside his new man of *The Wretched of the Earth*, who learns not to reintegrate with preexisting forms of cultural tradition, but to work militantly to create a new community modeled on the socialist values of national consciousness.

Now, I don't intend my critique of the psychoanalytic or psychiatric Fanon to suggest that a more accurate reading of the mirror stage concept, for example, might redress the errors that mar Fanon's application of it, as if Lacan holds the key that, inserted into the lock of Fanon's writing, opens the door to the correct interpretation. My view is rather that Fanon's development in *The Wretched of the Earth* of his anticolonial theory of national consciousness resonates in remarkably suggestive ways with the authentic Freudian message that I tried to outline in chapter 1. Whereas the ego-psychological influence plainly detracts from the political impact of Fanon's work, making manifest in the process its transferential symptoms, Lacan's theory of the unconscious subject provides an alternative perspective. This perspective radicalizes Fanon's theory by capturing the underlying coherence of the anticolonial desire that it so memorably but inconsistently evokes.

To support this argument I am no doubt required to examine ego psychology's impact on Fanon in more detail. The pervasive influence of Octave Mannoni—member, though clearly not the most insightful one, of Lacan's circle in the early 1950s, and whose text on the psychology of colonialism has been translated into English as *Prospero and Caliban*—has not thus far been sufficiently appreciated in Fanon studies. Indeed, the array of post-Freudian authors cited in *Black Skin* is virtually identical to the one in Mannoni's work. The long shadow that Mannoni casts over Fanon's first book is only darkened by the passion with which Fanon denounces its central thesis. This now somewhat notorious thesis holds that the Malagasy population's collective psychology is characterized by a dependency complex that has made it complicit with the French colonial project on the African continent and beyond.

Mannoni worked in Madagascar for the French colonial administration during the late 1940s, immediately prior to his involvement in the Lacan circle in Paris. *Prospero and Caliban* sees Mannoni develop his theory of colonial dependency by telling the story of an incident involving his tennis coach, a member of Madagascar's dominant Merina ethnic group. As the episode is related in the text, Mannoni arranges to have some quinine sent to his coach and friend after diagnosing him with malaria on the occasion of a medical consultation. The Frenchman immediately senses a change in the young Merina's attitude toward him. Before Mannoni offered his "gift," the coach's manner had been formal and distant: the Merina "had not been in the habit of seeking favours from me," Mannoni writes, and "off the courts he would bid me a rather shy good-day whenever we met in the street." Afterwards, by contrast, the "native" begins to expect regular gifts and favors from his student, to the point where Mannoni begins to interpret these requests as demands.[15]

From Mannoni's point of view, the tennis coach acted in an inappropriately dependent fashion in that he "failed to appreciate" the "objective and impersonal nature" of his gift (43). By way of offering an example of the coach's demanding behavior, Mannoni recounts that his instructor would repeatedly complain that "he was in need of cigarette papers" even though, Mannoni assures us, "the young Merina earned enough at each lesson to buy several packets of them" (42). In the introduction to the American edition of the book, anthropologist Maurice Bloch makes what is no doubt the expected cultural-anthropological criticism of Mannoni's interpretation of the incident. Bloch argues that the Merina's behavior is not what Mannoni sees it to be: an overly subjective reaction to an objectively impersonal gesture. In Bloch's view, the coach's attitude is rather determined by a set of expectations inscribed within the social relationships that define Merina culture, expectations that seem perfectly normal when considered from within its terms.

In my view, however, Bloch's objection to Mannoni's patently ethnocentric consideration of the quinine incident relies too uncritically on its reference to a cultural context whose traditions it assumes are coherent, universal, and devoid of ambiguity or dissent. In this way, Bloch upholds the problematic ideological assumptions of standard-issue anthropological culturalism. But more germane to my immediate concerns is the way in which Mannoni derives the framework of his theory of colonial dependency from the tennis coach's change of conduct. In his psychologistic framework, behaviors such as the coach's sudden "demands" are to be explained with reference to "the persistence of dependence as an essential part of the native's personality" (47). This dependence stems for Mannoni from a fear of abandonment occasioned by the native's excessive respect for authority as incarnated in the ancestral tradition. Unlike the European male—note the sex-specificity of Mannoni's outline of what distinguishes the native subject from the European—who enters into an agonistic Oedipal rivalry with the paternal figure, eventually achieving autonomy by murdering the father in unconscious fantasy and assuming his place, the Malagasy man never suffers from the guilt of patricide, which compromises his ability to achieve social and intellectual independence, or to individuate, as a sympathetic liberal psychology would want to phrase it.

In his failure to protest that "he is a man like his father," the colonized man views all other men as children like himself, since only the ancestors have paternal status according to Mannoni. For this reason, the colonized "projects his own dependence on everyone else" (60). The European man's Oedipal rivalry gives rise to an inferiority complex, which not only causes him to seek through the subjection of others the confirmation of his masculine authority, but motivates according to Mannoni the entire European colonial initiative. At this juncture, the least one can say from a Marxist perspective is that this dramatic thesis cavalierly jettisons the then-existing economic theories of imperialism, both Leninist and otherwise. For Mannoni, the dynamic of colonial culture is fully determined by the meeting of two pathological psychological profiles: the European's, characterized by the inferiority complex, and the dependency complex of the native.

Though the reductive scope of Mannoni's argument is surely quite scandalous, it is actually more shocking to note that Fanon's appropriately harsh criticism of the idea of a colonial dependency complex in *Black Skin* is not targeted at the complex as such. Rather, Fanon reproaches the psychoanalytic theorist of colonialism for the ahistorical character of his views; for his failure, more precisely, to appreciate the concrete situational causation of colonial psychopathology. Fanon argues that the dependency complex does indeed describe with alarming insight the psychology of the native subject under colonial rule. "I can subscribe," he writes, "to that part of M. Mannoni's work that tends to present the pathology of the conflict [between colonizer and colonized]."[16] Like the good Sartrean existentialist that he in many ways was, Fanon claims that the problem with Mannoni's work lies rather in its assumption that the psychological complexes preexist the colonial encounter. "Why does he try," Fanon asks of Mannoni, "to make the inferiority complex [of the white colonial] something that antedates colonization?" (85).

Mannoni goes wrong for Fanon where he assumes that inferiority and dependency are latently active in, respectively, colonial and native cultures *generally conceived*. According to Fanon, these complexes are, rather, products of the situation that a racialist European culture creates in the geopolitical space of colonialism. Instead of attacking the alarming level of generality on which Mannoni discusses the psychology of colonialism, or else decrying the reduction of the interaction of two complex societies to an encounter between abstract character types, Fanon chooses to reproach the European theorist for an insufficient appreciation of the role played by the situational specificity of the history of colonialism, whose civilizing mission he quite incredibly fails to question, at least on this level of his argument.

The emphatic, certainly passionate language through which Fanon criticizes Mannoni's thesis contrasts sharply with the comparatively minor reach of his reproach. Though Fanon will go on to reconfigure the terms of Mannoni's theory by re-attributing the inferiority complex to the colonized black Antillean, adamantly declaring that "a white man in a colony has never felt inferior in any respect" (92), it is clear that Fanon does not have major reservations about Mannoni's psychological portrait of the colonized. In essence, Fanon agrees with Mannoni that the colonized subject does in fact harbor something akin to a dependency complex. What is offensive for Fanon about Mannoni's argument is that it fails to recognize that the colonizer quite literally makes the dependent colonized through the virtually omnipotent and nefarious influence of a racially supremacist European culture. To modify Simone de Beauvoir's precisely analogous feminist existentialist axiom, for Fanon one is not born, but rather becomes, a dependent and inferior colonized subject.

It is therefore not an exaggeration to say that Fanon swallows Mannoni's theory of the colonial complexes more or less whole, with their heavy voluntarist ego-psychological baggage intact. Fanon's refutation of Mannoni's theory that the colonial project is motivated by the European subject's sense of inferiority in fact only underscores the extent to which Fanon's reading is marked by the effects of a defensive transferential idealization. Fanon's inability in *Black Skin, White Masks* to conceive that the European colonial project might be informed by a sense of inadequacy or deprivation on the side of the *colonizer* highlights the role played in Fanon's argument by the fantasy of an omnipotent white colonial master whose command over the field of culture and power relations is seamless and total.

No doubt a product of his French colonial education in Martinique, Fanon's ego structure at this early juncture is clearly dependent on a rather extreme unconscious idealization of France and the prestige of its colonial enterprise. Unready at this stage to draw the conclusion that the future of the colonized population lies in its own hands, Fanon's critique of Mannoni instead reproaches the Frenchman for failing to acknowledge and take responsibility for colonialism's devastating psychological effects.

The unfortunate impact of ego psychology extends even to Fanon's influential footnote on Lacan. Fanon refers to Lacan's mirror stage theory in the context of his discussion of the difference, as he sees it, between the psychodynamic motivations of anti-Semitism and negrophobia. The footnote is intended at least in part as a response to Sartre's noteworthy discussion of racism in his book *Anti-Semite and Jew*. Fanon argues that the white racist imaginary corporealizes and sexualizes the black subject to a greater extent than it does the Jew. In short, the former is closer to the animal than the latter. In consequence, the disruptive figure of the black man haunts the European subject's sense of corporeal integrity. "The Negro," Fanon writes, "because of his body, impedes the closing of the postural schema of the white man" (160). The mere presence of a black body in the colonialist's field of vision will interfere with his self-image, instigating aggressive racist behaviors designed to defend the white colonial ego against the intrusion of an unsettling alterity.

The interest of Fanon's intervention into Lacan's mirror stage discourse, which remains entirely silent on the question of race, lies in the suggestion that the white subject in colonial space racializes his body image differently than does the black subject. The colonialist's ideal ego is unambiguously white, according to Fanon, and the threatening otherness that haunts it is clearly racially different. In contrast, the black subject's alienation in and by colonial culture causes him to elaborate a white, or at any rate neutral, body image that for Fanon betrays a pathologically weak sense of self. To illustrate the effects of this inaccurately racialized body image, Fanon cites the output of black Martinican schoolchildren asked to write about their vacations. As Fanon recounts, they react "like real little Parisians," writing of running through wintry fields and returning home with "rosy cheeks" (*Black Skin*, 162n). Fanon develops in more theoretical terms this theme of the colonized's alienated selfhood in his comments on Anna Freud's notion of ego-withdrawal.[17] Here, Fanon claims that the black subject's inability to develop proper ego defenses gives rise to a "constant effort to run away from his own individuality, to annihilate his own presence" (60).

Though it would clearly be a mistake to minimize the impact of the kind of racial alienation that these passages memorably evoke, it is nonetheless necessary to point out that the premise of Fanon's discussion of the topic works at countermeasures to his more general argument, highlighting once again the effects of his colonial transference. More precisely, Fanon's statements judge the black Caribbean subject's Europeanized bodily ego as alienated in comparison to that of the white colonizer, who is presumed to enjoy a racially authentic imaginary schema that creates a secure sense of self. In contrast, Lacan's point was rather that the body image as constructed by the ego system is alienated *as such*. Put simply, the experience of imaginary alienation does not depend on the appearance in the field of vision of the phenomenon of racial difference.

Though it could very well be true that the racial misidentification of which Fanon speaks exacerbates the nefarious impact of imaginary alienation, it remains the case that Fanon's ambition is to provide the black subject with the self that he lacks, the healthy ego put to ruin by colonialist racism and the hostile field of vision it constructs. The aim of this aspect of Fanon's argument is therefore the construction of a strong black ego that has secured a recognized position for itself in the field of colonial relations. In this way, Fanon makes the colonized black subject depend on colonial culture for the acknowledgment of the value of its racial difference. It is at minimum difficult to square this Fanon with the one who declares provocatively that, in obeisance with *The Wretched of the Earth*'s universalizing anticolonial nationalism, he "does not have the right" to be a Negro (229).

I suggested at the outset of this chapter that there is a latent coherence in Fanon's work taken as a whole. If this is indeed the case, then the claim about the need for a legitimized racial identity can only be a symptom of Fanon's colonial transference. In fact, there is ample evidence in the mirror stage footnote and elsewhere that Fanon on some other level fully recognizes that the subject's attachment to its ego structures breeds hostility and frustration of a sort that can only impede the progress of the colonized toward a politicized anticolonial consciousness. It is also clear that in Fanon's view the white colonial's defensive buttressing of his bodily ego is the primary cause of colonial racism, indeed, an important motivating factor for the colonial project as such. Under the threat of a racialized alterity, colonialism endeavors to purify its collective self-image of this "extimate" danger. Yet this danger can never be entirely eliminated, since its apparent externality is in fact the very essence of the collective colonialist psyche. Logically, then, Fanon should be forced to admit that the development and reinforcement of an analogous but compensatory ego structure on the part of the black Antillean can only produce the very same tendency to erect a rigid and defensive racialist identity complicit with the nefarious colonial enterprise.

Even more importantly for my purposes, however, Fanon also explores in the mirror stage footnote the role that the structure of identification plays in the clinical manifestation of psychosis. Referring to the imago in which the infant situates the self, Fanon claims that "in mental pathology, when one examines delirious hallucinations or interpretations, one always finds that this self-image is respected" (*Black Skin*, 161n). Not only does the primacy of the imaginary structure in psychic life lead to racialist aggression and phobic avoidances, but it also bears a direct link, Fanon here admits, to the occurrence of parapsychotic hallucinations. Though on one level Fanon clearly regrets that the black subject in the colonies does not have access to the pacifying narcissistic structures that the colonial subject is meant to enjoy, his application of Lacan's concept of the mirror stage unambiguously characterizes the primacy of these structures in psychic life as pathological, certainly not the optimal model for postcolonized subjectivity. Thankfully, then, in some of its elements *Black Skin* flagrantly contradicts the argument elsewhere upheld that what is desirable is the colonized's development of an ego structure capable of making up for the narcissistic wound inflicted by colonial relations.

In keeping with my intention to read Fanon's work as a whole, I wish now to argue against the grain of contemporary postcolonial discourse that Fanon's early analysis of racial alienation in the Caribbean can be radicalized in the interests of the more explicitly political project of the later work. The colonized subject scorned by the colonial imaginary in fact acquires *an advantage,* at least potentially, over the white colonial in the struggle for political hegemony. To be sure, this advantage has nothing to do with the socioeconomic privileges that the colonial regime doles out to a pale select few.

However counterintuitive or even dangerous the contention might appear, we must grant that if for both Lacan and Fanon the primacy of the imaginary in psychic life is alienating and conducive to symptomatic acts of aggression, and if the power of colonial discourse over the Caribbean field of vision works to undermine the narcissism of the black subject, then this subject is conveniently placed to diminish the imaginary's powers of frustration and thereby actively to engage in the struggle against colonialism and its legacy. The lack of correspondence, which to be sure Fanon on one level laments, between the black Antillean subject's actual or objective body and this subject's unconscious identification as determined by colonial discourse makes the distant alterity of the body image more tangibly acute. In this way, the black subject's racial alienation makes manifest the noncultural truth that the investment in desirably racialized body images is necessarily alienating and defensive and therefore can only work to suppress the manifestation of emancipatory desire.

To be clear, I am not arguing that the black subject's bodily alienation as described by Fanon carries unambiguously positive consequences for the nonwhite subject of French colonialism, whatever one might understand those consequences to be. Indeed, there is no reason to take issue with the evidence Fanon himself provides to the effect that the racial and cultural confusion of black Antillean subjects features an important experiential element of painful absurdity. Yet in another sense, the absurdity of the Antillean's alienation—the very fact, for instance, that the young Martinican will write about returning home from a wintry outdoor ramble with rosy cheeks—surely works to create subjects who can potentially contest not only the colonialist command over the field of vision, but more generally the very political hegemony of racist colonial discourse itself. By virtue of colonialism's polarizing psychosocial law, the "us and them" Manicheanism that Fanon elsewhere so expertly describes, the colonized tends toward one of two extremes: either debilitating social alienation and abjection, or alternately self-destructive and emancipatory forms of political and cultural agency.

The colonized's unlivable conditions of existence render him more likely than the favored to revolt against the facts of colonial life, preparing him to embark upon the kind of exemplary political and theoretical trajectory that Fanon so inspiringly traveled. That colonialism and its contemporary derivatives inflict an extreme dehumanization that many live as a fate worse than death is a truth demonstrated daily even in today's condition of so-called postcoloniality. Indeed, this truth is everywhere available for all to discern despite the best efforts of the Western discourse on terrorism to convince us that terrorist actions are always and only motivated by a pathological hatred of life, at least as "we" construe it.

The preceding analysis suggests that two forms of the (anti-) colonial subject can be discerned in the early Fanon, only one of which is worthy of the term *subject* in the psychoanalytic sense. To make this distinction we must pay close attention to Fanon's description of the varying attributes of the object that animates desire among the colonized and all those who engage with their cause. Indeed, the main argument of this chapter is that it is possible to trace the ambivalence of Fanonian theory—the fact that it valiantly struggles, but sometimes fails, to express the anticolonial desire that it wants to theorize—to the ambivalence of the object relation in its mediation of the subject's engagement with its particular historical sociosymbolic formation, including the one Fanon so memorably evokes in *The Wretched of the Earth*: the society shaped by the French colonial regime in Algeria in its stubborn, sadistically paroxysmal death-throes.

On one level, the object appears in Fanon's texts in its narcissistic dimension as the ideal ego *i(a)* seen from the perspective of a privileged point of identification I, to refer back to the analysis of chapter 1. The object in this form takes on a variety of guises in Fanon: the colonial ideology that seamlessly saturates the field of Antillean power relations; the *pied-noir* settler who jealously hordes the objects of enjoyment denied the native: the fertile land and his alluring French wife; and the anticipated African culture of negritude, which would reclaim the continent's glorious imperial past, finally becoming capable of comparing itself favorably with modern European civilization at the summit of its colonialist "achievements."

The subject's relation to the object in this first guise features both a libidinous unconscious spontaneity of action—the one that Fanon will brilliantly dissect in *Wretched*—and a Hegelian logic of envy and desire for recognition. Here, the subject wants to take the place of the object, to apprehend itself at the ideal point where the elusive colonialist enjoyment might be secured. Within this logic the colonized finally acquires a proper position in the colonialist order of things: she is recognized by European culture and basks in the glow of a respected social position. This is the realm of the successfully assimilated native, the *évolué* of French colonial ideology. In the so-called Francophone world, the typical character here is the metropolitan-educated professional or intellectual who returns to the homeland either to milk what remains of the colonial apparatus or, alternatively, to conspire to establish a despotic bourgeois regime aiming to perpetuate the colonialist economic relation under an obfuscating discourse of postcolonial, often tribalist, nationalism.

In its contrasting second incarnation, however, the object-cause of Fanon's anticolonial desire is the wretched underside or residue of the first, more dignified object. Strikingly, Fanon pulls the aesthetic and ethical terms with which he evokes the object in this second mode from the discourses of ugliness and evil, the very antitheses of those consummately philosophical concepts of the beautiful and the good. This is the object that we can relate to Lacan's *objet petit a*: the traumatic real object that causes the subject's desire, the expropriating object that the reassuring ideal ego will eventually fail to dissimulate underneath its reassuring cloak. Fanon evokes the object in this second, real mode when he speaks of the downtrodden constituencies to whom the title of his most consequential work refers. We are now in a position to distinguish in its textual details the agency of these two incarnations of the object from the perspective of the role each one plays in the cathartic radicalization of Fanon's anticolonial subject.

The Metropolitan View

Not unlike the Freud I considered in chapter 1, Fanon manages despite his ambivalence to provide the tools needed to extricate from his texts a coherent theory, in this instance of a globalist anticolonial nationalism. The argument that nativist assertions of cultural particularity in the postcolony presuppose the legitimizing look of the colonialist who can bestow the elusive and long sought-after recognition, thereby reinscribing the native within the terms of colonialism, does in fact clearly emerge from a variety of spots in Fanon's writing.

In *Black Skin, White Masks,* for example, Fanon compares the situation of the black Antillean student in postwar France to that of his Russian or German counterpart. Though the former will demonstrate a higher level of competence in the French language than will the latter, it is the former who becomes the target of metropolitan condescension and stereotyping because the prestige of Russian or German culture will cause the French to attribute higher levels of cultural competence to their fellow Europeans. The nefarious effects of this archetypal "colonized student in the metropolis" scenario, memorably evoked in Bertène Juminer's novel *The Bastards,* for example, explains for Fanon the tremendous reserves of intellectual and creative energy behind the "striving of contemporary Negroes to prove the existence of a black civilization to the white world at all costs" (34).

The unconscious idealization that makes the colonized dependent on the judgment of colonial discourse also manifests itself in the form of a jealous and explicitly erotic identification which further illustrates the imaginary logic coloring Fanon's depiction of the colonial world. The celebrated passage I have in mind vividly foregrounds the polarized geography of colonial urban space. In characteristic Manichean fashion, the segregationist ethos of colonialism manufactures two utterly distinct environments: first, the "settler's town," with its brightly lit streets, sturdy stone and brick structures, tidy garbage bins, and well-fed, properly clothed inhabitants; and second, the "native town, the medina, the reservation" which, by contrast, is a "world without spaciousness" packed with "huts built one on top of the other" and residents "starved of bread, of meat, of shoes, of coal, of light." It is as if the colonized can only imagine the luxury of spatial extension in the place of the Other, a place from which he is of course excluded. The colonized's sector is a "world with no space," as Fanon succinctly concludes (*Wretched,* 4).

The revolting historical persistence of this spatial logic becomes disturbingly apparent if one thinks of the South African apartheid home-lands policy of not so long ago or, more recently still, the ongoing ethnic cleansing project of the Israeli state badly disguised as the reckless ideology of Zionist settlement. Yet for all the concrete political bite of the passage, Fanon places his emphasis not on colonial spatial organiza-tion objectively conceived, but rather on the native subject's properly psychical apprehension of the divide. In a captivating moment, when he could very well be describing the view from today's West Bank or Gaza, or even contemporary Beirut, surrounded still by teeming Palestin-ian refugee camps, Fanon evokes the inhabitant of the cramped native quarter casting an appetitive eye toward the adjacent colonial district:

The gaze that the colonized subject casts at the colonist's
sector is a look of lust, a look of envy. Dreams of possession.
Every type of possession: of sitting at the colonist's table and
sleeping in his bed, preferably with his wife. The colonized
man is an envious man. The colonist is aware of this as he
catches the furtive glance, and constantly on his guard, real-
izes bitterly that: "They want to take our place." And it's
true there is not one colonized subject who at least once a
day does not dream of taking the place of the colonist. (5)

The colonized subject whom Fanon describes identifies with the
settler's command over his comfortable home and sprawling land. Yet
the phrase "every type of possession" just intimates that what is owned
is more than simply a collection of objects, seemingly unlimited though
it might be. In this light, the reference to sexual possession of the
colonist's wife designates not an ordinary lustful sexual jealousy, that is
to say, a fascination with the obscene real of the colonist's enjoyment,
but rather a highly idealized, reflexive, or redoubled possession—a possession, you might say, of the very state of possessing itself. A logic of
substitution determines the dynamic of this patently imaginary structure: the colonized wants to eliminate the settler and take his place.
Hence, the pertinence of Fanon's reference to the Aristotelian principle
of reciprocal exclusivity: "It's either him or me," the fellah (peasant)
effectively says, "in the settler's bed." The concrete political implications
of this identificatory logic are easy to discern: the spontaneous action
of the anticolonial subject captivated by such a fantasy structure can
only effect—this is the best case scenario—the substitution of a national
elite for the colonial one, leaving intact a socioeconomic structure that
the interests of metropolitan capital will continue to control.

The colonized's spontaneous imaginary aggressiveness takes as its
object the figure of a rich settler endowed with an exaggerated mastery over colonial space. This object's powers of seduction threaten to
hold its subjects in its thrall, creating an atmosphere of competition
among the colonized from which colonialism has long since learned
to capitalize through its patented divide and conquer strategies. This
agonistic climate exacerbates historical ethnic resentments and rivalries
among the colonized constituencies, who are led to battle one another
for what few coveted positions of privilege might remain available. For
Fanon, of course, this dynamic inhibits the establishment of an authentic
and universal national consciousness, one that would have successfully

passed from retrograde ethnic particularisms to a politically unified and genuinely revolutionary anticolonial generality.

Fanon illustrates in compelling detail how this brand of imaginary passion most often results not in the targeting of anticolonial violence on the settler and his property, but rather in the revival of old intertribal hatreds. The libidinal energy released by the colonized's covetousness does not find expression in the appropriation of the land conquered by colonialism for the postcolonial nation. Rather, with devastating political consequences, it gives rise to divisive tribalization. Fanon draws attention to the inhibitory impact of the logic he describes: to be sure, the settler's masterful endowments are an object of fascinated aspiration, yet the structure of love that binds the colonized to this object effectively discourages him from conspiring to appropriate colonialism's possessions. Moreover, this inhibition sets in precisely at the moment when both the mounting social anarchy fomented by colonial decadence and the increasingly organized forces of anticolonial resistance actually make the prospect of reappropriation a concrete historical possibility.

Fanon elucidates the full consequences of the colonized's transferential idealization of the colonizer not in the problematic psychological, psychiatric, and psychoanalytic idioms of *Black Skin, White Masks*, but rather in the sociological and historical terms of *The Wretched of the Earth*. In this latter work, Fanon observes that the Manichean logic of colonial transference reappears during the initial postindependence period, only this time the constituencies in both camps are indigenous to the postcolonial nation. The positions formerly occupied by the European colonial elite are now taken up by members of the national bourgeoisie. It becomes apparent, in other words, that independence has failed to address the underlying structures that cause extreme material inequalities in the postcolony. Crucially, both for Fanon's purposes and my own, the frustration that this phenomenon inevitably fosters among the anticolonial agitators is followed in a second moment by an at once anguished and invigorating feeling of betrayal vis-à-vis the promise—false of course—of not only the European colonial project, but its bourgeois-nationalist reincarnation as well. This sense of betrayal is the same one that animates the desperate plea of *Black Skin, White Masks*. Only this time in *The Wretched of the Earth*, Fanon puts the desperation to practical strategic use.

In the controversial chapter "On Violence," for example, Fanon brilliantly depicts the situation of the anticolonial forces in the emerging postcolonial nation during the period of colonialist decadence following the end of World War II. The military expenditures made necessary by the increasing tensions of the cold war, the entrenchment of social-democratic interests stemming from the consolidation of the western European welfare state, and the demands of the industrial working class with respect to postwar economic growth all collude to convince the third world intellectual that the colonial powers are no longer materially in a position to sustain the collapsing colonial administrations. It is at this moment, Fanon sees, that the choice between socialist and bourgeois models for the new postcolonial nation must be made.

Fanon argues that despite the growing sense among intellectuals from both North and South of the historical inevitability of colonialism's demise, European modernity's cultural saturation of the colonized regions was so thoroughgoing that the emerging emancipatory movements begin to adopt—in a spontaneous, indeed unconscious, way—European modernity itself in all of its one-dimensional materialism as the object of their revolutionary subversions. Adopting a decidedly Enlightenment, Freudo-Kantian tone, Fanon notes that the colonized populations become painfully aware that they lack the accoutrements of industrial modernity so conspicuously on display before them in the colonial system. "By a kind of (infantile) reasoning," Fanon writes, "the masses become convinced that they have been robbed," their hopes "dashed" (34). Showing extraordinary historical foresight (much of it written during the previous two years, *Wretched* was completed during the summer of 1961, mere months after the majority of the new African nations gained independence), Fanon contends that this brand of transferential anticolonial infantilism accounts for the recklessly precipitous spontaneity of so much nationalist politicking, a spontaneity that inevitably engenders debilitating disappointment. "Two or three years after independence," Fanon writes, the colonized population asks itself "what was the point of fighting if nothing was really destined to change" (35).

Near the conclusion of *Wretched*, Fanon narrates a story from an unreferenced literary work by the Guinean poet and politician Keita Fodeba that surely resonated with his own experience in the French army during World War II. This narrative illustrates in brutal but poignant terms the kind of harrowing demythologization of colonialist ideology that the sense of betrayal evokes in the colonized. Moreover, the story unveils how the experience of colonialism's senseless violence traumatically awakens the indigenous subject from any unconscious dream she

might harbor of colonialist good will. Fodeba's poem tells the tale of
Naman, a West African man who, under the counsel of village elders,
leaves his tribe on the banks of the Niger to serve in the French colonial army as "the young man who best represents [his] race" (164).
After his release from a German prison at the war's conclusion, Naman
is decorated for his bravery on the battlefield and returns to Africa to
continue his military service in Senegal, where he is shot dead during
a racially motivated skirmish between African and French elements in
the colonial army.[18]
      In light of his own experience in the French military, one cannot
help but think that in recounting the poem Fanon also tells the story
of his own conversion to revolutionary anticolonial national consciousness; the story, that is to say, of the psychical event that forced him
painfully to come to terms with his transferential idealization of French
culture, including of course its long tradition of colonialist orientalism
and concrete wartime bloodthirstiness.

> There is not one colonized subject who will not understand
> the message in this poem. Naman, hero of the battlefields of
> Europe, Naman who vouched for the power and the conti-
> nuity of the metropolis, Naman mowed down by the police
> at the very moment he returns home; this is Sétif in 1945,
> Fort-de-France, Saigon, Dakar, and Lagos. All the "niggers"
> and all the "filthy Arabs" who fought to defend France's
> liberty or British civilization will recognize themselves in this
> poem by Keita Fodeba. (167)

The bleak outcome of Fodeba's narrative in all its devastating outrage,
symbolism, and typicality finally breaks the colonized's unconscious fascination with the prestige of colonial culture, putting a decisive end to
the demand for cultural recognition that motivates the lofty projects of
postcoloniality: the nostalgic rediscovery of long-lost African kingdoms
or the folkloric recuperation of authentic indigenous cultural practices,
for instance. The colonized finally abandons the project to establish a
cultural identity acknowledged by the European colonial Other, a project
that can only function as a politically inhibitory fetish.
      When Fanon writes that every colonized person will recognize
themselves in Fodeba's poem, he isn't evoking the kind of recognition
on which assertions of cultural identity depend. Recognition in this

instance rests instead on the identification of the self with the colonized subject *as he appears as an object in colonial fantasy*; as, precisely, the evil, immoral, primitive subhuman refuse that can be expediently discarded as a casualty of colonial progress or development. The transferential demand to be seen as one wants to be seen through the legitimizing eyes of the colonial master is now replaced by a confrontation with the brutal real of colonialism's death-bearing and ambivalent fascination with racialized alterity. Fanon mercilessly elucidates the seemingly paradoxical logic by which the political radicalization of the colonized occurs precisely through his internalization of the pathological, racializing images of colonialism itself. Unlike the consoling identitarian fantasies of postcoloniality, this wrenching subjective destitution holds within itself the power to wrest the colonized from his unconscious colonial dependency. The concrete suffering that it unveils persuades this subject to run the risk of a rebellion addressed not to the colonial authorities in all their idealized prestige and authority, but rather to her destitute peers among the wretched of the earth. These wretched are utterly empty of value in the colonial system and devoid even of any redemptive critical knowledge of the means of their own oppression.

A Pack of Rats

There is something in the shocking urgency of Fodeba's uncompromising poem that casts the retreat to an inward-looking culturalism as a patently empty and self-defeating gesture. The object of anticolonial investment in culturally predicated forms of praxis is an exalted and idealized one, which in psychoanalytic terms is constructed in the hopes of satisfying a transferential demand for love. Claims to cultural authenticity or value can only convincingly be acknowledged from "outside" the culture; they can only materialize in the colonial context as the product of a positive judgment from a recognized, that is to say Euro-American, authority.

In starkest contrast, narratives such as Fodeba's confront the colonized with the cruel realities of colonial history, foregrounding not only the hypocrisy of colonialism's false ideals, but also the colonized's unwitting complicity in his own victimization. It cannot be denied that the everyday functioning of the colonialist order depended in part not only on the colonized's belief, however unconscious, in the civilizing mission, but also on this subject's share, however meager, in the privileges of the colonial system. As Fanon makes abundantly clear, the colonized's oppression by the colonial regime does not go without a certain dividend in pleasure: idle lifestyle daydreams of the omnipotent settler who has everything, the exalted and exoticizing imaginings of a nativist past that was never lived, or the social-climbing and racially purifying fantasies of interracial bourgeois marriage as decried by Fanon himself in his prodigious misreading of Mayotte Capécia's novel of colonial alienation *Je suis martiniquaise.*

Fanon importantly implies that the subjective and material destitution of the native subject who has traversed her colonialist fantasy is what motivates her adoption of the radical anticolonial perspective that he wants to valorize. *The Wretched of the Earth* returns repeatedly to the fundamental Marxian principle that the only spontaneously revolutionary constituency in any sociosymbolic formation is precisely the one that has no place in it and in consequence has nothing to lose. The difficulty is that it is only by reaching that state of despondency and hopelessness—like the *Hilflösigkeit* of the Freudian analysand at the moment just prior to the termination of analysis—that the subject will accept the loss of all advantage, no matter how piddling, available in the colonial system. Only then will the colonized accept the necessity of radical risk—for Fanon, organized armed struggle against the colonial apparatus—to any lasting overthrow of an oppressive status quo.

Not until this crucial turning point is reached do the ideal objects of colonial transference—the authentic and harmonious precolonial tribal life, the Parnassus of negritude poets and the African cultural academy, or (for the heterosexual colonized woman) marriage to the appealing and prestigious colonial administrator—give way to another kind of object with highly contrasting attributes. This object resists all efforts at redemption through integration with the value system of colonialism. Fanon's text is at its most subversive and politically consequential when it evokes the powerful agency of this latter object which, in truth, is not a different object but rather the same one in an alternative guise, one that causes the emergence of an authentic anticolonial desire. In the Lacanian terms with which we acquainted ourselves in chapter 1, the ideal objects belong to the ego structure comprised of I and $i(a)$, whereas the latter bespeaks the agency of the partial object a.

The transition from one modality of the object to the other occurs in Fanon's writing as the colonized achieves a degree of autonomy before the pathologizing tropes and images of colonial discourse. The colonized gains access to this autonomy not by constructing an alternatively positive or more authentic image or discourse, but rather by adopting the objects of colonialism's scorn as objects of love. These objects in their very abjection begin to motivate the new humanity that for Fanon will be borne of organized militant anticolonial struggle.[19]

In his description of this process, Fanon employs the moral categorizations that structure the discourse of colonialism. Because the settler, for example, "turns the colonized into a kind of quintessence of evil" (*Wretched*, 6), the colonized must accept that anticolonial action must take this evil as its cause. This particular structure of desire determines the colonized's enunciation in such a way that it gives voice to the interests jettisoned from the field of possible representation under the colonialist status quo. The anticolonial proponent of national consciousness must come to the conclusion that the only truly subversive response to colonialism's pathologization of the colonized is to embrace these images precisely on the level of their pathology, to allow these abject quasi-objects to function as the catalyst for collective political action.

In this precise sense Fanon puts into practice the principle of literalism that characterizes psychoanalytic interpretation. As a means of clearing a path for alternative, more desirable representations, nativist responses to colonialist cultural oppression tend to respond to racist stereotyping by positing an ethnic reality steeped in cultural significance and meaning. The Mannoni example demonstrates that there is even a psychoanalytic version of this strategy: colonialism's racializing images of the native are in reality psychical projections that deliver the sordid truth of its own unconscious. In contrast, Fanon's anticolonial strategy simply accepts what is plainly and disturbingly visible on colonialism's Manichean surface, foregoing in this way the hysterical demand for more accurate or pleasing representations.

> The "native" is declared impervious to ethics, representing not only the absence of values but also the negation of values. He is, dare we say it, the enemy of values. In other words, absolute evil. A corrosive element, destroying everything within his reach, a corrupting element, distorting everything which involves aesthetics or morals, an agent of malevolent powers, an unconscious and incurable instrument of blind forces. (6)

My argument here is that for Fanon the colonized must reach the point where this kind of racist rhetoric no longer incites a desire to prove it wrong. The authentically subversive response is rather to say: "Yes, Mr. Colonialist, you're absolutely right; we natives are indeed a corrosive agent with respect to all that you hold beautiful, true, and good." At which point, of course, the colonized constituencies proceed to corrode the colonial order, in other words, to realize in concrete sociopolitical terms the fears that motivate colonial racism in the first place. However counterintuitive it may sound, for Fanon the colonial order blinds the colonized with the truth, which triggers an inhibitory and often reactionary project to set the record straight. This desire must be addressed to, and is therefore determined by, the authority of colonial discourse. Colonialism's explicit recognition of the potential destructiveness of the native populations is precisely what functions to inhibit these populations' militant politicization. It would seem illogical to think that colonial power on some level did not have some aware- ness of these workings.

Yet even more crucially, in my view, Fanon goes so far as to claim for this evil of the colonial order the status of a truth. Fanon's wretched humanity works as the object-cause of his revolutionary anticolonial desire. The abject truth of the colonial system becomes the national cause that rallies the people around it, allowing them to achieve an abiding solidarity, however temporary or fragile, through the transcendence of the small ethnic, linguistic, or tribal differences that sow division. The abject quality of this object—the fact, more precisely, that it cannot function psychically as an object of identification—enables the jump to the generic universal that unites the nation against colonialism. In other words, because the wretched of the earth cannot form the basis of a desirable, socially sanctioned identity, there is no sociologically defined limit—ethnic, tribal, religious, linguistic, sexual—on the possibilities for affiliation with the cause.

The relation between Fanon's enlistment of the category of truth and the problematic of representation is crucial in this context. For Lacan, the truth of desire is the fictional fundamental fantasy around which our symbolic universe orbits. But this universe achieves its organizing power only by virtue of the exclusion of the fantasy, its relegation to the unconscious. Truth in *The Wretched of the Earth* has a precisely analogous status: it designates not only the original criminally violent history of conquest, displacement, and dispossession on which the colonial order rests, but also the subjects who, as a result of that history, have no place, remain invisible, within the colonial order. For this reason, there are tremendous political consequences to be drawn

from Fanon's explicit qualification of the truth of colonialism as ontological. "The fellah, the unemployed and the starving do not lay claim
to truth," he writes. "They do not say they represent the truth because
they are the truth in their very being" (13).

We can begin to elucidate these consequences by referencing postcolonial theory's preoccupation with the relation between sociopolitical
marginality and representation as evoked, for example, by Gayatri Spivak's
famous question "Can the subaltern speak?"[20] The context for Fanon's
musings on truth is a discussion framed around precisely this question.
It is almost possible to imagine that Fanon anticipated the tortured
theorizations of some contemporary postcolonial theorists when we read
about the radical intellectual who, as he begins to associate with the
dregs of humanity whose interests he so dearly wishes to "represent,"
will get mired in a "curious obsession with detail" that causes him not
only "to forget the real purpose of the struggle—the defeat of colonialism," but also to "lose sight of the unity of the movement" (13–14).

This comment surely implies that Fanon would have considered the
problematic of the representation of subalternity that has preoccupied
a wide swathe of postcolonial work over the last three decades as an
indulgence in theoreticist and subjectivist obfuscation. He might even
agree with me that this obfuscation reflects the guilty ambivalences of
academic intellectuals more than it does the concrete realities of anticolonial or socialist struggle. Peter Hallward insightfully argues that
Spivak's discourse on subalternity features all the hallmarks of what he
calls singularity. "The subaltern is the theoretically untouchable, the
altogether-beyond-relation," he writes. "The attempt to 'relate' to the
subaltern defines what Spivak will quite appropriately name an 'impossible ethical singularity.' "[21] In my view, Fanon's desire lends itself to
expression in Hallward's idiom as the project to bring the singularity
of subalternity into the specific, relational field of historicity and politics. The bottom line, as Hallward would likely agree, is that Spivakian
postcolonial ethics is incompatible with Fanonian anticolonial politics.

The representationalist neurosis of mainstream postcolonial theory
fails to take account of the structural nonsimultaneity of truth and the
arena of presentation-representation; the fact that they are not "compos-
sible," to use Badiou's term, cannot be co-present on the same level
of being. The recognition of this disjunction has the effect of shifting
the problematic of anticolonial politics away from its preoccupation
with the capacity of the intellectual ("us") to represent the masses or

the subaltern ("them") toward a concern for the anticolonial subject's position of enunciation vis-à-vis the radical truth of which Fanon speaks, regardless of her objective position in the sociosymbolic formation. The crucial requirement of an authentic anticolonial strategy for Fanon is that it locate itself in the non-space of this truth of pure being that cannot be represented in such a way that its enunciation can bear witness to it with fidelity. The intertwined ambivalences and half-suppressed outrage of *Black Skin, White Masks* are perhaps first and foremost testament to the difficulty and considerable cost of this gambit. What matters to Fanon is precisely the adoption of this "impossible" point of enunciation, not the particular socioeconomic attributes or subject position of the speaker himself. The colonized or postcolonial intellectual is not absolutely, necessarily compromised by her privilege. But he is certainly required to subtract himself "self-destructively" from its considerable forces of attraction.

The alternative theoretical perspective that I am proposing implies a shift of focus with respect to the old problematic of the representation of the masses. Though no doubt the subaltern cannot speak, the voice of subalternity can most certainly make itself heard. Precisely because the wretched masses in their status as the Fanonian truth are situated on the ontological register, paradoxically, they do not really, that is to say objectively, exist. Banished by the logic of the colonial or neocolonial situation, they cannot be represented in the way that a left-liberal politician is meant to represent his more unfortunate constituents, for example. Subalternity should be viewed as a position of enunciation rendered possible by a gesture of subtraction from the social as such. This gesture is premised on a sort of immediate, unreflective "identification"—unreflective because it dissolves, rather than constructs, identity, and therefore a sort of nonidentification of which there can be no intentional consciousness—with what we might call the excrement of the colonialist-imperialist organism.

Though the voice of subalternity bears no necessary relation to any social constituency empirically defined, it can only be heard from the subject who has affiliated with that constituency which is objectively nonexistent, beneath the threshold of intelligibility legislated by the social formation in question. The Fanonian anticolonial intellectual does not *speak for* the masses. These masses, after all, are in this view indeterminate by virtue of the fact that they cannot on the level of their being partake of (re)presentation. Instead, she assumes, takes on, the truth and, as the self/other binary implodes, locates the masses in all their/our wretched abjection as object-cause of desire and as the truth of being. Then, quite simply, she speaks. The various criticisms of Fanon's involvement with the Algerian struggle—his Arabic was inadequate, he was insufficiently aware of Algeria's "Muslim reality," the FLN leadership never quite trusted him given his outsider status—are therefore simply instances of phobic skepticism about the very possibility of such a putatively impossible subjective commitment. These criticisms furnish an alibi that helps dissimulate the traumatic and disorienting realization that the skeptic might be capable of assuming such a commitment himself.

In 1961, Fanon quite naturally looked askance at orthodox Marxist political doctrine, because its privileged historical actor—the industrial proletariat—did not exist as such in postwar North Africa, nor was its formation at all discernible on the horizon of even the most ambitious fantasies of the ideologues of economic development. It is certainly true that Fanon in his work identifies the peasantry as the most spontaneously subversive group in the late Algerian colonial context. More specifically, he singles out those numerous peasants who abandon the relative security of tribal tradition in an unsuccessful attempt to integrate with the colonial economy in the national or regional capital. For Fanon, what is crucial about this constituency, to which he refers by the term *lumpenproletariat*, is that its angry anticolonial spontaneity stems precisely from its state of utter dispossession. The late colonial lumpenproletariat remains marginal to both what remains of the structures of precolonial tradition and the colonial system's waning material resources and privileges.

Fanon clearly departs from Marxist orthodoxy here as well, since the lumpenproletariat's very formlessness and unpredictability—the distance from industrial production's tendency in the right conditions to foster political organization, a distance which for Marx made this group especially prone to succumbing to the seductions of reactionary populist ideologies—is for Fanon the very source of its explosive activist potential. "The lumpenproletariat, this cohort of starving men, divorced from tribe and clan," Fanon writes, "constitutes one of the most spontaneously and radically revolutionary forces of a colonized people" (81). Ato Sekyi-Otu has provided the most concise definition of Fanon's version of the lumpenproletariat. "Faced with the most basic of human needs," he writes, it is "that class to whose members every access to the treacherous advantages of colonialism and modernity is barred, and who are the resentful witnesses to the privileged servitude of the national bourgeoisie and proletariat, the living accusation against the distributive injustice of the colonial order, the class in colonial society which has no place in its scheme of gradations."[22]

Yet from another angle Fanon remains close to Marxist-Leninist doctrine in his insistence that the authentically spontaneous potentialities of this lumpenproletariat only underscore the necessity of organization and leadership within anticolonial activity. The revolutionary elite perform a crucial pedagogical function that has them join the masses in the effort to build a national anticolonial consciousness. By emphasizing the importance of dialogue between leaders and led, and by dismissing the value of political rhetoric that resists popular understanding, Fanon's political theory desirably situates itself midway between what has been widely criticized as Leninist party vanguardism's doctrinaire and dictatorial underpinnings and the naive, feel-good horizontality of left postmodernism's rhizomatic, neo-anarchist, and autonomist imaginaries. The role of the anticolonial leadership for Fanon is simply to teach the lesson of collective agency. What the masses need to learn, as he succinctly puts it, is that "everything depends on them" (138). Leadership is responsible for communicating two fundamental lessons: revolution is indeed possible, but it cannot happen without everyone's participation.

Fanon's discourse on the colonized lumpenproletariat should be read in my view as a delineation of revolutionary anticolonial activity's subjective preconditions, "subjective" here understood in nonpsychological terms as the structural orientation of the colonized collectivity's desire vis-à-vis the colonial apparatus and its discourse. The prerequisite for radical anticolonial practice, or any other form of radical political practice for that matter, is the condition of utter dispossession in which the subject accepts its death with respect to the existing social order, dissolving its personhood in an immediate affiliation with the collective national cause as emblematized by this nation's most abject members. Far from romanticizing the wretched of the earth, or glossing over the brute materiality of their malnourishment, Fanon's theory targets the elimination of the distance between the revolutionary elite (which nonetheless remains, for the anti-anarchist Fanon, structurally necessary) and its subjects in such a manner that strategic anticolonial action eliminates at the moment of the act whatever remains of the distance.

The hunger of the masses becomes the hunger of all; the revolution is not complete until everyone is fed.

Fanon's anticolonial subject decisively steps out of the logic of demand and recognition that characterizes what Freud called transference love, the love that defines the colonizer-colonized binary and the entire edifice of colonial Manicheanism that Fanon so memorably describes. Fanon's most original insight lies in his acknowledgment that this extrication can occur only through the internalization of colonialism's insipidly pathologizing discourse. Within the terms of colonial transference love, only colonialism holds the power to acknowledge cultural worth. The true anticolonial politics is therefore secured through an unconditional affiliation with the masses, whose formless and unredeemable opacity can provide no reassuring self-affection, no affirmation of identity, no rationale for intellectual work or alibi for material privilege.

The masses belong to a category distinguished by its empty and universal attributes. This category is empty because the location of the masses beyond the limits of possible representation disallows the attribution to them of any determinate sociological content. They can only be discerned negatively through their nonappearance within the realm of acknowledged or identifiable political interest. Yet the masses are also universal in the precise sense that they designate the truth of the colonial regime considered as a material-semiotic totality. The masses are in this sense the absent cause of the field of political intelligibility, a cause whose subtraction from what can be recognized as a legitimate political interest ensures the field's closure and coherence, and hence its inherently exclusionary and ideological frame of meaning.

The Fanonian anticolonial subject undergoes a *conversion* through his submersion under the sovereignty of the national cause; in the process she is quite literally born again, reformed. Stripped of the characteristics assumed under the colonial sociosymbolic system, this subject acquires new life within the sphere of a general, global struggle against capitalist imperialism, a struggle that unites subjects in all their heterogeneous particularisms under the banner of a common fight against all those who would thwart the cause. Fanon's revolutionary subject therefore appears not under the poststructuralist sign of difference, but rather as inscribed within a sameness that effectively universalizes the externality of the lumpenproletariat with respect to the colonial system. The elimination of all points of contact with the colonialist status quo emancipates the anticolonial revolutionary, allowing him to step outside its field of signification, undermining in the process the very coherence and stability of colonialist meaning systems.

Now, it cannot be denied that Fanon describes this revolutionary renaissance through figures of purification and cleansing, and this redemptive element in his discourse, not unrelated to his existentialist humanism, merits considerable skepticism. Yet it is also clear that he recognizes that this purification in its psychical aspect involves both an assumption of shame and a dislocating yet emancipatory experience of defilement, of unification with the refuse of the metropolitan regime. In this precise sense Fanon's politics is premised on a refusal to seek a redemptive integration with the colonial order. This refusal cannot fully be reconciled with the official Sartrean socialist humanism that also, and more conspicuously, animates his text.

The object-cause of revolutionary anticolonial desire is finally for Fanon the lumpenproletariat itself: a "pack of rats" that goes on "gnawing at the roots of the tree" of colonialism; a "gangrene eating into the heart of colonial domination" (81). Consider now Fanon's description of the (anti-)heroic subjects of anticolonial struggle who collectively constitute the disavowed truth of European colonial history.

> The pimps, the hooligans, the unemployed, and the petty criminals, when approached, give the liberation struggle all they have got, devoting themselves to the cause like valiant workers. These vagrants, these second-class citizens, find their way back to the nation thanks to their decisive, militant action. Unchanged in the eyes of colonial society or vis-à-vis the moral standards of the colonizer, they believe the power of the gun and the hand grenade is the only way to enter the cities. These jobless, these species of subhumans, redeem themselves in their own eyes and before history. The prostitutes too, the domestics at two thousand francs a month, the hopeless cases, all those men and women who fluctuate between madness and suicide, are restored to sanity, return to action and take their vital place in the great march of a nation on the move. (81–82)

Yet it does not suffice to describe these agents in their unbeautiful abjection. The task of the anticolonial activist intellectual is precisely to eliminate the distance in her subjective economy between herself and "them," to recognize herself in these wretched masses, positioning this them/us as the root, as it were, of the national cause. Fanon readily admits that the lumpenproletariat's "lack of political consciousness and ignorance" (87) can lead it to fall into the hands of the colonial oppressors once their deadly reprisals against the spontaneous uprisings of the early days of anticolonial rebellion take the scene. The task of the anticolonial leader is therefore to "transform the movement from a peasant revolt into a revolutionary war" (86), to harness the energies unleashed by spontaneous insurrection among the abject masses in order to develop an organized armed resistance whose objective it is to bring the colonial era to a decisive close. The Fanonian anticolonial intellectual must ensure that this dynamic remains *indifferent* to the symbolic values of colonial discourse. The redemption of the wretched of the earth must be discernible not through the edifying eyes of colonial society, but rather from the earthly and unglamorous perspective of the history of basest humanity's progressive emancipation from oppression.

In the beginning pages of *The Wretched of the Earth*, Fanon describes what he bravely calls the "hysterical" qualities of a tradition-based African community "relegated to the realm of the imagination" (19) in ecstatic dances and mythologizing religious ritual, precisely the elements of indigenous cultures that Western New Age, cultural-anthropological intellectuals seek to preserve. It would be a grave, disastrous mistake, indeed a betrayal of Fanon's lifework, to link the "we" who observes these phenomena to the Eurocentric perspective of anthropological racism, which Fanon in this mistaken view would have symptomatically "internalized." Rather, Fanon's first-person plural designates the set of new men and women in the North and South united against both the forces of imperialist global capital and the obscurantism of indigenist, nativist, tribalist, and all other forms of culturalism. This is Fanon's desire, I want to contend, in its most authentically revolutionary form. The challenge before us today is to defend the legitimacy of its anti-identitarian socialist universalism against the dominant vectors of differentiating particularization that are mobilized in liberal multiculturalist discourses, which hide a secret complicity with the neocolonial logic of capital under the obfuscating cloak of antiracist tolerance and respect for alterity. This is the only way to bear faithful witness to Fanon's imperfect but immensely brave foray into the still uncharted territory that lies beyond colonial transference.

IV

Loving the Terrorist

Massacre and Subjectivation

During a two-year period beginning in October 1970, at the invitation of Mahmoud el Hamchari, the Paris-based PLO leader whose 1972 assassination at the hands of the Israeli secret service Steven Spielberg depicts in his 2005 film *Munich*,[1] Jean Genet spent a total of eleven months among the Palestinian refugees and resistance fighters in the northwest corner of Jordan. Following Israel's illegal 1967 occupation of the West Bank, Gaza, the Sinai peninsula, and the Golan Heights, the Palestinian refugees expelled from these regions organized an armed guerrilla resistance, establishing a handful of camps on the hills of the River Jordan's east bank between Amman, the Jordanian capital, and the Syrian border. Approximately five thousand Palestinian fedayeen were stationed in this region during that time.

In spite of its official endorsement of the Palestinian struggle's legitimacy, the Jordanian Hashemite monarchy grew increasingly wary of the refugees' powerful presence in the kingdom after the Six Day War. King Hussein began to fear that the political destabilization occasioned by the Palestinian presence might produce a military coup establishing Palestinian sovereignty In August 1970, under intense diplomatic pressure, Hussein signed in concert with Egypt a U.S.-sponsored peace accord with Israel, which the Palestinians understandably viewed as a betrayal of their cause. King Hussein's regime then instigated a brutal crackdown against the Palestinians, culminating in the infamous massacres of Black September[2] during which the Jordanian army, at this time composed mainly of Bedouins and Circassians, decimated the camps around Amman and Zarka, killing at least three thousand Palestinians. Genet arrived in Jordan roughly a month after these attacks. His arrival

at this fateful moment inaugurated a remarkable episode of revolutionary fellow-travelership which would fuel the fires of Genet's literary
and political passions for the remainder of his life. It also caused him
to question the value of the entirety of his prior literary production.

The massacres of Black September motivated Genet to return
to West Asia for the first time since his late teens, when he had been
stationed in French-mandate Syria as a member of the French Foreign
Legion. But it was an even more infamous tragedy that put a stop to
the ten-year period of creative procrastination that followed Genet's
first Palestinian sojourn. Obeying perhaps a prescient intuition of the
Palestinians' dark destiny in the Lebanese war—his instincts on political developments in the region were nothing if not prescient—Genet
returned to Beirut in September 1982. There he witnessed firsthand
the events leading up to the massacres in the Palestinian camps of
Sabra and Shatila where armed fighters, outfitted in the uniforms of the
Israeli-allied right wing Lebanese Christian Phalangist militia, slaugh-
tered a significant portion of the refugee population, much of which
had been forced to relocate from Jordan to Lebanon in the aftermath
of the Black September massacres twelve years before.

Prior to the savage attacks on Sabra and Shatila, the Israeli Defense
Forces had put in place a military installation at the camps' entrances
to monitor goings-on within. Though the extent of Israeli involvement
in the massacres has never been incontrovertibly established, it is clear
that at minimum Israeli soldiers stationed at the installation observed
the carnage and did nothing to intervene or to sound the alarm. Witnesses reported that the Israelis lit up the sky above the camps with
flares, one can only assume to facilitate the slaughter occurring below.
Outrage at Israel's complicity stretched well beyond its established Arab
enemies. "The connection with the I[sraeli] D[efense] F[orces]," Israeli
historian Ilan Pappe observes, "was clear enough to convince 400,000
Israelis to protest against the massacre, and led to the establishment of
a commission of inquiry." Israel's own Kahan commission eventually
"dismissed several senior officers involved," Pappe drily adds, finally
ruling "that [Ariel] Sharon, [then Israeli] minister of defense, was unfit
to serve in such a high position."[3]

As Robert Fisk notes in his essential *The Great War for Civilization*, the Kahan commission went so far as to hold Sharon "personally
responsible" for the killings, underlining how the minister spuriously
proclaimed PLO responsibility for the assassination of Phalangist leader

Bashir Gemayel, who had just been elected Lebanese president, immediately before he issued the directive to the Christian militia to enter
the camps.[4] Clearly, however, the stinging indictments of numerous
compatriots were not enough to prevent Sharon from being elected
Israeli prime minister eighteen years later when, after years of systematic
expropriations and forced expulsions of Arabs from East Jerusalem, he
undertook a heavily guarded and provocative foray onto the grounds
of the al-Aqsa mosque, unleashing a protest that predictably produced
four Palestinian victims of Israeli sniper fire and inaugurating what
became known as the second intifada.[5]

The number of dead at Sabra and Shatila, which the most reliable
sources estimate at around 1,500 ("up to 1,700 Palestinian refugees"
perished, Fisk writes [505]), remains indeterminate today. This is
largely due to the fact that the Israeli army held control of the camps'
entrances in the days following the killings, preventing authorities from
establishing and communicating the extent of the carnage. Also, there is
evidence to suggest that a large number of prisoners were surreptitiously
moved to other locations to be more discreetly murdered. It was not
until September 19, a full three days after the massacres, that Genet,
posing as a journalist, managed to enter the camps, in fact becoming
the very first Westerner to do so.

Wading through a devastated landscape littered with corpses rot-
ting under a blistering sun, Genet spent an afternoon observing the
massacre's gruesome outcome.[6] Afterward, Genet immediately returned
to Paris where, in a sudden spurt of literary creativity, he spent the
month of October writing the harrowing and unforgettable "Quatre
heures à Shatila," which would appear for the first time in the *Revue
d'études palestiniennes* the following January.[7] Relieved, it would seem
definitively, of the debilitating depression that he had been suffering
on and off for years, Genet at last set to work on the text that would
become *Prisoner of Love,* a text that he had planned to begin ever since
his first return to West Asia twelve years earlier, and which he had
been urged to write by no lesser a figure than Yassir Arafat, the iconic,
recently departed leader of Fatah and tarnished post-Oslo symbol of
Palestinian aspirations.

The most insightful of Genet's critics will on occasion refer to
Prisoner of Love, which treats his sojourn not only with the pre-intifada
Palestinian resistance, but with the American Black Panthers as well, as
his most significant work. Yet, with surprisingly few notable exceptions

the text has received scant critical attention, particularly among critics writing in English, and remains to this day scandalously under-
read. Speculation about why this has been the case yields a variety
of factors: widespread support for Israeli policy among the dominant
English-language media, or at least its ownership; the thoroughgoing
delegitimization of Marxian revolutionary movements since the collapse
of the Eastern bloc; the ideological overdetermination, especially since
the World Trade Center attacks and subsequent Anglo-American occupation of Iraq and ISAF-NATO presence in Afghanistan, of engagements
with the Arab and Muslim worlds; and finally, perhaps especially, the
literary difficulty and historical density of the text itself.

Doubtless each of these factors is at play. Yet it is also possible to
view *Prisoner's* relative nonreception as a continuation of the unsettled
response that Genet's numerous scandalous crossings have elicited
from a *bien-pensant* reading public ever since the appearance of his
earliest work. This chapter's premise will be that Genet's later writings, culminating in *Prisoner of Love*, offer an exemplary demonstration
of what can occur when an artist takes the risk of going beyond the
transference, that is to say when he pursues desire beyond the limits
that guard against the disruptive agency of the real. This pursuit has
the capacity fleetingly to unveil the veritable and scandalous cause of
desire as well as the seemingly impossible possibility of the unforeseeable effects to which this cause can give rise. The boundaries that
Genet sets himself the task of transgressing are not merely the ones the
subversion of which is ordinarily celebrated in comparative literary and
cultural studies, namely, those between cultures, ethnicities, and races;
socioeconomic classes; languages or dialects; genders and sexualities.
Rather, like Lacan's Antigone, Genet sets himself the task of breaching
the frontier that demarcates the field of intelligibility of life as such,
the line that implicitly sets down the very terms by means of which
cultural comparisons are customarily drawn.

Indeed, I would suggest that the subversions that *Prisoner* puts into
effect violate so systematically the West's latterly precarious hegemonic
idea of itself—white as against nonwhite, occident as against orient,
masculine as against feminine, civilization as against barbarism, freedom as against fraternity, order as against violence, sexuality as against
incest—that the very conditions of possibility of this idea, along with
the various differentiations that form its ground, are dramatically torn
asunder. In the process, Genet's violations uncover the acts of ideologi-

cal and epistemological violence that take place unrecognized before
the work of standard-issue comparative cultural analysis can even begin.

In fact, Genet's transgressions articulate a veritable ethics of revolt
so challenging that even those among his readers most well disposed to
his later work—notably biographer Edmund White and the late Edward
Said, the former with respect to a perceived low-grade anti-Semitism,
the latter on the topic of Genet's notion of ecstatic betrayal—have felt
obliged to maintain their distance from certain of its aspects. While
commenting on a 1971 Genet essay that appeared in a French photog-
raphy magazine in tandem with Bruno Barbey's images of Palestinian
refugee camps, White advances the view that "although the editors of
Zoom were careful to point out that Genet was anti-Zionist but not
anti-Semitic, the question remains an open one."[8] As expressed in his
biography of Genet, White's position on Israel and its critics rests on
the overfamiliar and patently illogical assumption that an anti-Zionist
argument can only with extreme difficulty, if at all, be extricated from
the charge of anti-Semitism.[9] Brought to its conclusion, this ideological
conflation of Israeli policy with the Jewish religion or ethnicity refuses
outright to entertain the legitimacy of any Arab claim to historical
Palestine. A key component of the cynical post-holocaust blackmail
from which White fails to extricate himself, this staunchly tendentious
argument can in my view accurately be qualified as racist.

But to do it justice a closer look at White's commentary is no
doubt required. Paraphrasing Genet's *Zoom* article argument, White
writes that "after two thousand years of the humiliating Diaspora and
ten years of the Nazi extermination campaign, Jews ha[d] taken on the
inhumanity of their former masters," adding that "although Israel was
conceived as a refuge for European Jews," for Genet "it ha[d] become
the bastion of Western imperialism in the Middle East." White takes
issue with these contentions, averring that such views result from what
he calls Genet's "highly coloured version of Jewish history" (558). Yet
White's position conveniently exonerates him from the obligation actually to consider the substance of Genet's perfectly legitimate criticism
of not only political Zionism's self-justifying manipulation of the Jewish holocaust's terrible tragedy, but also its consistent complicity with
European, and more recently American, strategic interests—classically
colonialist in nature—in the West Asia region. This history goes back
most significantly to the days of the post-Ottoman British Mandate,
whose generally friendly policies toward Zionist colonization—the

notorious 1917 Balfour Declaration is the best example—were surely a historical condition of possibility for the advent of the Jewish state. As is widely and duly recognized, Said's work on Palestine represents one of the best and most heroic attempts to defy the manipulative *Denkverbot* that prevents White from accounting with integrity for Genet's position. His laudable "On Jean Genet's Late Work" article is chock full of illuminating insights on the singular courage shown in both Genet's embrace of progressive politics in the Arab world and the literary manifestation of this politics not only in *Prisoner*, but in his ultimate dramatic piece *The Screens* as well. Without question, this is literary criticism of the highest order. Yet even though he proves unusually penetrating in his analysis of the uncompromising negativity and anti-identitarianism of Genet's concept of betrayal, carefully distinguishing, for example, Genet's always sociopolitically situated ethics of revolt from a conservatively and metaphysically nihilistic doctrine, Said in one particular passage awkwardly and indeed violently minimizes the weight of Genet's challenge by qualifying his ethics as "dubious, even repellent, on moral and political grounds." Though he warmly identifies Genet as an effective advocate for the Palestinian cause, Said ultimately propones the confinement of Genet's idea of betrayal to the "tolerable," decidedly bourgeois terrain of an "aesthetic or rhetorical credo" (Said 237).

There is something notably symptomatic about the contrast—contradiction, rather—between, on the one hand, Said's sensitive and more or less ringing endorsement of Genet's partisan enthusiasm for Arab sovereignty in Algeria and Palestine and, on the other, his cagey self-distancing from Genet's desire to systematize his musings on ecstatic betrayal and the import of evil into a sort of ethical conceptuality. For Said, Genet's concrete political positions on Arab-Israeli and Arab-European politics are one thing, but his general conceptual-poetic framework, it would seem, quite another. In the last analysis, Said proves reluctant to take on the full consequences of Genet's disruptive sensibility, as if doing so might commit him to undefined causes and positions that threaten to compromise the respectability of his own work. One senses that Said might have wished to reproach Genet for what he calls his solitude: the sense in which the Frenchman's ethics of revolt proves tricky to reconcile with any familiar notion of collective anticolonial national sovereignty, or even arguably of national culture in the properly Fanonian sense.[10] Curiously, however, Said's underdeveloped reservations never reach such a substantive level. His reader is left with the nagging sense of a promising opportunity missed.

With these examples in mind of his tendency to elicit anxious responses in even his most sympathetic readers, it comes as little surprise that Genet's later work also sheds an oblique, unsettling, and surely counterhegemonic light on dominant assumptions and methods in contemporary Anglo-American literary and cultural studies. In the same way that it fearlessly exposes *avant la lettre* the shortcomings of even its best-placed commentators' readings, Genet's later work also lays bare the inherent limitations of a wide swathe of contemporary humanistic inquiry. I propose now to survey these methodological implications of Genet's move beyond the transference before engaging in a more detailed discussion of exactly how Genet orchestrates this move in *Prisoner of Love*.

One especially illuminating example of Genet's potential disciplinary impact relates to the question of culture and interpretive method. As a Frenchman, albeit one decisively alienated from his nation and its traditions, Genet engages with the Arab-Muslim world in the wake of a long and by now exhaustively interrogated tradition of European orientalisms and exoticisms. As is well known, Said's rightly acclaimed work on this topic, along with the entire critical tradition that it has helped to inspire, has spelled out how European representations of non-European realities have served to justify claims to Western cultural identity and its inherent superiority, and thereby to grant spurious ideological legitimacy to centuries of intensely exploitative imperialisms and colonialisms.[11] In response to this unseemly history, critics have justifiably striven to produce more contextually situated analyses of "other" cultural artifacts. More specifically, in the best examples of comparative work in this tradition, complex patterns of cross-cultural, transnational, cosmopolitan, and interlinguistic influence have been suggestively charted and theorized.

Yet I want to argue that Genet's Palestinian calling is born of a different desire, one that perhaps calls into question a predominant culturalist assumption underlying much of even the most sophisticated comparative work. This assumption holds that the crossings of cultural travelers such as Genet destabilize or even dissolve borders between cultural contexts or systems which, in spite of their varying degrees of complexity, hybridity, internal antagonism, or even self-contradiction, remain more or less fully chartable, wholly available to cultural-interpretive inquiry. Numerous diagnostic claims about Genet's Arab adventures could be made in this regard. Disgusted with French and/or Judeo-Christian traditions, Genet seeks to reinvent himself, along with his literary initiatives, in alien cultural territory, seeking inspiration or renewal in radical alterity. A more critical version of this same assumption might run as follows: in the outright rejection of his French childhood and adolescence, Genet turns to Palestine in a gesture of symptomatic compensatory revolt, failing in the process to appreciate, through projection or ignorance, the authentic cultural nuances of his new surroundings.

The more obvious shortcoming of the brand of comparativism that produces such (far from irrelevant) insights is that it culturalizes what is first and foremost a patently *political* mode of solidarity or affiliation in Genet. To be sure, Genet's later texts are rife with pronouncements on the repressiveness and hypocrisy of a surely undernuanced notion of Judeo-Christian morality. Yet Genet is at bottom as little concerned with the cultural or racial identity of the Black Panthers (though he is certainly intrigued by their politico-aesthetic mobilization of blackness) as he is with the Arabness of the Palestinians, except insofar as these can be negatively mobilized as weapons against racializing colonialist European universalisms. Never is Genet "anthropologically" fascinated by cultural, ethnic, or religious differences for their own sake; never do such differences become a key component of his political thought.

A second and, in my view, more significant drawback of the culturalist-comparativist approach that I have sketched out here is its inherent inability to recognize that what captures Genet's interest within his political movements—the Palestinian resistance and the Black Panthers, but also Baader-Meinhof (the German Red Army Faction)—what veritably transforms him into a *captif amoureux* (the English translation fails to convey the sense of capture or captivation), is their thoroughly immanent yet negative-impossible status within the political, cultural, and historical contexts in which they erupt. The acts performed by these groups momentarily uncovered the repressed, unconscious element of the sociopolitical worlds from which they were necessarily forcibly excluded, the element that very precisely could not be thought within available cultural and ideological systems. In the reading of *Prisoner of Love* that I undertake in later sections of this chapter, I aim to show in what ways this alternative assumption is essential to a proper understanding of Genet's ultimate text.

Now, my reference to the unconscious also necessarily leads onto the terrain of sexuality, which—nothing is more consistent in his perpetually morphing work—is surely inextricable from Genet's singular ethico-political orientation. Despite his iconic status as a twentieth-century homosexual writer, on the biographical level Genet's influential and pioneering imaginative exploration of marginal sexualities notably failed to lead him to adopt a "political" view of homosexuality, one comparable to those that emerged during the post-Stonewall decades, from the activisms that arose in response to the HIV/AIDS pandemic to the sometimes confusing deconstructive-cum-Foucaultian articulations of queer theory. Though there is little question that Genet's sexual sensibility, so dramatically shaped by his experiences in the French correctional system's so-called colonies, impacts heavily on the political engagements that mark his creative maturity (indeed, Genet himself repeatedly spells this link out), it is equally clear that the logic of Genet's work firmly resists any attempt at rendering his treatment of sexuality as anything remotely programmatic. Whatever sexuality may be for Genet, it most certainly is not, as it nearly universally has been in the various strands of sexuality studies, a substantive category of difference that features either necessary or desirable political consequences.

As my own reading of *Prisoner of Love* will try to show, Genet conceived of sexuality not as a function of psychological identity, and therefore as a term through which claims for recognition might be made within a liberal political framework, but rather as the mode of this identity's impossibility and ensuing unavoidable failure. In this precise sense, sexuality acquires in Genet a properly ethical dimension: it signals the terrain of the unthinkable, the unintelligible, the excluded. It is for this reason that sexuality plays a privileged role in Genet's assault on the hegemonic expression of power and its properly metaphysical pretensions.

A Century of Violence

The 1961 publication of his play *The Screens*—the disjointed, Algeria-inspired meditation on colonial savagery and decadence—together with the 1964 death of his Moroccan acrobat lover Abdalla Bentaga, saw Genet fall into an acute affective and creative slump. During this period Genet repeatedly renounced his previous literary output, becoming increasingly pessimistic about the value of literature in a world permeated by extreme racial and socioeconomic injustice. Intriguingly, however, Genet's disenchantment with the powers of literature came hand in hand with his political radicalization. This radicalization caused him to embrace an utterly singular affiliation with his favored causes, a paradoxical identification with the unidentifiable located beyond the transference which I will attempt to theorize throughout the remainder of this chapter.

Genet's commitment to these causes enabled him not only to continue living—he made what White calls a "serious" (496) suicide attempt in 1967—but also to effect a definitive psychical separation from the dominant Euro-American identity formation and its various epistemological frameworks, indeed, with the entire network of symbolic and imaginary structures associated with Freudian transference love, as we saw in chapter 1. Breaking with the unconscious demand underlying this mode of love, Genet's amorous passions—drives, to call them by their psychoanalytic name—consistently address themselves to those barely discernible objects forcibly excluded from political and cultural intelligibility. In so doing, Genet enjoins us gleefully to betray, violently if necessary, the censored *brutality* that guards the frontiers of worldly power. What has consistently proven so indigestible in Genet is his unswerving fidelity to those events of the latter half of the twentieth century that have most destructively shattered the self-image of what is called the West. The love of which Genet becomes the captive is therefore the active, self-dislocating love that emancipates the subject from the demand of Freudian transference love. The paradox of an act through which one becomes captured nicely conveys the nonintentional brand of agency beyond the limits of amorous gratification that emerges in Genet's later texts.

Genet's lifework can be viewed as a protracted preparation for this ultimate rupture. From his 1970 introduction to *Soledad Brother*, the collection of George Jackson's prison letters, to 1986's spellbinding *Prisoner*, surely the culmination of the process, the late writings document the trajectory of an exemplary ethico-political journey. The singularity of this journey is to be found in its amalgamation of two interrelated psychical gestures. First, a selfless and unconditional embrace of the (political) cause enables a complete divestiture from worldly interest. This involves a post-transferential subtraction of desire from its captivation by hegemonic ideals: in psychoanalytic terms, an encounter with the self-expropriating jouissance of the drive. In a more philosophical idiom, Genet's transformation by his political causes, most especially the Palestinian one, serve as the events, understood in Alain Badiou's sense, that effectively re-subjectivate Genet, allowing him to rediscover the consistency of his fidelity to the series of properly revolutionary subversions that characterize the radical, distinctively twentieth-century tradition of principled violence. The traversal of the unconscious demand for symbolic accommodation enables in Genet a critical self-reflexivity which impedes the contamination of the insurgent *militancy* of desire (in its real, "beyond" dimension) by the dependent, transferential *adherence* of identification.

Somewhat surprisingly, however, this reflexivity emerges as a result not of some neo-Brechtian gesture of distancing or Shklovskyesque formalist defamiliarization, versions of which are almost without exception mobilized in the methodological interests of critique, but rather as a self-violating immersion in the quasi-object of revolutionary desire, an immersion that does violence to the self by disaggregating the psychical points of reference—ego ideal and ideal ego—from which the self can be discerned, as I explored in detail in chapter 1. This dynamic, in my view, distinguishes Genet's Palestinian advocacy from so many instances of twentieth-century radical-political fellow-travellership, whose effectiveness is paradigmatically sabotaged by a familiar pattern: the neurotic alternation of exoticizing idealization and frustrated or melancholic disillusionment.

The workings of this dynamic also enable Genet to mount a remarkably prescient critique of those tendencies in Arab and Palestinian politics, both (Arab-) nationalist and more recently Islamist, that have effectively betrayed the cause Genet supported in such exemplary fashion during the last two decades of his life. Tragically, these tendencies have perverted so much of contemporary Palestinian and Arab World politics, threatening to transform them into the mirror image—though one deprived of any substantive political or military power—of the racist, classically colonialist political Zionism to which they originally stood opposed.

The framework I bring to my reading of Genet carries the assumption that he may in fact be the literary figure who best exemplifies the quintessential passions of the twentieth century. I would even suggest that, as we negotiate the contemporary global political and economic reality that Hardt and Negri have termed empire,[12] our challenge is to remain faithful to those convulsive and indigestible political traumas, supremely vulnerable in their near unintelligibility, to which Genet became unconditionally attached. In this light, it is tremendously à propos that in his book *The Century* Badiou refers to *Prisoner of Love* in a footnote at the outset of his study.[13] Against the standard-issue conservative and pseudo-ethical narrative of the preceding century as the story of universal liberal capitalism's victory over totalitarianism and fascism, in other words, as the triumph of an ersatz idea of freedom over "crime," Badiou proposes to conceive of it rather as a sustained sequence of radical posthumanist experimentation, as a string of attempts to transcribe the real of the Idea—communism and the new socialist "man" in politics; the subtraction of sex from meaning in psychoanalysis; the decommodification of the work as irreducible *act* in avant-garde art—onto the very materiality of history.

The defining feature of the past century for Badiou is therefore a passion for the real: a dedication to those evanescent scenes of violent rupture that produce effects of subjectivation by subtracting participants and witnesses alike from the everyday circulation of values, meanings, and ideas—opinion, in Badiou's vocabulary. Politically, this requires in Badiou's view an adamant refusal to succumb to the moralistic blackmail of the dominant democratic ideology that desires above all else to cast the eruption of political, scientific, and artistic *violence*, regardless of its means of self-justification and concrete sociopolitical impact, as the very incarnation of evil. This idea of evil can then predictably serve as the negative value against which a (bourgeois, liberal) Good can be defined. For Badiou—for whom the paradigmatic political events of the century are the Russian Bolshevik revolution, the Chinese Maoist revolutions, the various anticolonial nationalist revolutions of the 1950s and 60s, as well as the Euro-American student and worker revolts of 1968—the primary function of such judgments is to eradicate in advance the tenuous possibility of the emergence of genuine, unforeseen, "impossible" alternatives; to foreclose on the difficult work of bearing witness to happenings that occur beneath the threshold of social and historical intelligibility. The violence that tends to accompany such scenes of rupture is therefore the *good violence* that would destroy the mechanisms of exploitation, thereby clearing a path for what Badiou inspiringly describes as the "advent of another humanity, of a radical change in what man is" (22).

We must be careful, however, to distinguish Genet's consistent and unambiguous hostility to any construct whatsoever of the Good (he shares this stance with Lacan, incidentally) from Badiou's attempt to rescue the Good from the morass of its simulacra, to link strategically this ethical concept to the normative ideals of revolutionary or anticapitalist politics. Notwithstanding this considerable difference, however, Genet and Badiou hold in common the key notion not of a *redemptive,* but rather an *emancipatory,* violence, which can fruitfully be compared to the Fanonian position that I examined in chapter 3.[14] For both Genet and Badiou, the violence of a genuine event enables no elevation of a sinful or unworthy humanity to a state of divine or transcendental grace. This is the feature that distinguishes their views from strands of contemporary Islamic and Christian ideologies, for example, which promise to the martyr heavenly compensations—often manifestly erotic in the Islamic versions—for his acts of earthly sacrifice.

Rather, violence reveals to humanity what Badiou calls its immortal essence. By this he means its capacity to move "suicidally" into a realm beyond mere animal or egoic interest; its ability blissfully to embrace death rather than succumb to servitude and humiliation but, crucially, without the distracting and obfuscating promise of otherworldly reward. Indeed, Badiou refreshingly recasts the transcendental beyond inherent in redemptive ideologies as an immanently infinitized worldliness: the divine promise is (potentially) intrinsic to the here and now. This is the line of argument that leads Badiou to make the "scandalous" claim that even victims of torture and prisoners in concentration camps cannot be reduced to their victimization without doing violence to thought. "In his role as executioner," he writes, "man is an animal abjection, but we must have the courage to add that in his role as victim, he is generally worth little more."[15] This is the premise on which Badiou elaborates his trenchant critique of both human rights discourse in general and, in particular, the mobilization of the Jewish holocaust in Zionist (and more generally dominant Israeli) political discourse and culture.[16]

For his part, Genet conceptually differentiates the liberating violence of the powerless from the repressive brutality of bourgeois and colonialist forms of exploitation. Eventually published at Éditions Maspero as a preface to a collection of writings by members of West Germany's Red Army Faction, but appearing originally in September 1977 as a front page feature in the Parisian daily *Le Monde,* "Violence and Brutality" is likely the most controversial piece ever written by Genet. It was in fact rejected for publication even by René Andrieu, editor of the communist organ *L'Humanité,* where most of Genet's political prose of this period appeared. According to Albert Dichy, Andrieu feared that this provocative article's publication would link the French Communist Party to the unanimously denounced terrorist violence of the notorious Baader-Meinhof group, many of whose members were by that time being held in solitary confinement in German prisons under reportedly atrocious conditions.

The publication of "Violence and Brutality" generated veritable heaps of outrage. For days the editorial offices of *Le Monde* were flooded with denunciations of Genet's argument, to which a wide array of respectable French intellectuals felt obliged to respond. Two days prior to its French publication, the essay had unleashed an even more uproarious furor when excerpts were printed in *Der Spiegel* a mere three days following a deadly Red Army attack, which resulted in the kidnapping of Hanns-Martin Schleyer, president of the German Employers Federation. The Red Army militants had held Schleyer's life against the release of its imprisoned members, whose desperate hunger strikes had met with only studied public indifference. Though submitted in ignorance before the incident occurred, Genet's piece was predictably received as an official sanction of the controversial Baader-Meinhof action.

But surely all of these conspicuous denunciations should not dissuade us from actually reading Genet's provocative piece. Its main point is to define violence as a benevolent underlying life-force which seeks to act freely against outward constraints—"violence and life are virtually synonymous,"[17] writes Genet—and then to characterize brutality as that which opposes this force. After decades of laboriously hyperskeptical poststructuralist critique, there is to my eye a disarming elegance in the simplicity of Genet's quasi-physical binary opposition. By way of giving examples of his general idea of brutality, Genet alludes to everything from "the architecture of public housing projects" to "the condescending speech of police addressing anyone with brown skin"; from big city traffic congestion to the American "bombing of Haiphong" during the Vietnam war. "Violence alone," Genet concludes, "can bring an end to the brutality of men" (172).

No doubt, one aspect of Genet's discussion of violence is to be situated on the level of politics and history. Ever the contrarian—more precisely, ever the pitiless denouncer of naive liberalist phantasms, even and perhaps especially those of socialist discourses—Genet resolutely affirms the value of postwar Soviet support for the third world (he likely had the Arab world in particular in mind), and this at a time when such affirmations—this is 1977, remember—had become anything but fashionable across the widest swathes of the left. Additionally, Genet refreshingly contrasts the legacy of May 1968, which he acerbically qualifies as "a sort of lacey fringe, an angelic, spiritualist, humanist lace" (174), with the austere anti-individualist Maoist group discipline of the Red Army Faction, whose heroism for Genet consists primarily in its suppression of all idiosyncratic whim and particularistic desire under the secular-sacred sovereignty of the collective cause.

Genet's embrace of this brand of militant heroism features a further crucial element, which speaks to the more conceptual or philosophical timbre of his discussion. Echoing the paradoxes of Freud's classic essay *Beyond the Pleasure Principle*, Genet in this second mode explicitly associates the life-affirming catharsis of violence with the approach of what he terms "the limits of death" (174). To be sure, Genet partly means that to act genuinely in the world is to risk power's murderous wrath. All the principal Baader-Meinhof militants (Andreas Baader, Ulrike Meinhof, Holger Meins, Gudrun Ensslin, and Jan-Karl Raspe) died in incarceration, some under circumstances many still consider suspicious. Yet there is another, more theoretically consequential level to Genet's discussion. If hegemonic power works to suppress the life force of violence, then the liberation of this force requires the affirmation of death, since death is precisely the name of the place where life seeks refuge in a world of brutality. The death-bearing morbidity of the terrorist or suicide bomber, the evil that seeks only death and destruction, as we are constantly told, may then be recoded as the very incarnation of vitality, as an authentic means of resistance to the truly death-bearing brutality of bourgeois and imperialist social relations.

Such a superficially destructive life-passion makes manifest what Genet memorably calls "the hidden generosity and tenderness of every revolutionary" (176). For Genet, the inhuman evil of Baader-Meinhof is in reality the insurrectionary rupture of life in the zone of death. This means in part that the militants' shocking acts of violence are a necessary consequence of the ruthlessly exploitative essence of imperialist capitalism. "It is the very brutality of German society," Genet asserts, "that has made the violence of the RAF necessary" (174). Recalling Fanon, who characterizes anticolonial violence as the redirection of the violence of colonialism itself—the colonized population's refusal, in other words, to interiorize that violence, to submit to its blows—Genet insists on theorizing the violence of the Red Army Faction's kidnappings and targeted assassinations as the life-affirming deflection of capitalism's repressive brutality. Such acts in truth transform freedom-negating hegemonic forces into vectors of egalitarian collective liberation.

This consideration of Genet's theory and practice of ethico-political rupture has set the stage for the reconfiguration in precise psychoanalytic terms of the confused and underdeveloped reception of *Prisoner of Love*. It would be a grave mistake in my view to link this text's various literary idiosyncrasies—sudden spatiotemporal shifts, the absence of a dominant narrative thread, complex interweaving of political and historical analysis with oneiric-surrealistic and mythopoetic passages—with a subjective, or more properly psychological, function. These numerous apparently postmodernist techniques result rather from a thoroughgoing authorial self-expropriation. The superficially subjective workings of this process dissimulate a fundamentally antipsychological—objective, concrete, sociohistorical—volitional core. As I argued at length in chapter 1, the reaching of this sociohistorical goal requires the isolation of what is irreducibly of the order of the psyche, of the unconscious.

In this sense, Genet's self-immolating textual movement closely parallels the development of the end of analysis thematic in the later Lacan. The analysand is called heroically to traverse the unconscious fundamental fantasy that undergirds her entire sociosymbolic reality and to withstand the traumatic and disorienting jouissance of the subjective destitution to be found beyond the transference. This is to say in more ordinary terms that in addition to being a carefully, albeit idiosyncratically, contextualized presentation of the Palestinian resistance at two specific moments of its history, *Prisoner* is in an important sense the record of Genet's analysis of what we might call his object relation, in other words his relation to the very unconscious fantasy-kernel that incites his literary and political passions. Such an analysis involves the interpretation of the various forms of transferential resistance that aim to keep this kernel beneath the threshold of consciousness. To claim, therefore, that Genet's text performs a kind of self-analytical work analogous to the sort that Freud performed in *The Interpretation of Dreams*, say, is therefore anything but an inappropriate banality. The analytical mode of his textual practice is in fact what permits Genet to divest himself of the amorous demand that he would otherwise place on his privileged political agents, from the warm and graceful

Palestinian fedayeen to the provocatively and poetically attired Black
Panther militants. In the process Genet grants himself the capacity to
view these historical actors through a lens only minimally distorted by
the idealizing deformations of transference love.

Dominant modern epistemologies since Descartes and Newton
have associated such objectivity with scientific detachment, that is to
say, with both the dissociation of the perceptual and intellectual facul-
ties from the determinations of the object, as well as the separation
of the observer from the empirical field of observation. In Genet's
later writings, in contrast, we discover what I wish to argue is a truer
objectivity, one that couples an acute, even merciless, critical faculty
with the self-transcendent passion of partisanship. This is the underlying
lesson of *Prisoner of Love*: genuine critical engagement follows from a
thoroughgoing post-transferential immersion in the object, one which
abandons the reassuring and illusory distance of perspective—the hysterical, denunciatory, and hypocritical perspective from which the object
can repeatedly be judged unworthy of desire.

In this precise sense, authentic subjectivity is to be located on the
side of the (partial) object, in the leap of faith by means of which the
subject abandons himself in a kind of self-immolation in the object, not
in the sublimity of its seductively narcissistic ideality, that is to say, from
the edifying perspective of the ego ideal, but rather in the shapeless,
opaque, and uncanny features of its properly traumatic mode. Far from
clouding his political judgment, Genet's self-abandonment to the subjec-
tivating, at once death-bearing and life-affirming, energies of the cause
is precisely what enables him to uncover its corruptions and deficiencies
without succumbing to disillusionment. It also permits Genet to resist
the temptation of retreating to the exalted and treasonous perspective
that would seal him off from the imperfections he would otherwise
denounce in order to buttress the precarious structure of self-regard.

A Begging Bowl Made of Flesh

I propose to begin exploring this underlying dynamic in Genet by considering some textual evidence of the object's transition from its specular
and narcissistic aspect to its second, partial, and opaquely uncanny one.
The passage I have in mind has the added benefit of making explicit
the connection between this transition's properly psychical level of

determination and the concrete historical problem of the oppressive polarization that structures (neo-)colonial space. In these evocative pages of *Prisoner of Love*, Genet explores the tension between the egoic ideality that underpins claims to determinate hegemonic identity and the subjective destitution that results from what Genet describes as the treasonous and ecstatic abandonment of those claims.

Genet's depiction of an imaginary cityscape presented as Amman circa 1970 hearkens back to Fanon's memorable analysis in *The Wretched of the Earth* of the Manichean or polarizing spatial organization of the colonial capital, which I considered in some detail in chapter 3. The Jordanian capital at this time was beset by increasing political tension between the exiled Palestinian resistance fighters and a Hashemite monarchy that had begun strategically to align itself more closely with Israel and the United States. According to Edmund White, Amman in 1970 featured no *quartier réservé*—no disreputable neighborhood of brothels, illegal gambling halls, and black markets—like the one Genet describes; White speculates that Genet likely drew from his memories of Morocco while composing this key passage (579). Yet, to concern ourselves with Genet's geographical inaccuracies would surely be tanta-mount to imposing inappropriate criteria of sociological or geographical exactitude on an aspect of his text that in my view features an entirely different intention: to illuminate the underlying fantasmatics of colonial power and class oppression and to spell out the means by which these forces give rise to their own self-defeating, identity-predicated negations.

Genet poetically describes an urban space divided into two dis-tinct zones. The first is a luxurious palatial quarter inhabited by King Hussein, his Bedouin and Circassian military supporters, and other members of the Jordanian elite. This district jarringly abuts a teeming, insalubrious shantytown housing an assemblage of the desperate and the weak, including, significantly, the most subaltern segment of the Palestinian refugee population. My claim about this passage will be that Genet's disturbing oneiric imagery figures the polarizing logic by which an assertion of identity supported by colonialist power creates a realm of social abjection, which may then succumb to the transferential temptation of issuing a defensive and pseudo-symmetrical (because issu-ing from powerlessness) counter-identitarian response. In consequence, Genet suggests, a screen emerges in the liminal space between the two opposed constituencies—the hegemonic and the potentially revolution-ary—on which the spectacle of unconscious colonialist fantasy may then be projected. This spectacle not only betokens the function of the exoticized repressed as an excluded object of desire for the hegemonic social class. It also presents for both sides an occasion for what Genet throughout his work consistently calls *betrayal*: the traumatically pleasurable dissolution of identity's alienating reflectiveness; the disorienting renunciation of the ego's sociosymbolic points of anchorage.

For the privileged members of the Jordanian elite, the shantytown offers the prospect of escape from "moral and aesthetic effort."[18] It is the place, in other words, where tribal chiefs, military generals, senior government officials, and their respective entourages go slumming. Adventures here promise an earthy release from demanding ideals of morality, religion, and decorum. Genet's description makes clear that the underlying attraction of such frolic is the means it offers to divest oneself of the properly symbolic accoutrements of membership in the privileged classes. Outside palatial space, Genet writes, the courtier can throw off "the pride of self" that comes along with "having a surname, a family tree, a country, an ideology" (61).

In Lacanian terms, the shantytown's dens of iniquity grant access to the self-expropriating experience of the symbolic order's suspension; the intoxicating feeling of liberation from the burden of social visibility that usually accompanies positions of material privilege and symbolic capital. The courtier succumbs to the attractions of that part of jouissance excluded from the terms of membership of the elite. The exalted Other that reflects back to the deserving sheikh an image of his enviable status disintegrates under the shattering force of proscribed pleasures. Yet, Genet also emphasizes that this excess pleasure can be purchased only at the cost of effectively disappearing, as it were, from one's own psychical map.

On the other side of the divide, by contrast, everyday life is marked by precisely this kind of official nonexistence. This invisibility naturally gives rise to a wish for the same legitimacy, however repressive, from which the privileged seek relief. The material anguish of deprivation, in other words, is compounded by a properly psychical desire for recognition. The protestations of dogmatic materialists will not suffice to reduce the cause of this desire to socioeconomic marginality. Genet's shantytown is the realm of the Fanonian lumpenproletariat, that great aggregate of subjects, as I developed in chapter 3, whose vague existence lies beneath the threshold of historical and political representation, but whose revolutionary potential in the (post-)colonial mode of production, motivated not only by material need but by sociosymbolic invisibility as well, Fanon firmly defends against Marxist orthodoxy, which by omission reduces the latter to the former.

The Palace's formality and ceremoniousness issue to the socially abject the prospect of sanctioned *being*: the assurance guaranteed by a social position recognized by the Other and thereby reflected back to the self. The considerable force of this legitimizing power leads Genet to evoke the symbolic value of commodities signifying social position and prestige. The "scarves, shirts and watches" (58) that circulate in the shantytown are acquired by those applicants to the royal court who wish to graduate to more comfortable life circumstances. Genet specifies that these would-be social climbers are also more than willing to offer up voluptuous erotic transgressions in exchange for access to the presumed refinements of the court. The paradigmatic significance of the Manichean social organization that both Genet and Fanon find in proto-revolutionary colonial space is no doubt attributable to what here appears at first glance to be a smooth exchange of equivalent values in enjoyment. While the slumming Hashemite courtier is accorded a fleeting release from the demanding renunciations of elite social identity, the ambitious but subaltern Palestinian *arriviste* is granted at least the tokens of social belonging to the hegemonic class.

Intriguingly, Genet's evocation of Amman's sociospatial structure focuses specifically on the body and its image. Indeed, the passage lends itself to interpretation through the lens of Lacan's well-known idea of the specular construction of the alienated self in the space of the Other, a thematic that I explored in detail in chapter 1 in my analysis of the inverted vase experiment. The Lacanian reference will allow me to show that what initially seems to be a fair exchange dissimulates an entrenchment of political asymmetry.

According to Genet, the young and ambitious Arab men of the shantytown discover a completed image of their own bodies in the desiring reflections of the Jordanian court. But the participants in the sexual exchanges in the brothels, in sharp contrast, undergo an actual corporeal *experience,* one that proves to be unmediated by the specular and is lived in consequence as disassembled and decomposed. Indeed, Genet's presentation of sexual life on the other side of neo-feudal privilege offers a dense and disturbing weave of images evoking body parts and secretions. The reader discovers astonishing libidinal intensities grafted onto corporeal fragments disaggregated from any discernible shape or form. While the aspirational body image of the dreamy Palestinian boys betokens the ideality and personhood of the corporeal ego, among the shantytown's less respectable denizens we find only disembodied organs and desubjectivized pulsations, which begin in fact to converge with the nonhuman organic matter lying beneath. These structures correspond respectively to I and *a*, the ego ideal and partial object as discussed in chapter 1.

> The shanty town, a medley of monsters and woes seen from the Palace, and in turn seeing the palace and its woes, in turn knew pleasures unheard of elsewhere. One went about on two legs and a torso, around dusk—a torso from which a wrist stuck out with a hand on its end like a stoup, a begging bowl made of flesh that demanded its mite with three fingers you could see through. The wrist emerged from a ragged mass of crumpled, worn-out, dirty American surplus, merging ever more completely with the mud and shit until it was sold as rags, mud and muck combined.
>
> Further on, also on two legs, is a female sex organ, bare, shaven, but twitching and damp and always trying to cling on to me. Somewhere else there's a single eye without a socket, fixed and sightless, but sometimes sharp, and hanging from a bit of sky-blue wood. Somewhere else again, an arse with its balls hanging bare and weary between a pair of flaccid thighs. (59–60)

Genet's startling vision of social and sexual abjection pays testament to the mutual implication of acute poverty and the bodily ego's collapse. The commercialization of sexual exchange in the shantytown deprives its residents of the luxury of idealization that frames erotic life in the Palace and entrances the excluded who succumb to its lure. It cannot be denied that there is an important sociological point to be made here: Genet wishes to draw his reader's attention to the intimate link between material desperation and the sexual depersonalization that occurs in tandem with the sex trade as it develops in such circumstances of extreme material penury.

Yet, I want to suggest that this key passage's emphasis lies instead on the symbiotic relationship, to use Genet's biological metaphor, that inheres between the two locales; as Genet himself puts it, there is a conspicuous lack of "friction" between them. Considered as a totality, the Palace and shantytown function for Genet as a kind of ecosystem in which a libidinal balance, however fragile or deceptive, is achieved through the apparently equal exchange of fantasy-investments—cathexes, as Freud translator James Strachey would say—that I have already spelled out. What is crucial to note, however, is that whereas the exchange itself is fair in the sense of bidirectional—a quantity of (presumptive) jouissance travels from one side of the screen to the other going both ways—the contents of the exchange are logically contradictory. This contradiction ensures that the encounter between courtier and hustler at the nexus of the two spaces will be *missed*: the prestigious visibility that the shanty-dweller seeks in the Palace is for the courtier the source of the demanding "sublimation" that he must escape; conversely, the ecstatic self-dispossession that the courtier seeks in the brothel is for the shanty dweller the source of his social nonrecognition and material plight.

Not unlike Hegel in his justifiably celebrated dialectic of lord and bondsman, Genet underscores the dependence of each constituency on a view of life on the other side. Each locale's inhabitants become entranced by what they (imagine they) lack, such that Genet can write that "the two powers [are] so evenly balanced you wonder if it wasn't a case of mutual mesmerism, that familiar, flirtatious but bitter confrontation linking the two [places]" (58–59). Also like Hegel, however, Genet implies that the relationship of the two parties is only deceptively symmetrical, for he stresses in another, apparently contradictory passage that "the splendour of the Palace is a kind of poverty," its status "purely mythical" (61). Disrupting the exchange of libidinal equivalents between naughty notable and provocative prostitute is the immanence of disintegration, which Genet evokes as the "inexplicable lull" that deflects the mirror reflections bouncing to and fro between the locales. This lull corresponds precisely to a distinctly negative and unreflective spatiotemporality in which, Genet provocatively asserts, "nothing survive[s] but bodily functions" (60). Here all subjects lose their self-images, however tenuously constituted or seemingly well established, and corporeal wholeness entirely unravels. But this unraveling gives rise not to a Deleuzo-Guattarian body-without-organs, much celebrated in contemporary cultural theory, but rather to a non-denumerable series of organs that cannot be unified within any recognizable bodily shape, figure, or form—organs without a body to enclose them, that is to say.[19]

The libidinal link joining the two spaces ultimately privileges neither one. Genet, rather, draws our attention to a species of ecstatic encounter, one that effectively sabotages the self-interested and quasi-commercial exchange that takes place between the two groups. I write "sabotage" because the eruption of enjoyment in the shantytown that Genet so memorably evokes does not merely reveal that the Palace's glamorous lure is an empty sham, for it also denounces as vain the efforts of the ambitious to penetrate into the courtly habitus by means of sartorial conformity or erotic seduction.

An example from the text will weave together the strands of my argument. Genet alludes to the "beauty" of "a few handsome" shanty-town boys whose desire for social mobility comes into being through an identification that he qualifies quite explicitly as alienated and virtual. Given as children mirror fragments in which "they trap a ray of the sun and reflect it into one of the Palace windows," these boys "discover bit by bit their faces and bodies" through these reflections, anticipating in this way a bodily completion seemingly denied them by material hard-ship and the pain of exile (62). Genet here formulates a textual image of the corporeal form available only as a mirror reflection directed into the space of an idealized Other. By asserting that the Palace "consumes a great deal of youth" (62), Genet also ensures that his reader is not misled as to the destiny of these beautiful Arab boys: captivated by an illusion, they lose themselves amid the corrupting shenanigans of court life, lured by the empty promise of conspicuous wealth and devoured by the erotic appetites of the kingdom's most powerful.

For all the intensity of its abject imagery, then, Genet's strange imaginative vision of 1970 Amman would remain disappointingly descriptive if we were to conclude that its ecological dimension is its final word. What is required at this juncture is a return to Genet's key notion of betrayal, for it becomes possible to understand the term in this context as the subversion of the false harmony between the two locales, as the shattering of the specular binary relation constructed by each side's anticipation of the enjoyment to be had on the other side. "Anyone who hasn't experienced the ecstasy of betrayal knows noth-ing about ecstasy at all," writes Genet and, suddenly alluding to the Abbot of Cluny's desire to understand Islam by ordering the translation of the Quran, he links this ecstasy to the kind of desanctification that occurs in consequence of the fact that "in passing from one language to another the holy text [can] only convey what can be expressed just as easily in any tongue—that is everything except that which is holy" (59). Translation, transgression, betrayal, *déclassement*: each of these motifs in Genet's text evokes the scandal of disintegration that occurs when the fantasy propping up a structure of psychosocial meaning collapses. Just as the fascination the abbot harbors for the Islamic faith evaporates with the translation of its holy text into familiar, pedestrian French, so does the ambition of the Arab boy who, having gained entry to the Palace's confines, is brought to nothing by the cynicism and hypocrisy in circulation among the court's familiars.

But I must add a crucial nuance to this analysis, for surely Genet is not trying to persuade his reader that the inevitable frustration of the desires that fuel social ambition and erotic fantasy should lead the inhabitants of his imaginary Manichean Amman simply to stay home. Rather, Genet wants to *valorize* the moment of voluptuous negation that subtracts us from our familiar psychosocial standing, but without adducing a redemptive or compensatory quality, without actually delivering the idealized or domesticated enjoyment that ostensibly caused the desire to betray in the first place. Genet's text implies that the release of jouissance takes place not when social identities are formed and class and ethnic differentiations established, but rather when these constructs shatter and come to ruin. Genet's point can be clarified with reference to Lacan's distinction between desire and drive: whereas the subject derives its aspirational raison d'être (desire) from a transferential idealization in fantasy of a forbidden enjoyment, one that serves to buttress its reassuring ego structures, satisfaction (drive) can only occur by means of a radically decentering self-dispossession, one that staunchly resists all attempts at integration within the realm of possible social meanings and identities.

This transition from desire to drive involves a move beyond Freudian transference love because it requires the subject to withstand the collapse of its Other. While the subaltern Arab youth discovers only treachery behind the seductive facade of courtly prestige, the courtier must recognize the hidden truth that the desiring dynamics of palatial life depend on an unmentionable eroticization of the strife on which its privilege depends. Genet's concept of betrayal merits the epithet *ethical*: indifferent to any communicable moral maxim, the ethics of betrayal enjoins us not only psychically to inhabit the space of radical social abjection and invisibility, but also to resist the temptation to

domesticate or elevate this space, to render it respectable by integrating
it with an existing or nascent discourse or ideology.

We can understand in this light Genet's numerous claims in *Prisoner of Love* that he will abandon, *betray* the Palestinian cause when
it becomes fixated on territoriality and nationhood (clearly Genet was
able to discern already in the early 1980s the signs of this growing
tendency); after it becomes, in other words, something more norma-
tively positive than a radical negation of the values of Euro-American
capitalist-colonialist modernity and its enviously dutiful political-Zionist
offspring. Today one needs to go far into the obscurest Marxist margins
of the Palestinian resistance—beyond Hamas, Islamic Jihad, even and
especially Fatah—to find elements that remain faithful to the fleeting,
now barely discernible cause that Genet so exemplarily embraced.

Of Grey Hair and Treachery

The importance of *Prisoner's* Amman-set passages lies in its suggestion
of a kind of psychodynamic sociology of colonial space. Genet uncovers not only how the binary specular logic that undergirds colonialist
social relations rests on the oppressed's identification with an image,
pregnant with fantasy, of the power that oppresses, but also how this
logic is inherently vulnerable to collapse, a collapse catalyzed by the
ecstatic passion of betrayal. Yet, the strange power of a different but
not unrelated motif overshadows the reader's immersion in the world
of *Prisoner of Love*. Despite the scattered and insubstantial space that
its account in the text takes up, Genet's remembrance of his encounter
with a young fedayee and an elderly Palestinian woman—Hamza and
his mother as they are called in the text—plays the most central role in
his interpretation of his attachment, necessarily colored by transference,
to the Palestinians and their cause. These two figures, in fact, become
the very cornerstone of Genet's autobiographical architecture; they take
center stage in the drama of the author's curiously disaggregated textual
reconstruction of his experience in the Jordanian camps.

My argument in this last section will be that the recurring image
of Hamza and his mother functions in a manner analogous to the
Freudian screen memory, though one that has been identified as such
and analyzed through Genet's textual work.[20] Situated at the point

where the sociohistorical real is reshaped and distorted by the psyche, Genet's hybrid memory-fantasy both protects him from and threatens to expose him to the real of his desire vis-à-vis the Palestinians. The properly psychical nature of this image—its function, very precisely, as an indication of the fundamental fantasy's structuring power—is most strikingly revealed when Genet makes the patently illogical claim that its construction predates his Jordanian sojourn. It is as if, in other words, the image of Hamza and his mother provides Genet with retroactive compensation for his abandonment in his infancy at the hands of his own biographical mother to the care of the French public services. Linked in the text, naturally enough, to the Pietà tradition in Christian art and iconography, the incestuous figuration of Hamza and his mother is the signifier that knots together Genet's psychical structure. This knot is the place where the subjective specificity of Genet's fantasy—a fantasy that, no doubt unsurprisingly, gives pride of place to a phallicized maternal imago—grafts itself onto sociohistorical objectivity, that is to say, onto the concrete vagaries of the political struggle that defined the last two decades of Genet's life.

It makes tremendous sense, therefore, that in its function as psychical pivot point the image of Hamza and his mother features in its various incarnations all of the ambivalence that characterizes, as psychoanalysis argues, the object of love. In a first light, one shed by the demands of narcissistic idealization, the image $i(a)$ stands for the paradoxical transgressive purity of the revolutionary impulse as Genet perceives it. This purity is characterized by a combination of elements: the sacrifice of the self for the good of a fraternal cause; the absolute negation of bourgeois materialism or, put in more positive terms, the triumph of ludic, death-defying spontaneity over the calculated discipline of joyless economic productivity; and perhaps most crucially, an incest-tinged enjoyment linked to a youthful and homoeroticized male sociality placed under the sign of a maternal, rather than a paternal, normative authority. Indeed, as if to underline his marginal status within Genet's fantasy-memory of mother and son, the text hardly mentions Hamza's father. As readers we remain barely aware even of his absence throughout the entirety of the work.

It is not until "reality" intrudes—during his 1982 return to Jordan Genet obtains Hamza's telephone number in West Germany, where he is now exiled, married, and working in a factory of the Ruhr—that the sublimity of this emblem of insubordinate masculine Palestinian dignity collapses under the unsupportable weight of West Asian history and Arab dispossession. Though he scatters contradictory intimations of Hamza's fate across his text, Genet provides in the final pages a more or less straightforward narration of this crucial telephone conversation. In keeping with the merciless analytic acumen of *Prisoner of Love,* Genet shows himself to be deeply conscious of how his depiction is necessarily distorted by fantasy and desire. Indeed, he wonders aloud in the book's final paragraphs if it was "a light of [his] own that he threw" on his cherished Palestinian icons (374). This unflinching self-criticism leaves its mark on the portrayal of the resistance movement as a whole. For example, on several occasions Genet comments ironically on the disharmony between his homoerotic figuration of the sexy young fedayeen—Genet's homosexuality seems more than anything to be the object of playful teasing among the fighters, most of whom, incidentally, are portrayed as devout Muslims—and the fedayeen's own (almost exclusively) heterosexual and patently adolescent romantic yearnings.

On the narrative level, Genet's account of his return to the Palestinian camps a full decade after his initial sojourn is shot through with the anticipation of his reunion with Hamza and his mother. In light of the discussion thus far, however, it should come as no surprise that what Genet eventually finds in Irbid contrasts sharply with the too perfect image that Genet himself readily admits is more akin to an imaginary construction than a reliable recollection. In a general sense, Genet's depiction of Hamza and his mother by means of literary techniques designed to subvert authorial mastery conveys the author's cognizance of the impossibility of the autobiographical project: the unavoidability, more precisely, of the considerable supplement that fantasy adds to fact. Yet the intention behind the Irbid passages surely moves beyond this postmodernist commonplace. More consequentially, Genet shows a deep awareness that the recognition, indeed, the *betrayal* of this fantasy—the traversal that produces what Lacan calls subjective destitution—is a condition of possibility for the ensuing, deeply insightful (auto-)critical evaluation of both the Palestinian cause's unfortunate vicissitudes and Genet's own "personal investment" in them.

In a second light, Hamza and his mother become in *Prisoner of Love* metonyms for the Palestinian resistance's various treacherous compromises of its revolutionary ideals, first nationalist and bourgeois, then later Islamist. Before at long last narrating his reunion with the mother, Genet evokes a number of rumors circulating among his Palestinian contacts concerning the destiny of the son, all of which—torture, imprisonment, assassination at the hands of Mossad, the Israeli intelligence agency— carry strong intimations of heroic martyrdom. When Genet evokes his phone conversation with Hamza, however, now exiled on German soil out of harm's way, he remarks that his young friend's voice is "full of real despair" (330). Asked if he anticipates ever being able to return to his "own country," a country alongside which his refugee mother still resides in the destitution of her camp, Hamza responds with a despondent "Which country's that?" adding, in a movingly desperate attempt to conjure a horizon of hope, that his own son in some vague future will return to Palestine on his behalf. Devastatingly, Genet informs his reader that "the despair in [Hamza's] voice was greater still" (330) in this last response, betraying to the Frenchman's ear the guilty, mutely exasperated melancholy of a revolutionary dream crushed under the weight of Zionist propaganda and U.S.-abetted Israeli military power. As Genet draws it, the contrast could not be starker between the youthful and exuberant Hamza of 1970, who disappears in the middle of the night to join a dangerous commando offensive in the Israeli-occupied West Bank, and the mournful, exiled Hamza, who complains that he's "done for," casually referring to "grey hairs" which betray the stresses of displacement and premature old age (330).

This central grey hair motif recurs in Genet's climactic narration of his return to the Irbid refugee camp, specifically when he relates his awkward reunion with Hamza's mother, whose hair has now lost all its former color. The repetition is likely a symptom of the quasi-incestuous intimacy that permeates what Genet knowingly describes as his subjective representation of mother and son. More certainly, however, Genet's text links Hamza's abandonment of the resistance—albeit after imprisonment and torture at the hands of not the Israelis, but the Jordanians, as Genet finally discovers from his informants—with not only the mother's deep despair at the resistance's protracted decline, but also with her mounting hopelessness in the face of Israeli intransigence and military force.

The grey hair shared by mother and son therefore hints at a sense of guilty complicity imperfectly laid to rest. Though by all accounts each did all that was "humanly possible" to resist the occupation—to the point, in Hamza's case, of being subjected to torture—one cannot help but sense that the hateful vitriol Hamza's mother directs toward the Israelis is partly directed against herself. It is as if the limits of the humanly possible dissimulated another, only vaguely discernible possibility, one that would succeed in negating, against all odds as it were, the Israeli negation of the Palestinians' collective humanity.

Offered directions by a friendly young refugee, Genet immediately recognizes the courtyard of the house in which he had been a guest more than a decade before. There he meets "a frail woman whose white hair [is] just visible" (349), deciding after much consideration that she is in fact Hamza's mother. When she asks Genet if he held a camera among his possessions at the time of his initial visit, Genet senses that the question is a test, telling us that he remembers full well that he had no camera with him at the time. Now apparently secure in the knowledge of her European visitor's identity, the mother grabs Genet by the hand, leading her guest into the bedroom where he slept and pointing out the hole in the wall in which he was to hide in the event of an attack by Hussein's Bedouin soldiers and Circassian generals. Despite the apparently hospitable reception that greets both him and his translator-companion, however, Genet detects a strange reticence in the old woman when she insists, for instance, that it was tea, not coffee, that she brought him during the night. Compounding this impression of ambivalent suspicion are the repeated interjections of one of the old woman's grandsons, who joins the group mid-interview to learn of any news of his uncle which Genet might have brought. The grandson proceeds to scold his grandmother sharply for her seeming cooperation with outsiders whose motivations, Genet surmises, surely at best seem unclear.

As the conversation unfolds, Genet gains a more vivid sense of the depth of Hamza's mother's bitterness. He begins to discern the resentment coloring her response to his attempt to recapture through an effort at collective reminiscence a time when the resistance, still ingenuously referred to as a revolution, was young, carefree, and brimming with hope. Twelve years earlier, the Palestinian movement was no doubt rationally cognizant, especially in the aftermath of the devastating Six Day War, of the slim odds of victory against the massive weight of U.S.-backed Israeli military power and the seductive pull of Zionist ideology in the wake of the Jewish holocaust. Yet the sober realism of the earlier era was nonetheless superseded, Genet implies, by the anything-can-happen zeal of what he wishes after all to depict as an authentically revolutionary moment. Though Genet assures himself that the woman before him is indeed Hamza's mother, the radical change in her appearance—she was once the spry, Kalashnikov-toting paragon of militant Palestinian femininity, surely idealized, as Genet himself readily admits, through the synchronous and inextricable agencies of memory and fantasy—has brought to the fore a hardened and argumentative old woman whose hair is so white and thin that a casual glance reveals henna stains on her scalp. Indeed, the metamorphosis is so thoroughgoing that it calls into question for Genet whether the subjective representation of his entire Palestinian adventure corresponds at all to anything that actually took place.

> After it's been used in the bath for a long time and dwindled to half its original size, a piece of soap, amazed at the change in itself, might exclaim, 'It's not possible!'

> Before, my memory had been firmly imprinted with the image of a woman strong enough to carry a gun, and to load, aim and fire it. Her lips weren't thin in those days, nor faded to the same pallor as the trace of henna on her dandruff. I hadn't been present at the debacle; I could measure its effects all the better. Hamza's mother had become as thin and flat as all the other two-dimensional shapes you saw in Jordan. (407)

Foreshadowing the destiny of Arafat himself, Hamza's mother becomes for Genet a tarnished icon for the sorry fate of the Palestinian resistance as a whole. What is so significant about Genet's consideration, however, is the acuity of his awareness of the dangers of succumbing to the aridly nostalgic reverie that had already so dishearteningly cast a pall over the Jordanian camps at the moment of his return. Indeed, the paradox revealed by the Hamza and his mother motif is that the depressing realism of Genet's depiction of the Palestinians' bitter destiny is precisely what allows him to maintain his fidelity to that aspect of the resistance that he wishes so passionately to defend.

Genet's militant sobriety prevents him from demanding, in a symptomatic manifestation of transference love, that the youthful and heroic image of the Palestinians come together with the tired and cynical one to form a reinvigorated pseudo-revolutionary idealism, hopeful but ultimately fake. In effect, the memory-images of the despairing Hamza in his pathetic German exile and his balding mother in her anti-Jewish vitriol become through his textual self-analysis the true objects of Genet's love, the true cause of his authentically revolutionary desire. Crucially, Genet doesn't reject them, but instead effectively internalizes them as the truth of his desire for Palestine.

Genet's de-idealized images of Hamza and his mother perform precisely the same function as the lumpenproletariat images in Fanon's *The Wretched of the Earth*. Both sets of images allow their creators to pursue desire to its logical conclusion, beyond any transferential demand for accommodation with existing cultural structures or integration with established political ideologies. In Lacanian terms, Genet manages to keep separate his I and his *a*, his ego ideal and his partial object. No doubt it is this success that made it possible for Genet finally to complete, after a decade of melancholic procrastination, what is surely the most arresting, challenging, and politically disciplined memoir in all of twentieth-century literature.

V

For the Love of Cinema

In some respects, cinematic identification is similar to transference in analysis, though this analogy should not be taken too far.

—Peter Wollen, "Godard and Counter-Cinema: *Vent d'est*"

To be a theoretician of the cinema, one should ideally no longer love the cinema and yet still love it.

—Christian Metz, *The Imaginary Signifier: Psychoanalysis and the Cinema*

Imaginary Signifiers?

Much of the lingering ambiguity surrounding Christian Metz's influential, though now decidedly out of fashion, psychoanalytically inflected work can be traced to his question-begging coupling of the terms "imaginary" and "signifier." To open this chapter I will introduce these two key notions in the context of film theory for the benefit of nonspecialists before relating the chapter's general argument to the transference problematic. Both the linguist of structuralist persuasion and the psychoanalyst of Lacanian orientation will insist on the properly semiotic meaning of "signifier." If we define the signifier as a conventional linguistic unit (acoustic image or sound pattern) positioned in a network along with other signifiers and partaking thereby of a process of differential signification, then this signifier would appear to have little bearing on the question of the image and the associated notion of the imaginary. On the condition that we set aside the quality of arbitrariness intrinsic to the signifier concept as Saussure originally defined it,[1] the Metzian

159

film theorist might submit that the classical definition in structuralist linguistics need not necessarily rule out the cinema. After all, what is a film text if not a network of signifying elements—shots, as the concept is usually retooled for cinema—which compose a meaning-making system equivalent to the totality of their various interrelations?

Though we can surely grant this counterpoint, it fails nevertheless to resolve the lingering uncertainty. Indeed the linguist, not to mention many a semiotician and semiologist, will distinguish the functioning of the linguistic sign properly speaking from that of other signs, such as the image or icon, for example, as defined in semiotic schools such as C. S. Peirce's which, unlike the Saussurean tradition, explicitly include nonverbal signs within the strict purview of semiotics.[2] Moreover, the Lacanian theorist will remind us that from the earliest seminars the signifier concept works to distinguish its objective role in the signification of unconscious desire from the misleading and narcissistic seductions of an imaginary—and thus alienated—corporealized ego. To be sure, the Lacanian will insist on separating the work of the signifier out from the lure of the image, at least insofar as the mental construction of the body image, for not only Lacan but also his phenomenologist interlocutor Maurice Merleau-Ponty, is a condition of possibility of perception as such, of our very capacity psychically to draw a line between what belongs to the body and what does not. We are therefore left to wonder in what precise sense the cinematic signifier—aural (in both linguistic and nonlinguistic forms from the beginning of the sound era) and visual, or rather almost always both at once—can be qualified as imaginary.

Now, Metz makes clear in *The Imaginary Signifier* that the term carries two distinct meanings in the intellectual context into which his text intervenes.[3] First, it refers to the fictional status of conventional narrative cinema and its far from necessary dominance over alternative cinematic forms. This of course is the meaning normally implied in ordinary conversation when we want to distinguish the world that a science fiction film depicts, for example, from the purportedly more real one that a documentary on health care politics is meant to show. More consequentially, however, Metz also connects the imaginary to Lacan's teaching, more specifically to his early notion of the mirror stage and its role in the formation of the ego. Readers conversant in film theory will recall that Metz's project to bring cinema discourse into dialogue with Freudian psychoanalysis helped generate a veritable raft of commentary in the 1970s and early '80s in France, the United

Kingdom, and beyond. Indeed, for what now retrospectively seems a mere fleeting moment, psychoanalytically informed analyses of the apparatus and spectatorship, of widely divergent levels of rigor and interest, held pride of place among the then-available theoretical approaches of cinema studies.

Despite the admirable perseverance of a few diehards, however, this moment of psychosemiological hegemony over the discipline now seems ephemeral and decidedly lost. Most certainly, it never threatened to form the insular and doctrinaire establishment that David Bordwell and company conjured as late as the mid-1990s in a crescendo of overblown rhetoric designed to banish psychoanalysis from the disciplinary territory of film studies.[4] Still, it must be granted that a significant portion of the work Metz helped to inspire quite unhelpfully lapsed into undernuanced ideological or symptomatic readings which jettisoned the dialectical complexity of the original elaborations in favor of a vulgar Althusserianism premised on a distorting simplification of the idea of the cinema screen as a "new kind" of mirror, one that, Metz felt compelled to insist, is nonetheless "very different" from the mirror of the Lacanian mirror stage (45, 49). For this reason the "post-theoretical" critique of psychoanalytic film theory, despite its polemical tendentiousness, cannot be dismissed entirely out of hand.

Indeed, it cannot be denied that influential voices within the Althusser-influenced "Metzian" current elaborated a view of the cinema spectator as the more or less satisfied recipient of subjectivity-effects (or positions) held to emanate unilaterally from the cinematic text. This construction conceived of the spectator as a mere receptacle into which the ideological messages of the film were directed and in which, to risk an understatement, they gained determinative subjective purchase. What resulted was a simplistic and univocal picture of both the cinema and its reception, in the worst cases guilty as charged by the Bordwellian post-theorists. The least one can say in defense of his complex work, however, is that despite the (modified) screen-mirror analogy for which he has been criticized even by avowedly Lacanian theorists, for Metz the route from film to viewer is decidedly *not* a one-way street.[5]

It is clear today that the familiar and easily dismissed construal of the spectator as a virtual, dyadic, exclusively imaginary reflection off the screen-cum-mirror regrettably stood as the straw figure against which the reaction against psychoanalytic film theory could strike what proved to be devastating blows.[6] In my view, this reaction was at least as indicative of a general backlash against politicized theoretical initiatives coming out of French structuralism in the humanities at large as it was specifically against psychoanalysis or Lacan.[7] No doubt, little is to be gained by revisiting in detail the low points of Metz's reception in the English-speaking world in the view of specifying how it went wrong: a soul-deadening prospect if there ever was one. Still, despite indisputable areas of weakness in Metz's grasp of psychoanalytic concepts,[8] his psychosemiology of the apparatus—the primary text as it were—continues to offer tremendously fertile ground for work in cinema theory today. Indeed, it is my contention that the complexities and ambiguities inherent in his account of cinematic spectatorship suggest paths of inquiry that have yet adequately to be mapped out. When properly explored, these paths have the potential to wake cinema studies up from its moribund and contextualist post-theoretical pedestrianism. Especially overlooked, in my view, has been Metz's provocative exposure of the collusion of a certain enthusiastic brand of spectatorship with the profit motive of entertainment capital. Today a return to Metz is therefore in order.

This chapter aims to show how a fresh reading of Metz through Lacan can help us understand how certain films—my example will be Chantal Akerman's stunning and unexpectedly hilarious Proust adaptation *The Captive* (2000)—can bring to our reluctant awareness as spectators the complicity of our transferential demand for love, what Metz himself calls our "love of the cinema," with the mindless profit machine of capitalism in its properly cinematic manifestation and beyond. Throughout the previous chapters I have distinguished in various ways between the event of transference as the encounter with the real of desire and the resistance to that encounter, which Freud termed transference love and Lacan discussed under the rubric of demand. This chapter will argue that if we understand cinematic spectatorship—more specifically, the two distinct levels of identification that Metz elaborates in his psychoanalytic work—as an instantiation of Freudian transference love, then we must conclude that Peter Wollen's cinema-clinic analogy cited in the first epigraph may not in fact have been taken far enough. Overlooked in Metz's text have been those indications of a *failure* of spectatorship, the significance of which is illuminated by the notion of transference that this book aims to put to work in literary and cultural studies.

I have risked the claim that Metz's psychoanalytic work on cinema has yet properly to be engaged with. The first task on the agenda must therefore be to assemble an original argument for what Metz actually set out to say in *The Imaginary Signifier*. I have also averred that a further clarifying reference to Lacan (though a later Lacan than the one Metz relies on) can make Metz's theory of spectatorship at once more convincing and more faithful to the Freudian ethos.

The benefits of this additional filtration through Lacan are twofold. First, it destabilizes, makes precarious, the levels of identification that Metz discerns in the cinematic apparatus by adding to his references to the symbolic and imaginary a more explicit acknowledgment of the agency of the real—the real of unconscious desire that both transference love and spectatorship seek to keep at bay. Now, Metz already argues in his own terms for the properly *dialectical* character of what I will insist on calling authentic psychoanalytic cinema theory. By dialectical, I here mean to suggest that the relation between the cinema text and the spectatorial function is minimally bidirectional, conflicted, ambivalent, and therefore dynamic. As Metz figures it, the viewer is at the same time point of origin and recipient of the cinema text and therefore something other than the actualization in the psyche of its meaning or content. This premise entails that the text-viewer relation is subject to a complex brand of ideological articulation that, first, cannot be summarily rendered in a formula generically applicable to the medium as such and, second, therefore varies in tandem with techniques of montage and subjective suture: the means by which the apparatus, in a specific but commercially hegemonic subset of films of the narrative sort, can establish point of view.

Second, the supplemental Lacan reference I bring to my reading of Metz has the added benefit of fleshing out the significance of his neglected Platonic-Cartesian, properly antiphenomenological orientation. This orientation's importance gains in significance by virtue of its dramatic incommensurability with dominant contemporary discourses on cinema. At the present moment, cinema discourse foregrounds a phenomenology of technological specificity based on the assumption that spectatorship is more or less fully technologically determined and therefore varies experientially with the specific sort of audio-visual apparatus with which the spectator is engaged. What has never to my knowledge been properly brought forward in readings of *The Imaginary Signifier* is the notion that Metz's discernment of the element of cinematic subjectivity that is *not of the level of experience* helpfully uncovers the inadequacies of the general phenomenological approach to film viewing. Long after André Bazin's pre-Marxist *Cahiers du cinéma,* this approach has not only attracted a number of prominent proponents over the last two decades, but has also been offered up as a corrective to perceived deficiencies—ahistoricism, inflexibility, excessive generality, intellectualism, decorporealization, for example—within Metz's psychosemiological approach.[9] These finer and admittedly somewhat technical details of Metz's discussion call out to be revisited because their significance can now be reconsidered in light of the discipline's ascending orthodoxies of both the pragmatically antitheoretical and anti-intellectually phenomenological and technologicist varieties.[10]

To lay what few cards I have left on the table, I hold the view that the full significance of Metz's cinematic antiphenomenology only becomes clear if we go beyond the modified mirror stage analogy to consider in more detail than does *The Imaginary Signifier* the disruptive agency of unconscious desire in spectatorship, more specifically the transferential ruin of cinematic identification in the form of what Metz himself calls filmic "unpleasure" (111). Metz's notion of unpleasure no doubt lends itself to comparison with the neo-Brechtianism of Peter Wollen's old idea of counter-cinema, by which he meant to differentiate, among other things, the "identification" and "pleasure" inherent in Hollywood and Zhdanovite socialist realism from the "estrangement" and "unpleasure" of the avant-garde tradition he then sought to valorize.[11]

The ineradicable prospect of spectatorial unpleasure—it is inherent in the apparatus as such, I will argue in contrast to Wollen—is what most clearly distinguishes cinematic spectatorship generically conceived from perversion in its strong, diagnostic, or clinical meaning: perversion as psychic structure, that is to say.[12] In this precise sense, the analogy between film viewing and voyeurism suggested by Laura Mulvey and others has been significantly overstated, though they are certainly not unrelated. As a rule, filmic pleasure is essentially perverse only in the sense that human desire itself is generically perverse. Having dispensed with the preliminaries required when one ventures onto well-trod and discipline-splitting ground, we are now free to engage with the substance of Metz's contribution to the study of the apparatus. I will begin by considering how Metz differentiates cinematic identification properly speaking from the generic psychical variety that caught Freud's attention as he sought after the cause of his patients' resistance to the cure.

Species of Identification

The opportunity is ripe at this juncture to revisit the Freudian origins of a distinction I made in chapter 1 between the two functions that Lacan designates as *i(a)* and I: the partial object enveloped in the cloak of idealization required for integration with the ego system, and the privileged symbolic point, ego ideal, from which this object can be psychically perceived. This background material will serve to contextualize Metz's main contention about the specificity of the forms of identification he sees at work in the cinema.

Freudian metapsychology makes reference to both a narcissism and an identification—the two terms are so closely intertwined that it can be difficult at times to distinguish between them—that he explicitly qualifies as "primary." As regards the former term, Freud writes that for the subject "one part of self-regard is primary—the residue of infantile narcissism," while "another part," never explicitly qualified as secondary, arises out of the omnipotence that is "corroborated by experience (the fulfillment of the ego ideal)."[13] Freud links primary narcissism to the formation of the ideal ego (*Idealich*) in contrast to the ego ideal (*Ichideal*), the source of the omnipotence of which Freud speaks. Freud memorably describes the primary narcissism that he locates in infancy as a "real happy love" in which "object-libido and ego-libido cannot be distinguished" and the ideal (or "infantile") ego and ego ideal are not yet differentiated (100). Note that according to Freud's own definitions, the ideal ego/ego ideal and ego-libido/object-libido pairings are not rigorously synonymous, since the notion of object-libido in this essay vacillates between two different meanings, which are clearly distinguished in Lacan. More consistently than does Freud, Lacan differentiates between the idealized symbolic mechanism of self-regard (ego ideal or I) and the real partial object of the drive *a*, which is very precisely not an ideal, nor is it amenable to idealization.

Lacan's development of the interrelation of the imaginary and symbolic dimensions of narcissism explicitly denies that Freudian happy love was ever actually experienced, arguing instead that the two functions remain part of the same libidinal system beginning with the subject's most primordial identifications. From this same perspective, Freud's view that the ego ideal can be fulfilled in experience is also modified by Lacan's more dialectical view that the accomplishment of the ego system can only ever be precarious, that it depends on the subject's success in repeatedly coaxing an anxiety-eradicating sign of confirmation from the Other. It is crucial to note, however, that Freud also mentions almost in passing that there is a "third part" of the mechanism of self-regard which "proceeds from the satisfaction of object-libido" (100). However obscurely, Freud insinuates here that there is a third category of object in the relation of narcissism, one whose power to deliver satisfaction would seem to distinguish it from the objects at work in the ego system, and therefore from the logic of neurosis and resistance that the ego is designed to enforce.

Freud's discourse on identification exhibits striking parallels with his discussion of narcissism. Observing that the ego's "object-identifications," if "they obtain the upper hand and become too numerous," can produce grave neurotic symptoms, Freud in *The Ego and the Id* differentiates these iterations of the ego ideal from what lies "behind it," namely, the subject's "identification with the father in his own personal prehistory." Going on to call this latter identification "primary," Freud avers that it is "not in the first instance the consequence or outcome of an object-cathexis," but rather "a direct and immediate identification," which "takes place earlier than any object-cathexis."[14] In a footnote, however, Freud casts doubt on his reference to the father, suggesting that this identification is so original that it must precede all perception of sexual difference. Freud's commentary on identification tends to stress the subject's alienation in external forms, either the ideal of "experience" or the more immediate pre-object. In contrast, the discourse on narcissism hints at the prospect of reconciliation, at a completed or realized selfhood embodied in the ego entity. Freud remains unclear, however, on the question of whether we are to regard such completion as futilely aspired to or rather concretely to be realized.

Though these nuances are indeed intriguing in themselves, what is important to retain for my purposes in this chapter is that both terms, identification and narcissism, imply a binary that fixes the before and after of an event of mediation or alienation that separates the subject from itself, that makes the subject dependent on an alien object without which it remains unable to apprehend itself. As we await Lacan's clarification, we can record two noteworthy opacities in Freud's thinking. Is the primary stage ever actually experienced or is it rather a mere logical precondition of our capacity to think the secondary moment? Also: How are we to understand the nature of this obscure "third" object to which Freud gestures, the "part" that provides a satisfaction apparently beyond the constraints of the ego, seemingly beyond the transferential amibitions of desire itself?

Freud's apparent attachment to the highly dubious notion of an infantile happy love should not prevent us from grasping his main theoretical point. As speaking subjects, our desire to construct a satisfying mental representation in which the self might take shelter is diffracted across two conceptually distinct but psychically interrelated modalities. The first of these, however dependent on the second, implies a direct, immediate, pre-objectal identity that is logically, if not temporally or developmentally, prior to relationality and difference. In question here is a static dyad devoid of an outside from which it might be separated or distinguished. In contrast, the second modality of the ego features an entity or form ("object") chosen from among a class or selection of such forms. It serves as the standpoint—often psychically associated, as we saw in chapter 1's analysis of the Freudian *einziger Zug*, with characteristics of specific persons—from which the first ego entity can be beheld. My sense is that the paradoxes that beset the Freudian iteration of these ideas are to be retained rather than rationalized away. The unmediated feature of primary identification is inconceivable for the subject in the absence of the mediation performed by the secondary form. And despite its secondary status, this latter form has in turn always already conditioned the primary mode of identification that Freud associates, however misleadingly or ideologically, with the presumptive full happiness of our earliest infantile experience.

Now, Metz's discussion of identification in the cinema shows that he understands Lacan to have clarified the ambiguities of Freud's treatment by qualifying the ideal ego of primary narcissism as a function of the imaginary register and the secondary identification with the ego ideal as a function of the symbolic. These two levels for Lacan are more intricately intertwined than they are for Freud, even at the level of infantile experience. As I also explored in chapter 1, Lacan chooses to emphasize the virtual and erroneous qualities of identification: the fact that the subject can situate its ego outside itself (or, in the presence of a nonmetaphorical mirror or movie screen, outside the three actual dimensions of geometrical space), and therefore quite literally sees itself where it is not, does not prevent this misrecognition from functioning as a condition of possibility for perception as such.

Lacan's gloss on Freud's ego ideal concept emphasizes that the subject's self-perception is always externalized, routed through an ideal symbolic point. This routing has the effect of extending, or more precisely of *perforating,* space in such a way that an immanent beyond of the three geometrical dimensions is opened up. This virtualization of space—the idea that space somehow contains within itself its own ineffable beyond—can take place in the absence of an actual mirror. This is so because perception as inflected by desire already functions as if the phenomenal world were a semi-opaque surface that haunts us with the question of what there could be on the other side. As far as Metz is concerned, the significance of his qualified mirror stage analogy is that narcissism and cinematic spectatorship share an investment in a properly virtual spatial extension, in a kind of trompe l'oeil. Spectatorship is indelibly marked by so-called primary identification insofar as the impression of reality intrinsic to the apparatus is dependent on the cinema screen's function as a kind of window which opens up onto the virtual world of diegetic space: the fictitious story-world of the cinema, in other words, at least in its narrative forms.

Now, *The Imaginary Signifier* sees Metz base his differentiation of spectatorship from the Lacanian mirror stage dynamic on the fact that the spectator does not see his own image on the screen. For Metz, this in itself justifies the reference to the specifically secondary aspect of cinematic identification.[15] Contrary to what Metz here assumes, however, spectatorship in its generic form (as opposed to the specific form that creates point of view; see below) is secondary not because the viewer is absent from the screen, but rather because subjectivity, never fully trapped in the imaginary, is always marked by lack, by desire. Still, it is my contention that we would be mistaken to dismiss Metz's elaboration of cinematic spectatorship on his erroneous, overly literal reading of Lacan's mirror stage argument.

Indeed, Metz's reference to Lacan's early work on the ego is otherwise admirably nuanced, for he acknowledges elsewhere that identification at the level of the mirror stage is already traversed by the symbolic function. This is demonstrated for Metz by the fact that the infant must be taught to recognize itself in its mirror image. The discourse of a second party (mother, father, caregiver, etc.) indexes—the medium here, to be perfectly explicit, is language—the identity of the virtual body reflection. In this way, the infant's primary identification must be propped up by its inscription within a network of relations which are symbolically articulated. The construct fabricated in this pri- mordial scene—the adult attributing the infant's name to the image in the mirror, implying that the infant "is" that image—functions as the very prototype of the ego structure. The adult, or rather a signifier representing him or her, stands as the infant's original ego ideal, the point from which the infant's own image becomes intelligible as its "self."

The conclusion to be drawn here for cinema spectatorship is that no theoretically significant distinction need be made between the subject's "natural" relation to the field of vision in general—that relation unmediated by image technology, that is—and its specific relation to this or that cinematic image considered in isolation. This is to say, against the discourse of technologicism, that *the phenomenal world is already a screen that separates us from desire's realization.* Therefore, the addition of an actual screen which frames represented moving images does nothing in itself to alter the fundamental conditions that structure our relation to the field of vision in general. As we are now in a position to explore, the difference between unmediated and technologically mediated perception only emerges in cinema when it begins to subjectivize the image, to attribute point of view to it by means of editing, or what the classical film theorists called montage.

We have seen that primary identification for psychoanalysis is always accompanied by the introjection of a properly symbolic relation, by the detour taken by the path of our relation to the self's construction through a particular signifier. To this basic psychoanalytic premise, however, Metz importantly adds the argument that the cinematic equivalent of this secondary identification is mediated—secondarized, if you will—to a further degree. Cinematic spectatorship is split (minimally, as we will shortly see) between two modalities: first, the diegetic stand-ins through whom the spectator includes itself in the story at a (spatial) remove from the screen, and a logically prior totalizing function of identification that Metz famously associates with the viewer's idea of the camera or projector. This latter modality is an abstract, indeed disembodied, properly transcendental instance of identification, which Metz is at pains to stress is *not* equivalent to the sum total of the spectator's secondary identifications, the ones through which this spectator vicariously participates in the action through the mechanism of point of view. This transcendental identification therefore has no analogue in so-called naked perception; it is therefore particular to the cinema, or more precisely to the technology of the moving image generically conceived.

Integral to Metz's intervention is the key notion that the two levels of identification that Freud first theorized and Lacan sought to clarify cannot be directly mapped onto spectatorship in the cinema. In Metz's view, *primary* cinematic identification correlates to *secondary* narcissism in Freud, that is to say with the subject's identification with the ego ideal or I. This identification fully admits of the subject's dependence on a network of signifiers in order to include itself, however problematically or imperfectly, within that network. The seldom remarked-upon corollary of this distinction, however, is that secondary cinematic identification for Metz must be medium-specific: it does not exist among the forms of subjectivity that occur independently of the brand of mediation effected by the cinema, alongside all the other proliferating forms of moving image and virtual reality technologies.

To anticipate, I will suggest when we finally arrive at my reading of *The Captive* that the disjunction between, first, the suturing that undergirds the properly vicarious, experiential dimension of spectatorship, and second, spectatorship's contrasting and more fundamental nonphenomenal or transcendental register makes it possible for filmmakers to intervene technically on a level corresponding to the cinema's enunciative, and consequently broadly political, potentialities.[16] Put in less technical language, the cinema allows for a kind of subjectivity framing—a foregrounding of the function of unconscious fantasy in subjectivity—which is not, strictly speaking, possible outside the apparatus's conditions.

Due to its inherent precariousness, this framing function calls into question the pleasurable, ego-propping effects of the cinematic image and, risking the failure of spectatorship as such, potentially lays bare the properly symptomatic dimensions of the cinema industry, including most importantly its complicity with the profit-making motive of capital. The cinema's tendency to establish a specifically neurotic dynamic that aims to buttress the ego's powers of resistance—Freudian transference love, that is—is precisely what motivates the saturation of cinematic production by the profit motive. As is the case everywhere else, in the cinema neurosis and capital work in perfect harmony with one another. Before expanding on these admittedly ambitious contentions, however, I am first required to examine in more detail how Metz presents spectatorship's nonphenomenal element through his crucial notion of *le sujet tout-percevant*, the all-perceiving subject.

With his idea of a cinematically primary identification with the camera, Metz describes a spectatorial function that remains unbounded by the experiential constraints of space and time. This level of cinematic subjectivity, Metz argues, is the condition of possibility for spectator-ship as such. Without this underlying identification, the spectator is incapable of establishing the various logical connections between the shots and sequences that comprise the narrative of fiction film, which remains as a result entirely unintelligible. Nor would the spectator be able unconsciously to internalize what we might call the cinematic contract: that tacit agreement—neither necessary nor socioculturally universal, mind you—thanks to which the viewer can sit back, relaxed and immobile, and remain both intellectually unperturbed and kineti-cally unmoved by the contradiction between its own bodily immobility and the spatiotemporal fluctuations on display in the composite vistas visible onscreen.

Metz sheds further light on this unintuitive condition of spectator-ship by distinguishing it from what it is not, namely, the perspectival interface between spectator and diegesis to which we refer in ordinary language as point of view. The explanation begins with a disarmingly simple assertion: "[I]n a fiction film the characters look at one another" (55), writes Metz. One can, of course, add that the spectator looks at these characters looking at one another, and one can instantly grasp the distinction between these two separate levels of looking. Crucially, however, what Metz calls the subjective image—his term for a point of view shot—depends on a third, intermediary perspective that can only be created with an edit. More precisely, Metz argues that the viewer is incapable of attributing an image with subjectivity—not its own, but that of a character, or rather more precisely a fusion of the two—in the absence of a reference within the image to off-screen space.

Classically, of course, we see the character looking in the first shot and what the character sees in the second. Metz's observation here is that this edit establishes a virtual point (fictional space extends out into "real" space) *in front of the screen* where the spectator's and the character's respective looks meet. This point is the mechanism that sutures the spectator to a character's visual, and in this sense subjective, perspective. This virtual space must be in front of the screen simply because the spectator must see the character looking in order to get a sense of the direction of the character's line of sight. Though Metz does not make this point explicit, it should be remarked here that this virtualization of space in front of the image further distinguishes the cinematic screen from the mirror, which of course can only create imaginary space "behind" itself.

Technically speaking, the fusion of spectatorial and story-world functions in this secondary modality of cinematic identification occurs through the association of the angle of the subjectivized character's perspective within a shot's composition with the angle presented in the ensuing shot. The impression of subjectivity, in other words, would fail to arise if what we see in the second shot could not logically be visible to the character seen in the first, with the exception, of course, of dream sequences and the like. Clearly, the character whose point of view is being represented must necessarily be absent from the second shot in order not to violate the spatial logic being established.

Two main consequences follow from this basic convention for Metz. First, there is no inherent limit to the number of diegetical points of view that can be established by means of this off-screen "obligatory intermediary," as Metz refers to it (56). Second, the power of montage to attribute subjectivity to individual shots in the cinema-text manifests the first level—there is another, as we shall see—of what I call spectatorial splitting. The spectator witnesses the film's story-world from a series of "objective" (diegetically non-subjectivized, more technically) perspectives while at the same time seeing the film vicariously through the eyes of a theoretically unlimited number of character-intermediaries. "As we see through him," Metz writes of the self-effacing offscreen agency he is theorizing, "we see ourselves not seeing him" (56).

The point, to be sure, has its paradoxical aspect: the cinema text becomes subjectivized when the character whose visual point of view is being represented is in fact missing from the image, and thereby not an object of the viewer's immediate visual awareness. Equally paradoxically, this form of subjectivization, in spite of its vicariousness, lays bare *our own* agency as spectators, engages us more intensely in the experience of viewing the film. The subjective image pulls us in precisely at the moment when our own perspective is fused with that of the character to whom we are sutured, a character who must nevertheless disappear from view. This fusion retains the traces of the contradiction it never fully resolves: we are and yet we are not the subjectivity concretized in the sutured image. For Metz, as cinema-subjects we cannot place ourselves within the fiction film's story-world without the mediation of this identificatory mechanism. Indeed, we hardly need be aware of our virtual intermediary in front of the screen to sense that what we are seeing both does and does not "belong to us."

Beyond the Phenomenon of Cinema

My aim in this section will be to argue in detail that Metz's idea of primary cinematic identification is best understood through the lens of the transference as Lacan defines it. Film studies readers well know that the other, secondary dimension of spectatorship discussed above has had the most conspicuous afterlife in film theory discourse. Feminist film theory, for example, became concerned with the ways in which sexual difference is inscribed within cinematic subjectivity, arguing that dominant cinemas set up a dynamic of viewing pleasure that facilitates the expression of male heterosexual desire. Laura Mulvey's early work is of course the classic reference here.[17] As far as Metz is concerned, however, the point to be made in response is that the visual pleasure scenario remains limited to the secondary level of spectatorship. The consequence for Mulvey's argument of Metz's thesis about a primary identification with the camera is that the spectatorial function can never be reduced to any particular instance of perspective or suture within the film's story-world. Nor can it be reduced to the sum total of such perspectives and sutures. The question of who gets pleasure from what images in narrative cinema cannot therefore be translated in such brusque fashion into the terms of sexual difference.

That this secondary level of spectatorial identification is the more empirically and therefore intuitively self-evident of the two is surely not unrelated to its relative theoretical success. As I have already intimated, however, the aspect of Metz's theory that will prove of greater signifi-cance to my own argument relates, rather, to the other level. This more primary level of splitting manifests itself underneath, if I can put it this way, the other, properly diegetic or narrative level. More precisely, this primary splitting occurs in consequence of a disjunction between the first level of splitting just discussed—the suture mechanism effected through Metz's offscreen intermediary—and the underlying perceptual synthesis responsible in the first instance not for point of view, but rather for the cinema's foundational but precarious impression of reality: the perpetu-ation of its counterintuitively successful optical illusion. Parenthetically, if we were to acknowledge only the secondary mode of identification, it would prove impossible to account for our capacity to sustain our interest as viewers in films that do not represent images of human (or humanizable) actors—abstract films, for instance—since these films are by Metz's definition incapable of creating the properly subjective effect of suture on which narrative cinema commercially depends.

But Metz's framework puts forth that the subjective shot is not the only form of identification in the cinema. The oft-misunderstood "identification with the camera," the function that creates an all-perceiving subject unshackled from spatiotemporal constraints, cannot therefore be reduced to the sequence of objective and subjective images that, when editorially arranged, give rise to point of view. Primary cinematic identification does not operate on the level of the alternation of shots in the cinema text and therefore does not partake of the differential logic generically inherent in semiotic approaches to cinema, including Metz's own. Simply put, Metz's original concept rests on the assumption that the sequence of shots comprising the film must be assembled into a totality in order to become intelligible to the viewer and give a persuasive impression of reality.

This assemblage of shots rests on a function of identification within the spectator situated somewhere other than the level of perception properly speaking, in a "place" associated with the conditions of possibility of the apparatus as such. My suggestion here is that though Metz does indeed name this mechanism, *The Imaginary Signifier* never fully spells out its consequences. We are now in a position to pay closer attention to Metz's criticism of the phenomenological study of cinema to discern the finer points of this difficulty in his work, and to suggest how a further reference to Lacan might help to flesh out the implications of Metz's discussion of primary cinematic identification.

Metz openly admits that the onus is on him to identify with precision the blind spot within phenomenological film discourse on which he thinks psychoanalysis can shed light. Emblematized for Metz by the influential work of André Bazin,[18] cinematic phenomenology succumbs to the seductive pull of the image by exclusively emphasizing the *experience* of spectatorship. It devolves in consequence into an enthusiastic and uncritical celebration of the cinema's subjectivity-effects. This is the "love of the cinema" (14), as Metz aptly puts it, that today still not only fuels the commercial film industry's formidable profit machine, but also motivates vast swathes of film criticism both within the academy and outside in the film media.

More significantly for both Metz's purposes and my own, however, the phenomenological framework proves incapable of coming to grips with the functioning of the apparatus: how the cinema grafts itself onto the human perceptual faculty by redoubling its basic structure through technological means. Indeed, phenomenology's main drawback is that it leaves unexamined what for Metz remains the cinema's underlying mystery, namely, the force of its seductive pull. Why does the apparatus of cinema work so effectively? Why does it go on producing ever more sophisticated technological means of creating virtual realities? In asking the former question—though the latter, in my view, is thoroughly Metzian, it was never posed by Metz himself—Metz implicitly returns to the Platonic origin of the idea of a perception-projection apparatus.

In an allegorical representation of the powers of human intellection liberated from the shackles of sense perception, Plato in Book 7 of his *Republic* famously describes chain-bound cave-dwelling prisoners whose only perceptual reality is a band of shadows cast on the rocky wall in front of them.[19] The duty of the philosopher according to Plato is not only to liberate himself from the spectacle of the simulacra projected onto the cave wall and climb up to the sunlit world of clear and distinct ideas, but also to plunge back down into the cave to convince the remaining reluctant prisoners to follow suit. My Metzian questions can be translated into the terms of Plato's allegory. Of what compelling essence do the prisoners' chains consist? If a decisive exit from the cave is finally possible, as Plato himself insisted on believing, then can we envision an analogous exit from the cinematic apparatus, at least in its industrial-cum-corporate incarnation as a pure profit machine for capital?

The analytical work of cinematic psychosemiology depends for Metz on the prior diagnosis of the cinema's properly symptomatic element. Metz discerns that the pleasures to be had in film viewing feed off the same misrecognition upon which the human ego is constructed; the ego and the cinema are both engaged in forms of hallucinated virtual satisfaction. The cinema strives to indulge the human desire for an idealized, narcissistically gratifying mastery over both space and time, a mastery denied to a speaking subject who is castrated: separated from a (perceived) part of itself through its problematic insertion into language. But symbolic castration also features a properly visual-perceptual consequence: we are haunted by the troubling dissymmetry between, on the one hand, the unfailing constancy of our demand for full command over space and time and, on the other, the suspect or ambiguous reality of what is presented by way of objects in the visual field, whether these appear through the intervention of image technology or more simply "in reality" *tout court*. In short, the cinema holds forth to the subject the promise of a perceptual omniscience which, however precarious, elsewhere this subject can seek only in vain.

Surely, among the most innovative and seldom-observed aspects of Metz's cinematic psychoanalysis is that it foregrounds the material, properly socioeconomic implications of this last observation. Today, these implications are mistakenly considered even by many within the Freudian and post-Freudian traditions to lie beyond the purview of psychoanalytic inquiry, properly speaking. The film industry effectively exploits the same imaginary anticipation of perfection that mediates the infant's representation of space during the Lacanian mirror stage. For Metz, this is the imaginary plane on which cinematic phenomenology remains trapped. More precisely, phenomenology's emphasis on the experience of spectatorship stays blind to the abstract or transcendental perceptual synthesis that conditions the apparatus's effectiveness, that is to say, its very capacity to create a more or less convincing image-world by involving us experientially in what takes place onscreen.

The pinning down in thought of this nonempirical synthesis is for Metz what makes possible the apparatus's conceptualization; it provides the "impossible" intellectual perspective, abstracted from space and time, from which the phenomenon of spectatorship might be conceived as if from outside itself. If spectatorship were entirely subsumed by the cinematic experience, then it is not clear how we could capture our captivation by the apparatus *in thought*. That Plato was able effectively to conceive of the cinema over two millennia before the medium's technological realization lends further support to the claim that the cinema, by which I mean to include our very experience as viewers, depends on the agency of what can only be called an idea, however unconscious it might be. Metz's Platonic-Cartesian wager is that we *can* indeed think the function of the apparatus because the perceptual-ideational synthesis that lies at its base does not form part of the cinematic experience properly speaking. In short, what makes possible the experience of cinema is never experienced as such.

Given its unfamiliarity in contemporary cinema discourse, it will be wise at this juncture to consider in greater detail Metz's own evocation of this nonexperiential element of cinematic subjectivity and to inquire more deeply than Metz does himself into its dependence on unconscious fantasy. In order for the apparatus to function, the spectator must "withdraw into himself as a pure instance of perception," according to Metz (53). This spectator "identifies with himself as look,"

Metz continues, and "can do no other than identify with the camera" (49). Metz's terminological choices suggest an affinity shared by the apparatus's underlying synthesis and Kant's notion of transcendental apperception. This is the synthesis in Kantian epistemology that allows the subject to unify the disparate and unorganized information received by the senses into a single and continuous experience which this subject can view as her own.[20] Metz's "identification with the camera" notion performs the same totalizing function. It does so only from an abstract point outside or beyond the diegesis, beyond even the virtual point in front of the screen that serves as the axis for the point-of-view effect that defines secondary cinematic identification.

Metz's argument therefore makes the Kantian assumption that a function outside experience must be presupposed in order to explain why my experience as a sensate subject can become intelligible as a unity, as a totality of interrelated impressions which reflect the particularity of my own personal engagement with the world. This is the function that is effectively taken over by the cinematic apparatus, which, having incorporated one or several spectators, similarly needs to identify with itself in order to become a technology of subjectivization. To clarify his admittedly difficult notion, Metz compares this empty, self-relating operation to the viewing subject of Renaissance perspective, who projects himself into the picture at the perspectival vanishing point. This point is figured in the image-space only virtually as the impossible meeting point of (subjectively) parallel lines located well beyond the limits of two-dimensional pictorial space, "deep inside" the canvas.

In similar fashion, cinema's primary identification operates at a virtual point of pure self-relating consciousness, which the spectator unconsciously associates with the camera or projector behind it. Crucial to note here is the fact that this identificatory function is subtracted from the spectator's field of vision, unavailable not only to presentation as an object of experience, but also, at least while the technology is working smoothly, to consciousness as such. Though the camera or projector of which Metz speaks is not of course reducible to the actual machine in the projection room, it remains the case nonetheless that a mechanical failure or power outage, for example, will have the effect of bringing primary cinematic identification to ruin, destroying the alluring impression of reality on which it depends. The fact that Metz's function is psychical, and not technological, in nature rectifies the misguided criticism that DVDs and iPhones have rendered his theory obsolete. The projector at the back of our heads is simply the "place" in the psyche from which all the shots that make up a film can be viewed simultaneously as if assembled into one.

It now becomes clear why the underlying subjective instance of primary cinematic identification cannot be accounted for when we view spectatorship purely as passive empirical sense perception. In order to make sense of the story-world unfurling before him, the viewer must abstract himself from the body, from his concrete placement in space and time. The film-world we allow ourselves to be drawn into knows none of the limitations that circumscribe our experience of the world unmediated by image technology. In sum, the cinema puts to work a properly disembodied instance of perception which must remain unperceived in order for the viewer, cyborg-like, to effect an unconscious fantasmatic internalization of the apparatus, allowing it to function as a sensory-perceptual prosthetic.

Now, this last point—Metz's intimation, never explicitly argued, that the abstract synthetical apperception underlying spectatorship features a properly fantasmatic instance—is the one that can most helpfully be strengthened with a further reference to Lacan. It was Lacan, after all, who rigorously formalized the subjective function as the correlation between an absence of signifying material—a gap or failure in the signifying chain, but also an associated wavering, opacity, or de-realization of form or image—and an immaterial object of fantasy by means of which this gap can potentially be filled, this inadequacy rectified.

This, then, is my suggestion: the visual pleasure that film theory associates with spectatorship occurs in consequence of the gratification that we receive not only from the (secondary) vicariousness of point of view, but also from the apparatus generically conceived in its (primary) power to assemble or totalize a sequence of cinematic images in such a way that it becomes possible to anticipate an impossible transcendence of the limitations of space and time. This is to say that *unconscious fantasy is the condition of Metzian primary cinematic identification,* of the means by which a discontinuous succession of spatiotemporally bounded moving images is potentially assembled into a transcendental unity. By means of this primary fantasy, the apparatus tries to fashion a narcissistic or closed libidinal circuit whereby we see a projected manifestation of desire reflected back to us by the cinematic image in a way that promises to confirm our being, to consolidate our command over the conditions of desire. On this level, Metz's psychical projector at the back of the spectator's head is strictly analogous to Lacan's I (ego ideal)—the unconscious symbolic point from which we see ourselves as we wish to be seen.

Our susceptibility to being interpellated in this way—the Althusserian term is indeed appropriate here—enables the apparatus to work as an image-machine for the virtual satisfaction of "infantile" demands. To risk an understatement, there is no lack of evidence to support the claim that this machine spews forth an endless sequence of spectacularly antisocial fantasies which only serve further to subjugate its spectator-cogs under the cultural and political status quo. Yet it is also crucial to note that this economy is not a stable one. The apparatus—I use the term here in the broadest sense to include its socioeconomic dimensions—expends a tremendous amount of energy and capital trying to forestall the entropic collapse of its libidinal system. Surely, the increasing sophistication of computer-generated imagery and virtual reality technologies, as well as the hyperactive editing, accelerated camera movements, and multiplying perspectival fragmentation that together characterize so much of the contemporary commercial industry, are telltale signs that the cinema economy is responding, much in the mode of a Freudian obsessional, to fears of an impending failure of its capacity to entrance. Indeed, this is doubtless one of the more intelligent ways of interpreting the "death of cinema" motif that has been a feature of cinema discourse virtually since its inception, but that has witnessed a notable resurgence during the last decade or so in tandem with celluloid's imminent obsolescence.

In addition to offering this Marxian symptomatic reading, however, my qualification of Metz's idea of primary identification as inherently unstable has the added benefit of implying that spectatorship need not succumb to the transferential, ego-propping resistance toward which it tends. As countless films, including Akerman's *The Captive,* have shown, the apparatus has at its disposal a variety of means of approaching, indeed, of framing, the prospect of its own collapse, of playing with the image's powers of seduction in a way that exposes the limits of visual pleasure. This inherent virtue of cinema holds the power to produce not Althusserian ideological *interpellation,* but rather an authentic *subjectivation* (as opposed to the "subjectivization" I referred to earlier in the context of Metzian secondary identification or point of view).

By means of an initially unpleasurable failure of the image's seductive power, this subjectivation encourages the less passive and more critically hystericized brand of spectatorship that the commercial cinema works to forestall at all costs. Cinematic subjectivation occurs as we become aware of the fundamental disequilibrium between, first, the limitless demands we place on moving image technology for a spectatorial omniscience premised on the transcendence of space and time, and second, this same technology's ultimate inability to sustain the dynamic of visual pleasure, to forestall indefinitely the collapse of the image's enticing lure.

At these moments when the apparatus fails, the closed libidinal system of narrative and visual pleasure short-circuits, and the world-constructing Metzian projector at the back of our brains breaks down. Returning to my earlier discussion of narcissism, we can say that it is here where Freud's mysterious third agency of self-regard enters onto the scene of spectatorship. This agency in fact destroys the pleasurable amorous synergy by means of which we aspire to see ourselves, from the outside as it were, as both master of and participant in the cinematic diegesis. Indeed, I would suggest that the unpleasure occasioned by the failure of interpellation in spectatorship is a condition of possibility for what Freud calls the satisfaction of object libido. This means, in plainer language, that we experience drive satisfaction as spectators precisely at the moment when visual pleasure turns into its opposite. Spectatorial jouissance manifests itself as unpleasure precisely because the apparatus is primarily a mechanism of defense against unconscious desire. By holding out the promise of desire fulfilled, the apparatus in fact *protects* us from the dislocating and disorienting impact of true corporeal satisfaction, which, when it inevitably begins to appear, the viewer will in consequence, at least initially, experience as disagreeable.

This alternative view of spectatorship gives an intimation of a different modality of (un)pleasure the agency of which within cinematic spectatorship remains undertheorized. Pushing us out from the image and back into the social world, spectatorship's failure interrupts both the logic of vicarious or second-order visual perception as well as the sense of omniscience over space and time. In this way, cinematic unpleasure has the effect of reinserting our bodies into the here-and-now, causing space and time to unfurl with possibility in a way that cannot, however, be psychically mapped. The exposure of the apparatus's involvement with unpleasure gestures beyond the kind of spectatorship endemic to hegemonic masculine bourgeois cinema. This is precisely the kind of cinema the logic of which Akerman seeks to dissect in her film.

Proustian Obsession and the Failure of Spectatorship

We can now finally turn to *The Captive* to explore in more concrete terms—things thus far have remained perhaps irritatingly abstract—the inherent economic tension in the apparatus by considering how Akerman lays bare the ultimate emptiness of its narcissistic promise. In the terms of this book's theoretical framework, the topic of Akerman's film is a specifically masculine form of transference love, an obsessional and therefore futile attempt to solve the enigma of femininity through the extraction from Woman of a knowledge she does not have. The genius of Akerman's film lies in the way it links this transferential dynamic to the underlying mechanism of spectatorship I have identified in this chapter through Metz.

The film is a faithful but loose adaptation of the fifth volume of Proust's mammoth modernist classic *In Search of Lost Time*. Indeed, it is at least as intertwined with other, nonliterary texts—Mozart's comic opera *Così fan tutte* and especially Hitchcock's *Vertigo*—as it is with Proust's work. *The Captive* explores with painstaking analytical rigor the obsessive love of Simon (a stand-in for the novel's narrator Marcel, played by Stanislas Merhar) for Ariane (a double of Proust's Albertine, played by Sylvie Testud). The film covers the novelistic territory corresponding to the moment when the narrator has successfully wrenched his paramour from her pack of *jeunes filles en fleur* and confined her to the claustrophobic darkness of his staidly bourgeois Parisian apartment. My contention in this final section will be that by means of a subtle framing technique, the film presents the dynamic of Simon's voyeuristic epistemophilia as an allegory for the very cinematic apparatus by means of which it is represented. More precisely, Simon's repeatedly frustrated attempts to gain perfect knowledge of Ariane's feminine desire exactly parallels the spectator's ambition to live the identificatory spatiotemporal omniscience that the apparatus deceptively promises. This is the same omniscience I have previously linked to the aim of Freudian transference love and Lacanian love as demand.

With the help, more technically, of Akerman's trademark clinical style—minimal editing and camera movement, attention-trying extended takes devoid of significant action, and stylized, absurdist, ambiguously comic dialogue—the film draws attention to not only the neurotic foundations of our desire for a completed form of knowledge, but also the voyeuristic underpinnings of the resistance characterizing the forms of spectatorship generally available in dominant commercial cinema. Akerman's technique trains our perception to become cognizant of its dependence on an apparently missing or dissimulated object which makes impossible the prospect of perfectly knowing another being, particularly at the level of its fascinating yet forbidding jouissance. In general terms, the film lays bare the fundamental inadequacy of the cinematic image with respect to desire. Unafraid blatantly to frustrate the demands that we place as spectators on the image, Akerman forces her hystericized viewer to come to terms with the tragic pathos of Simon's obsession, and to participate vicariously in the unraveling of his desperately narcissistic psychic structure. Akerman carefully leads her viewer to the difficult but liberating conclusion that the dynamic of this obsession is a diegetical rendering of the truth of our delirious complicity with the apparatus, precisely what Metz disparagingly calls our love of the cinema.

Since Akerman expresses her thematic framing of the apparatus in the way she chooses to frame the film itself, it will be wise to examine in detail *The Captive's* crucial opening and closing sequences. As the opening credits disappear from the screen against a backdrop of moonlit ocean waves (which conspicuously reappear in the tragic final sequence), we witness a cut to faded film footage—we know it is footage from the flickering of the image, a subtle slow-motion effect, and the mechanical sounds of an offscreen projector—showing a group of young, carefree women frolicking in swimsuits on a beach. Proust readers immediately recognize the exuberant feminine collective the narrator encounters at the seaside resort of Balbec. In both novel and film, the band of women serves as a figure for a particular masculine fantasy of feminine enjoyment in all its unconquerable, non-phallic indistinctness, precisely the fantasy that sets off and sustains Simon/Marcel's all-consuming desire to flesh out with knowledge the innermost being of his beloved. The film-within-a-film singles out the woman we will come to know as Ariane as well as another woman, Ariane's friend Andrée who, apparently a bad swimmer, has run into difficulty in the sea and is being helped ashore by Ariane. Following a shadowy close-up of Ariane, a cut taking us away from the footage reveals to us the young man we will come to recognize as our antihero Simon.

Lit in vaguely ominous chiaroscuro fashion, Simon stands aside a projector replaying a segment of the footage while slowly muttering the words "*je . . . vous . . . aime . . . bien*" ("I like/love you very much").

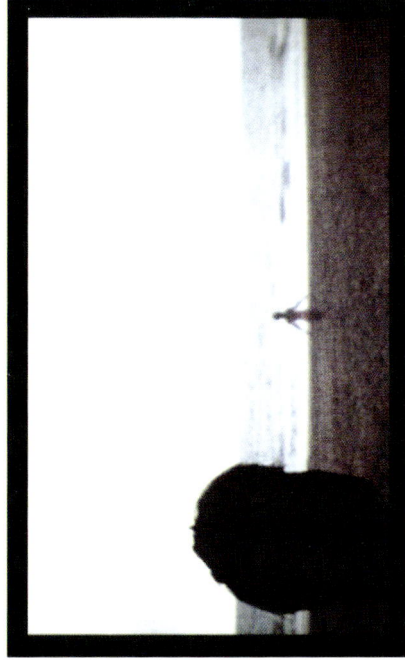

Figure 5.2. Chantal Akerman, *La Captive*, opening sequence (©2000 Gemini Films and ©2004 Kimstim, Inc.).

The film goes on to cut repeatedly between the footage—specifically a medium shot of Ariane alongside Andrée in which we can barely discern Ariane's lips move, uttering some indecipherable phrase—and shots of Simon at the projector who, as we begin to piece together, is trying to make his own declaration of love coincide with the movement of Ariane's lips onscreen. It is as if Simon were trying to establish an impossible symbolic exchange between himself and Ariane's image, vainly attempting to establish through the apparatus of cinema a seamless correspondence between the invocation of his desire for his beloved and this desire's imaginary-virtual materialization. Now returned to the beach footage, we see Simon's head appear in dark silhouette on the lower lefthand corner of the screen-within-a-screen, the one now seamlessly superimposed upon the other. Apparently satisfied, Simon has sat himself down to enjoy the film. In this final shot of the sequence, we observe Simon in yet another foreshadowing of Ariane's tragic end as he watches her image recede toward the horizon and into the sea.

   This subtle but crucial opening sequence sees Akerman make explicit to her viewer the two different levels of identification that Metz sees at work in the cinema. From here on in we will view the film simultaneously from Simon's perspective as well as, less consciously of course, from the abstract, disembodied and totalized perspective of the apparatus itself, the perspective provided by Metz's primary cinematic identification. We have been made aware of the metaphorical Metzian projector at the back of our heads because we have just seen a literal representation of it onscreen. In this way, Akerman draws an explicit comparison between the function of the apparatus in general and the desire, presented as increasingly jealous and obsessional as the film goes on, of a particular character in the story. By drawing our attention to this parallel throughout the film, Akerman cleverly underscores the neurotic underpinnings of not only Simon's creepy stalker behavior, but also of spectatorship's underlying dynamic.

   Significantly, the narrative tells us nothing about the origin of the beach footage. Is it Simon's? Was it shot by a member of the *bande*? To whom is Ariane really declaring her love? Yet the sequence also asks a more fundamental question about the relation between the dynamic of neurotic masculine fantasy and the means by which the apparatus is able to incorporate the spectator's subjectivity. *The Captive*'s opening sequence is allegorical both diegetically and generically. First, Simon's effort to ascertain via filmic projection that he is indeed the addressee of Ariane's message of love is a metonym for the story's central conflict: Simon's effort, ultimately unsuccessful, to reassure himself that he is the exclusive object of Ariane's love; or more precisely, that Ariane is not willfully withholding evidence of secret lesbian liaisons. In the clinical terms outlined in chapter 1, Simon's relation to Ariane is analogous to the patient in the transference whose emotional provocations aim to coax an anxiety-dispelling sign of love from the analyst. Second and more fundamentally, however, Akerman's decision to introduce her film through a representation of spectatorship foregrounds the medium's capacity to objectify the limits of the cinematic image with respect to both knowledge and desire. Indeed, this initial sequence institutes what we might wish to call a *meta-suture*: it frames, redoubles, the means by which the film visually grafts itself onto Simon's desire and by extension our own desire as viewers. It lays bare the obsessional logic by means of which this desire attempts a futile fashioning of the visual field in its own image.

The cut that brings us from the opening framing sequence to the film's story-world, properly speaking—we are taken from the unreality of Simon's screening room to the not-so-different unreality of the ultra-chichi Place Vendôme—therefore corresponds to the cut that separates the two different levels of what I have called spectatorial identification or splitting. Narratively, the sequence foregrounds the film's dependence—logical, diegetical, aesthetic—on Simon's all-consuming desire to gain perfect knowledge of Ariane. Generically, however, the sequence forces the spectator to come to grips with the subjective void underlying the fantasy of spatiotemporal mastery that structures not only this film, but also the very apparatus that makes it possible. Like the patient in analysis confronting the traumatic core of non-knowledge in the analyst, Akerman's viewer will eventually be forced to sustain an encounter with the visual unpleasure at the heart of the cinematic image.

The Captive offers a literal iteration of the intimate relation between fantasy and "reality" that structures perception even when it is not mediated by image technology. More precisely, it is not enough to say that the film is effectively Simon's personal movie of his jealous paranoia. Our relation to the world outside the cinema, it must be added, is similarly conditioned by the fantasy projections of desire. Contrary to what one might think, it is not at all clear that the movie has ended when we leave the screening room or turn off the monitor. *The Captive*'s basic argument is therefore not unlike the one we can

Figure 5.2. Chantal Akerman, *La Captive* (2000), closing sequence (©2000 Gemini Films and ©2004 Kimstim, Inc.).

ascribe retrospectively to Plato's cave allegory: the cinematic apparatus simply reduplicates and externalizes through technological means
the psycho-optical mechanisms of human perception and its necessary
distortion by desire. In this precise sense, our relation to the visual
field is always already virtualized: deformed, reshaped, perforated by
a perturbing and ghostly entity, which our desire projects onto the
world of appearances, but which the images that constitute this world
can only fail to display, even when these images result from the most
sophisticated, most "real" forms of technological mediation.

An inquiry into *The Captive*'s equally crucial concluding sequence
will convey the kind of subjective destitution beyond the transference
that Akerman's framing technique makes possible. As Simon's desperation increases in absurdity—he spends an evening chasing shadows
through dark Parisian streets and quizzes a lesbian couple to ascertain
if he has any chance with his beloved, who repeatedly denies that she
is *comme ça*—it becomes quite clear that the missing knowledge he
craves doesn't exist. My suggestion about the film's conclusion is that
Akerman's deliberate hystericization of the viewer leads us onto the
threshold of the apparatus's collapse, to the ruination of subjectivity
that leads to the transference's beyond. Whereas the function of the
opening sequence is to objectify in the image the mechanism of primary cinematic identification and the neurotic desire for mastery over
desire's conditions, the concluding sequence works to make manifest
the dislocating subjective void for which primary identification seeks to
compensate. The sequence exposes the disjunction between what we
desire to see in the cinematic image and what in reality it is capable
of showing.

The movement of Ariane's silhouette out toward the sea in the
opening sequence holds forth the promise of desire's potential fulfillment. The motion away from the spectator toward the shot's vanishing
point, along with the image of Ariane's shrinking and fading body,
hints at a virtual beyond of the image-space that invites the cathexis
of desire. Narratively, this sequence presents us with an intimation of
the beautiful, self-reflecting object to which Simon's desire wishes to
address itself: an Ariane, that is to say, who has fully disclosed herself
to Simon, finally satisfied his insatiable desire to know her most secret
and intimate self.

By contrast, an opposite movement back out from the sea in the
concluding sequence poignantly conveys the subjective destitution of the

analysand who has finally traversed the fantasy, accepted the challenge to confront the truth that the object's essence lies in its irreducible difference from everything that desire would have stand in for it. Unveiling the death-bearing real of Simon's desire, the sequence discloses that Simon has failed to grapple with the disjunction between what Ariane represents for his desire and what she is capable of offering him on the level of drive satisfaction. Indeed, the film has already made clear that Simon remains oblivious to what Ariane could provide him on this level: he is only able to engage with her sexually when she is asleep or else when physical contact between them is mediated by bed linens or mottled glass.

Just prior to the film's ultimate sequence, Simon and Ariane drive to a beautiful old seaside hotel in a desperate attempt to resume their relationship. As Simon awaits the arrival of their late-night supper, Ariane announces that she will go out for a swim. But something is amiss: Ariane is sullen and distracted (she wants her eggs both poached and scrambled), a strong wind has arisen, and the night is deep and black. When, after their food has been delivered, Simon walks out onto an elegant patio to see what has become of Ariane, he scans the water and panics, desperately running onto the beach, stripping, and diving into the ocean. Now out among waves only dimly lit by moonlight, we are shown what appears to be Simon and Ariane struggling in the water. But the weakness of the light and the uncharacteristic brevity of the sequence prevent us from drawing any reliable conclusion as to what is going on. Is Ariane resisting her rescue? Why would she need rescuing, anyway? Did she herself not rescue Andrée in the footage sequence? Is one of the members of our doomed couple trying to drown the other?

The Captive then cuts to its final shot. We are back on the shoreline at daybreak, looking out to sea at a small motorboat making its way with aching slowness to port. As we listen to the ominous crescendos of Rachmaninov's *Isle of the Dead*, a musical leitmotiv associated throughout the film with the unsettling desperation of Simon's pursuit, Akerman forces us to wait two full torturous minutes before we can discern with certainty who is in the boat. Did Simon rescue Ariane? Did he kill her? Did Ariane kill Simon? Discerning that it is Simon, apparently alone, in the boat, we wonder, Where is Ariane? Is her body lying in the hull? Is she unconscious? Dead?

The scene is patent Akerman. The sheer duration of the shot, the virtual immobility of the camera, and the lack of editing—her refusal to condense time or parcel up space—lend an excruciating quality to the suspense. There is no visual pleasure to be had anywhere in the image, and we suspect that the resolution we desire, like Simon's desire fully to know Ariane, will fail to materialize. In a quintessentially high-modernist gesture, Akerman brings bourgeois cinema's visual regime to its implosion. The seductive experiential vicariousness of the apparatus is revealed to be an empty sham. The beautiful cinematic window through which we seek escape from a pedestrian reality becomes the threshold of the death drive, here pushed by the dogged resistance of transference love down a path of sadistic misogynist destruction. As we finally discover, there is indeed nothing, no one in the boat except for a huddled and shivering Simon. "What are you thinking about?" Simon insistently asks Ariane throughout the film. "*À rien,*" she responds, echoing her name—nothing. "What *more* is there really to see in the cinema?" asks *The Captive*'s final sequence. The unsettling answer: a conspicuous absence, *a nothing.*

Throughout its course the film elucidates how the structures of cinematic identification parallel the amorous and defensive demands we issue to the field of vision to see our desire perfectly materialized. At its poignant conclusion, *The Captive* insists on leaving its viewer defenseless against the inevitable frustration of our love of cinema in its complicitous and transferential dimension.

VI

Naked Love

Bodies of Theory

There are three main groups of ideas about the body that circulate in cultural analysis today. To begin this final chapter, I will sketch a hasty preparatory overview of these ideas for more specialist readers and invite the others to hold their collective breath for a moment or two. The first idea, phenomenological and anti-Cartesian in inspiration, departs from embodied experience to make claims to knowledge. Rebelling against the Platonic dismissal of sense data as the seat of illusion, this tradition seeks to heal the rift between mind and body with the premise of an intentionality directed out into the world or, in its existentialist-Beauvoirian version, a concrete or material situation from which an individual volitional project can be launched. A poststructuralist and professedly antihumanist offshoot of this tradition, aiming to trace modernity's semiotic and psychoanalytic signifying structures back to the Platonic ideas, seeks to theorize a "body without organs." This body substitutes heterogeneous and nonhierarchical corporeal flows and intensities for, so it argues, the repressively normative and personalizing ("Oedipal") circumscriptions of desire and the signifiers through which it is viewed to be expressed

Now, the second approach, probably the dominant one in Anglo-American academic feminist and sexuality theories of the last few decades, takes its cue from deconstruction and a certain reading of later-period Foucault. While retaining the first approach's antinaturalist assumption concerning language's or discourse's construction of the body, it rejects the prior feminist differentiation between its cultural and biological aspects, offering as an alternative a theory of gender performativity that finds modest opportunities for subversion in the disjunction it posits between regulatory ideals of embodiment, as seen in the image repertoire of advertising, for example, and the actual behavior of bodies in the social world.

Less theoretically elitist and avowedly oppositional, but noticeably more ambient in popular culture, the third approach generally characterizes today's hegemonic ethos of liberal psychologism. This discourse enjoins us to cultivate a healthy body image in a culture increasingly beset by oppressively and unrealistically idealized representations. Replacing the unattainable airbrushed bodies of advertising with an immediate personal or proprietary body in need of continuous care or even worship ("Your body is a temple" is the familiar refrain), this approach conveniently sidesteps the fundamental question of how, under what forces of determination, we come to develop a sense of our own bodies to begin with. Moreover, as the project of caring for the body always requires a purchase or two, it turns a blind eye to its spectacular complicity with the saturation of late capitalist social space by all-pervasive forces of reification—the obfuscation, we may now need reminding, of concrete social relations of production by abstract networks of commodity valuation and exchange.

Though adherents of each of these approaches will doubtless object to aspects of my summary formulations, I maintain nonetheless that they paint an adequate general picture of the situation of body theory today. Against these three approaches, I will argue in this chapter that Lacan responds precisely to the questions to which none of the outlined theories of the body gives satisfactory answers: not only how it comes to be that we have a sense of the body in the first place, but also what it means precisely to live in a body, to have a properly corporeal *experience*. As is widely known, Lacan broaches these topics through his early concept of the mirror stage, underlining that the sense of the body is necessarily mediated, always and only constructible in the space of the Other. Less commonly acknowledged, however, is the fact that Lacan also presents an alternative view of the body as the experience of jouissance: a form of enjoyment that provides an intense rush of embodied pleasure. But for Lacan, this experience comes at a cost: the ego collapses, disassembling in the process the means by which we can attribute to ourselves an identity—from the outside, as it were—within the field of existing social relations.

Like his phenomenologist interlocutor Maurice Merleau-Ponty, Lacan wishes to reacquaint human embodiment with the category of experience, to think about what is so difficult, indeed traumatic, about living in a body, and to come to terms with the unsettling consequences of embodiment for thought. Unlike the phenomenologists, however, Lacan aims not to undermine the Platonic-Cartesian skepticism about the value of sense experience for knowledge, but rather to radicalize Descartes' thesis; to claim more precisely that, on the one hand, our *idea* or *image* of the body and, on the other, the *experience* of the body are incommensurable, separated by a disjunction that can never be rejoined.

In my view, psychoanalysis is the only discourse in the cultural theory repertoire that manages to disclose unreconstructed the disquieting truth that, with scant few exceptions, the representation or figuration of the human body functions psychically as a defense against the very experience of embodiment. This chapter will try to illustrate this thesis through a study of painting, beginning with Lacan's overlooked and sometimes sketchy theory of its practice. I will then examine aspects of the history of the nude, finally turning to the work of Lucian Freud as an example of a painting practice that moves beyond the transference by working against the collusion of corporeal idealism with today's ambient resistance to the challenge that genuine embodiment proffers to us.

Painting in Nature

No doubt the most unexpected element of Lacan's foray into the theory of art is that he bases it not on accumulated art-historical knowledge, but rather on discoveries in the field of natural history in their filtration through mid-century French thought. Though generally speaking his work unwaveringly draws attention to the radical break that separates the denatured human realm of the signifier from the instinctual life of animals, in this instance Lacan wants to suggest a fraternity linking certain "aesthetic" phenomena in nature with the distinctively human practice of art. In this connection, the major reference in *The Four Fundamental Concepts of Psycho-Analysis*, still largely unexamined to this day,[1] is to the work of Roger Caillois, co-founder with Georges Bataille of the influential Collège de Sociologie and idiosyncratic practitioner of "transversal science."

Lacan endorses the thesis of Caillois' 1960 book *Mask of the Medusa* (*Méduse et cie.*). In this book Caillois objects to the dominant functionalist and Darwinian accounts of nature's aesthetic splendors, arguing that neither the imperative of adaptation nor the logic of evolution can fully explain them. Caillois' vivid and copious examples of the aesthetic in nature range from the striking forms and patterns discernible in rock and mineral formations, through the kaleidoscopic "canvases" conspicuously displayed on the wings of numerous species of butterfly, to the phenomena of disguise (*travesti*), camouflage, and intimidation variously assembled by zoologists and entomologists under the rubric of mimicry (*mimétisme*).

Lacan extracts from Caillois' book the argument that "the facts of mimicry at the animal level are analogous to what among humans manifests itself as art, as painting."[2] Likely aware of its ambitious idiosyncrasy, Lacan prefaces his commentary by stating that it is intended neither as an art-critical or art-historical intervention nor as a theory of any particular tradition, school, or period. Nor is it offered as a psychobiographical outline of the repressed unconscious desires of this or that artistic personality, desires that could find themselves "sublimated," for example, in the form and content of the art object. Its purpose, he implies, is rather to furnish a general theory of painting's underlying psychical function. More precisely, Lacan wants to shed light on how painting provides the subject with a means to defend itself against the malevolence of an enigmatic agency of social visibility, one that unsettlingly resists localization within the field of vision. This agency—the gaze, that is—wields the uncomfortable power to make us visible while at the same time absconding itself from sight.

As far as Lacan is concerned, the central insight for psychoanalysis to be found in *Mask of the Medusa* relates to the splitting that Caillois sees at work in the natural as well as the human worlds, a kind of redoubling of being that takes the form of an extruded semblance functioning to lure, intimidate, or appease the Other. "Through this form cast off by the living being [*l'être*] the effects of life and death come into play" (107 TM), specifies Lacan. This comment likely alludes not only to the specific forms of display that condition reproduction among many species of insect, but also to the way the organism's various poses, gestures, and props serve to protect its own life and bring its prey's to an end.

I have stated that what is most intriguing and enigmatic about the phenomenon of mimicry for Caillois is how it shows that nonhuman aesthetic prowess far exceeds what can be explained with reference to natural selection or utilitarian functionalism. For his part, Lacan lends support to Caillois' thesis when he observes that the stomach contents of birds that prey on butterflies which themselves mimic toxic species reveal that these butterflies are no less well represented there than their non-mimicking cousins. Further, since the marks of mimicry in a given species are unchanging over time—they are "there from the start," says Lacan (73 TM)—they cannot be viewed as adaptive and therefore part and parcel of some evolutionary process. For Lacan as for Caillois, these facts demonstrate that "already in nature" (105) there is evidence pointing toward a nefarious agency in the visual field that cannot be reduced to any actually existing threat to species-life in the ecosystem. This agency causes the organism to engage in elaborate behaviors and displays seemingly as a means of self-preservation. I write "seemingly" because what is being guarded against cannot always be identified, and also because the protection from predators that mimicry would appear designed to furnish in many instances fails, casting doubt over the assumption that mimicry provides any survival advantage to speak of.

By now the reader may be wondering how all this information about insects could possibly bear on the question of painting. Yet this is the point where we can establish a link with Lacan's ideas about art in its relation to his theory of the field of vision. Caillois' evidence suggests that the organism's subjection to visibility instills a sense of vulnerability which exceeds any actual or potential threat to its survival. The *Arcturus* butterfly, for example, develops its non- or supra-functional "aesthetic" strategy not merely as a means of self-defense, but also to compensate more generally for its nonmastery of the visual field, for the fact that its appearance as a phenomenon in nature requires the construction of distractions and lures. From the mere fact of being present in space, it follows that a part of that space at any given moment is unavailable to vision, and therefore inherently dangerous. According to Lacan, the canvases that human beings cover in paint are analogous, though perhaps not strictly so, to the broad panoply of masks, cloaks, and disguises scattered across the insect world that seek, vainly it would seem, to defend against the supremacy of the living being's visibility—its subjection to the gaze—over and above its inherently limited capacity to see.

Lacan takes from Caillois a particularly striking example of mimicry in an effort to illustrate the function of what he calls the stain (*la tache*). A look at Lacan's commentary on the ocelli phenomenon will serve to make more concrete how the aesthetic realm in both nonhuman and human worlds can function as a defense against the gaze—to tame it, as Lacan on occasion will say. This in turn will prepare the ground for the argument I will later make about the significance of Lucian Freud's nudes for both Lacan's theory of painting and the conception of the body in contemporary cultural theory.

Ocelli are large, round, opaque and reflective shapes that pigment the surface of a variety of organisms from butterflies and moths to caterpillars. Eye-like in appearance, they are not, however, eyes, Caillois points out, either literally (they are not located on the organs of vision) or figuratively (it makes more sense, Lacan agrees with Caillois, to assume that eyes can intimidate potential predators because they resemble ocelli, rather than the reverse). Even so, the ocelli's "gleaming, enormous, immobile and circular" shapes "seem to look," as Caillois puts it, unveiling in the process the traumatic impact of a point in space from which we are implacably made available to sight.[3]

The fact that ocelli almost always appear in pairs has more to do with the inherent symmetry of insect physiognomy than it does with some presumptive entomological trompe l'oeil, according to Caillois, since "the condition of their efficacy" is "their excessively large appearance," in other words their unconvincing resemblance to actual eyes (120). The effectiveness of ocelli in intimidating potential predators therefore cannot be attributed to mimetic competence. One would be correct to infer that the ocelli's function is to scare off predators by causing them fright were it not for the fact that, as with the other forms of mimicry, ocelli seem to overshoot their species functionality with remarkable conspicuousness. *Smerinthus ocellatus* provides a typical example. At rest, this hawkmoth resembles a small bunch of dried-out leaves. It camouflages itself by echoing a pattern of irregular brownish shapes set against the shadowy surface of the forest floor. Then suddenly, Caillois writes, the "antennae stand up, the thorax inflates" and "the abdomen collapses" as the insect "brusquely unveils on its lower wings two large and transfixing blue eyes set against a pink background," and proceeds "to shake and vibrate its body," putting its terrorized aggressor into "a trance" (123). Not only would the camouflage in this instance already seem sufficient protection, but the entrancing effect of the hawkmoth's performance is at odds with what would seem to be a more obvious evolutionary aim: to cause the potential predator not to stop in its tracks, but instead to scamper away in fright, thereby efficiently removing the threat to its would-be victim's life.

A significant double temporality characterizes Caillois' example. At a first moment, the moment of camouflage, the hawkmoth blends in with the environment as it presumably appears to potential predators. In Lacan's view, the insect accomplishes this conformity not by disappearing into a two-dimensional surface marked by regularity of form, but rather by reproducing outward patterns on a mottled and multicolored space imbued with an ambiguous sense of depth. Counterintuitively, the mimicking animal integrates itself into the picture by drawing attention to itself, more precisely by imitating a zone of foreground opacity that calms and pacifies, Lacan insinuates, by inviting the look of potential prey and satisfying the appetites of vision. Against the ordinary understanding of camouflage as a blending into the background, Lacan argues that the organism disappears as it takes its place in the foreground as a kind of blur or anomaly of focus. Essential to the phenomenon of mimicry, in other words, is this bivalence of figure and ground, of ambiguous or vague appearances thrust out against more regular and clearly defined depths.

Not wishing to be outdone by Caillois in abstruse naturalist knowledge, Lacan draws attention to the small crustacean *Caprella acanthifera*, which, nestling in among bryozoa, otherwise known as moss animals, conceals itself by mimicking not the complete organic form of the species that surrounds it, but rather, as he puts it, "that which in this animal that is nearly a plant forms a stain": depending on what life phase the bryozoa concerned are in, anything from a "colored center" to an "intestinal loop" (99 TM). With this example, Lacan singles out the essence of mimicry that he wants to compare to the function of painting among humans. This essence involves the projection outward of an ambiguous foreground surface, which somehow disrupts the homogeneity or consistency of what we see, preventing the whole scene from appearing in focus all at the same time.

Now, the painter's canvas, or rather a specific zone within it, is analogous for Lacan to this appearance that the insect projects out into the world in order to protect itself from—to mediate—its own status as a being that is given to be seen. Like the mimicking animal, the artist casts off a mask that at once incorporates her into a picture (*tableau*) for the gaze, but also tames this gaze by creating a zone of opacity—screen or stain—that fascinates or pacifies by hinting that something might be hiding behind: *objet petit a*, that is, which, because veiled, always promises to be better than any fully disclosed object the heart might desire. Even more importantly, however, the artist's canvas-mask gives the Other an indication of something the naked subject knows in its heart of hearts it could never give, something actually worthy of the Other's desire. As we have seen in a variety of contexts throughout this book, the unconscious causes us to doubt that as subjects we can ever be worthy of love. Like the patient in the transference defending his symptom by withholding associations from the analyst, we resist unconscious desire by offering up the canvas as a dissimulation designed to coax a sign, a positive judgment, from the Other.

The effect of fascination or pacification that naturalists observe in predators confronted with the camouflaged moth does not tell the whole story, however. At the second moment of our hawkmoth's mimicking behavior, its appeasing camouflaged appearance vanishes as it stands erect to display its horrifying azure ocelli. Granted, Lacan never comes around in his seminar to demonstrating exactly how this double temporality—entrancement followed by terror—informs his theory of the gaze. We can surmise nonetheless that the properly Medusa-like properties of mimicry, those which Caillois puts under the rubric of intimidation, contrast sharply with the luring and disarming effects of camouflage. The two phenomena are in effect one another's opposites with respect to the function of the stain. Camouflage integrates the *creature* in the form of a stain into what Lacan calls the picture, paradoxically making the creature invisible by inviting and pacifying the predatory onlooker. By contrast, *Smerinthus ocellatus* shocks through its conspicuously hyperbolized representation of vision, transforming the unfortunate *predator,* now paralyzed by panic, into a stain. For Lacan, the field of vision can be neither uniform nor neutral: there is always the gaze as *objet petit a,* either veiled to entertain the infinite confabulations of fantasy—*i(a)* in the terms of chapter 1—or else revealed as the frightful, shame-inducing reminder of our all-pervasive and unconquerable visibility—*a* in its naked form as object of the drive.

Crucial to retain here for the purposes of my argument is that Lacan associates painting in general with the former effect of pacification and lure. At its most fundamental level, the practice of painting serves for the artist as a mode of defense against the power of the gaze. By putting paint to canvas, the artist provides the Other with an absorbingly enigmatic, opaque surface on which to rest and localize its faculty of vision, which then becomes preoccupied with fantasies of what might lie beyond. With the Other's expropriating gaze conveniently distracted, the artist gains a modicum of agency with which to mediate the terms of her own social visibility. In turn, the canvas's beholder enjoys the ennobling gratification to be derived from erecting in the field of vision a screen which fends off the gaze by providing a surface on which can flourish the play of (the Other's) desire. For Lacan, the canvas resembles the various para-aesthetic phenomena of the insect world in that it functions as a sort of protective mask, which shelters the artist from the shaming ravages of the gaze. As I will argue later on, however, not all canvases aim for this effect; indeed, Lucian Freud's nudes deviate radically from it.

Nude and Naked

Before turning to Freud's paintings, it will be helpful to take the opportunity this moment presents to relate Lacan's discussion of mimicry more explicitly to theories of the body and the history of the nude. This section will help situate Lacan's unfamiliar understanding of painting within a broader art-historical context, albeit with the proviso that Lacan's discussion broaches art as such, as opposed to any historical instantiation of its practice. I wish more specifically to examine Kenneth Clark's classic and valuable distinction between nakedness and nudity in Western art history, and also the critique of this distinction in the more contemporary poststructuralist discourse of visual studies.

In *The Nude: A Study in Ideal Form,* Clark fathoms the origin of the classical figuration of the human body in Western art, all pleasing proportion and flatteringly athletic fullness of form. He argues that the normative schemata for bodily proportion in ancient statuary, for instance, reflect a characteristically Greek passion for geometrical regularity, itself derived from Pythagorean arithmetical mysticism and its Platonic descendants. Changing social ideals of beauty determine later, contrasting proportions for the body in subsequent art-historical periods. The elongation and ballooning of the female torso in medieval art, for example, respond to the church's ideological subjection of women to their putative reproductive function. According to Clark, the general function of the nude is to reform the body, to redeem it from its embarrassing naked form by lifting it up to the ideal heights of art.[4] Though the ideological valences that transform the perfect human shape vary over time, the imperative of idealization itself, Clark's study suggests in agreement with psychoanalysis, remains a nonhistorical constant.

But how are we to explain the insistence of these bodily ideals? From the Lacanian perspective, we should resist the temptation to view this corporeal idealism merely as the effect of the anticipation of a perfected embodiment; as compensation through wish fulfillment, that is to say, for the limitations that living in a vulnerable, imperfect, mortal, and desiring body will necessarily impose. This view is incomplete because it is limited to the register of the imaginary, which is never experienced in isolation. In the broadest anthropological terms, human beings engage in the figuration of the bodily form not for their own pleasure, but rather for that of the gods, of the Other. Consider the edict of that primordial incarnation of the Law, the Hebrew God. Yahweh prohibits the worship of idols not as a means of curtailing human narcissism, but rather out of a violent jealousy. As self-professed sole legitimate god, He will brook no human attention paid to rival objects of divinity. The triangulating reference to the Other is significant because it shows that our relation to the body is always mediated by, alienated through, the field of social relations. Because the Other holds the power to remind us of the shame that is the objective correlative of genuine embodiment, this Other must be duped, distracted, lured by a fabricated appearance into which we project our aspirational self, to borrow a phrase from the idiom of lifestyle marketing.

Given postmodernity's chronic allergy to sweeping universalistic claims, it is hardly a surprise that Clark's ambitious thesis about the nude has come under considerable pressure in contemporary criticism. In his book *Ouvrir Vénus* (*Opening Venus*), for instance, the influential French practitioner of visual studies Georges Didi-Huberman protests that Clark's distinction between nudity and nakedness errs in its alleged neo-Vasarianism and neo-Kantianism. These reproaches gain in significance by virtue of the fact that they are emblematic of the general poststructuralist approach to the body. For this reason, a brief consideration of Didi-Huberman's critique will further develop the theoretical framework I will bring to the discussion of Lucian Freud's work.

Didi-Huberman's first allegation references Giorgio Vasari, the sixteenth-century Florentine luminary of the High Renaissance who founded the Accademia del disegno. Not only was this academy the fountainhead of the neoclassical aesthetic ideology that saturated Renaissance artistic

production, but it also originated the art-historical discourse—biographical, impressionistic, conventional—with which Didi-Huberman clearly
associates Clark's work. As Didi-Huberman construes it, the Vasarian
aesthetic credo pivots around "an implicit bracketing [*encadrement*] of
desire" and of "everything in painting associated with a phenomenology
of the body and of the flesh."[5] Clark's neo-Kantianism, for its part,
bases "the preeminence of aesthetic *judgment* on an avowed refusal of
empathy for the image." Clark's theory is decidedly old-fashioned in its
alleged antisensualist intellectualism; it remains complicit with the same
body-hating Platonism that Nussbaum attributes to Socratic teaching
in the *Symposium,* as we saw in chapter 2. For Didi-Huberman, Clark's
theory of the nude allows the beholder to "keep the judgment and
forget desire, keep the concept and forget the phenomenon, keep the
symbol and forget the image, keep the design/drawing [*le dessin*] and
forget the flesh" (15–16).

In my view, however, we should not allow Clark's frumpy art
historicism to persuade us to buy into Didi-Huberman's trendily skeptical assessment, for it quite egregiously projects vulgar neo-Platonist
dichotomies onto an argument that in actuality is not without subtlety.
Contrary to the tenets of Didi-Huberman's reproach, for example,
Clark's narrative of the nude's history does not in fact tell the story
of an idealist aesthetic asceticism, of a puritanical rejection of bodily
pleasure relentlessly imposed through the centuries. Rather, it portrays
a protracted and complex negotiation undertaken by individual artists
affected by dominant social values of the inherent tension between
the respective dynamics of nudity and nakedness in the history of the
human form's manifold representations.

More consequentially for my own purposes, however, Clark
insinuates an explicitly erotic conception of desire into the very heart
of classicism's ambition of corporeal idealization. "No nude, however
abstract, should fail to arouse in the spectator some vestige of erotic
feeling," he boldly writes, "and if it does not do so, it is bad art and
false morals" (8). As it turns out, it is the fashionable poststructuralist practitioner of visual studies, not the fuddy-duddy mid-century
Oxbridge art historian, who upholds the canonical "Platonic" distinction
between the hygienically airy heights of the idea and the body's lusty,
earth-bound sensuousness.

But there is an even more fundamental difficulty with the framework that Didi-Huberman brings to his revisionist study. It lies in the

assumption that the insatiability of human desire can be reconciled with the phenomenological fleshiness inherent in a bodily experience he construes as entirely unsullied by the abstraction of the idea. Interestingly enough, Didi-Huberman finds the exemplification of this potentiality in the "cruelty" depicted in Georges Bataille's erotic novel *Madame Edwarda*, as well as in Clemente Susini's quite gruesome late-eighteenth-century (female) anatomical models in colored wax, used for the education, and on this view titillation, of (male) Enlightenment medical students. These models feature three-dimensional pieces depicting the outermost tissues of the body which, when removed, reveal lifelike simulacra of the body's internal organs. Didi-Huberman gives this suggestive directive to the model's beholder: "Put your hands on the hips or breasts of the lady, lift them up, and you will suddenly find yourself before the blood-streaked ribs, the muscles' fibrous structures, the convoluted masses of this female body" (108).

The reader of such passages begins to sense how Didi-Huberman's self-described phenomenology of corporeal nakedness is founded on an admittedly sadistic fantasy, which aims to incite an experience of embodiment that somehow remains in synchrony with the ego-propping ambitions of desire. This fantasy's raison d'être is to defend the subject against the eclipse of self-consciousness that for Lacan inevitably accompanies jouissance. In short, by attempting to phenomenologize enjoyment—to bridge the unbridgeable chasm between intentional sensuous consciousness and the self-expropriating experience of the body—Didi-Huberman effectively dismisses the possibility of a jouissance without cruelty, a life of the body that would not subscribe to the sadomasochistic logic of perversion. Indeed, I suspect that the adoption of this perverse logic is the inevitable consequence of any theory of the body that seeks to reconcile raw embodiment with a notion of experience restricted to the level of conscious knowledge.

So Clark's canonical distinction between nakedness and nudity—it is so canonical that it is almost obscenely out of fashion—holds still today an elegant and illuminating power. Perhaps the most incontrovertible sign of Lacan's comparable dissent with respect to contemporary body culture and theory is his premise that the body, unveiled as it were, is always lacking. Because it is always found wanting as an object of the Other's desire, the true, naked body inevitably brings forth the affect of shame when it is subjected to the gaze—the condition, that is, of general visibility. Clark is therefore entirely correct to characterize the classical nude's idealized proportions as a defense against shame. "To be naked," he writes, "is to be deprived of our clothes, and the word implies some of the embarrassment most of us feel in that condition." Nudity, in contrast, "carries no uncomfortable overtone," as it projects the image "not of a huddled and defenseless body, but of a balanced, prosperous, and confident body: the body reformed" (3). From the Lacanian perspective, it is only necessary to add that this corporeal reformation can only be anticipated: our transferential ambition to elicit a sign of bodily acceptance from the Other must inevitably meet with disappointment. Though the young gym rat may reward himself for a good workout with an admiring self-inspection in the changing room mirror, a mirror that reflects not his own view but rather his construction of the views of those around him, he will be found before too long back among the machines and free weights, grunting as he strives for that next centimeter of rock-hard bicep muscle.

Clark's art-historical survey ably demonstrates that the function of the nude has never been to furnish a convincing representation of the human bodily form. From the perfect equilateral triangle of nipples and navel geometrically figured in Praxiteles' Knidian Aphrodite to the starkly contrasting pear-shaped torso of the medieval Memlinc workshop's Eve, the nude not only bears witness, as Clark himself will on occasion aver, to some innate human ambition of bodily perfection. More fundamentally, these figurations body forth social ideals, of gender, for example, which in essence serve as culturally dominant interpretations of what the Other wants; ambient collective efforts, in other words, to glean a reading of the Other's criterion for love. In this precise sense, Clark's underlying point bears a striking resemblance to the Caillois-Lacan thesis according to which the phenomena of mimicry in the natural world serve to placate, to disarm the gaze by creating an alluringly deceptive appearance that will finally give the Other, or so we infer, what it wants.

Tableau and Screen

Thus far, we have looked at how Lacan enlists Caillois' observations on mimicry to support his idea of painting as a trap for, or defense against, the gaze. I have also considered the canonical distinction between nudity and nakedness as well as a signal critique of this distinction in contemporary visual studies. In this section, the final stepping-stone before the discussion of Lucian Freud, I will be interested in exploring a key detail of Lacan's commentary on painting, more specifically the function of what he calls the *tableau*.

Lacan uses the term in a very precise sense: tableau designates the subjective function as it is captured by light. I should state parenthetically that for the most part I will retain the French term in my discussion to convey both English equivalents: picture and painting. Against the tradition of classical or geometrical optics, which associates a light source with a point in space, Lacan links light with the agency of the gaze, which always resists being fixed to a single point. He places his tableau (picture) on the second of three diagrams, the first of which represents the space of geometrical optics as it has been conceived since the Greeks. This modality of space is constructed by means of the infinite quantity of straight diverging lines on which light is viewed to travel. These lines connect the "geometral point" at the spatial apex to the set of points that comprise the illuminated object, forming the first triangle in the series of diagrams.

Lacan defines the image, also depicted on this first diagram, as "a point by point correspondence of two unities in space" (86): the sum total of points, in other words, on any (two-dimensional) plane that bisects geometrical space. Now, the main point of Lacan's discussion is that the field of vision is a more ambiguous and elusive space than the one defined by geometrism's hermetic, self-sufficient three-dimensionality. As subjects of the unconscious—subjects subjected to the gaze—we are something more opaque and dialectical, less unambiguously ideal, than the point at which all the rays of light in the optical paradigm converge, as one might think takes place at the aperture of our ocular apparatus, for example.

Light, as Lacan defines it, indexes not the point from which a spatial geometry may be fully constructed through the application of mathematical law, but rather the point of space's externality to itself, an uncanny gateway to a paradoxical spatial excess that lies within an internal but indefinable beyond. Unlike geometry's fully illuminated space, the field of vision contains zones of opacity that dissimulate immanent yet hidden virtual arenas, rather like the extra-spatial dimensions that string theory posits to reconcile quantum mechanics with the theory of relativity.

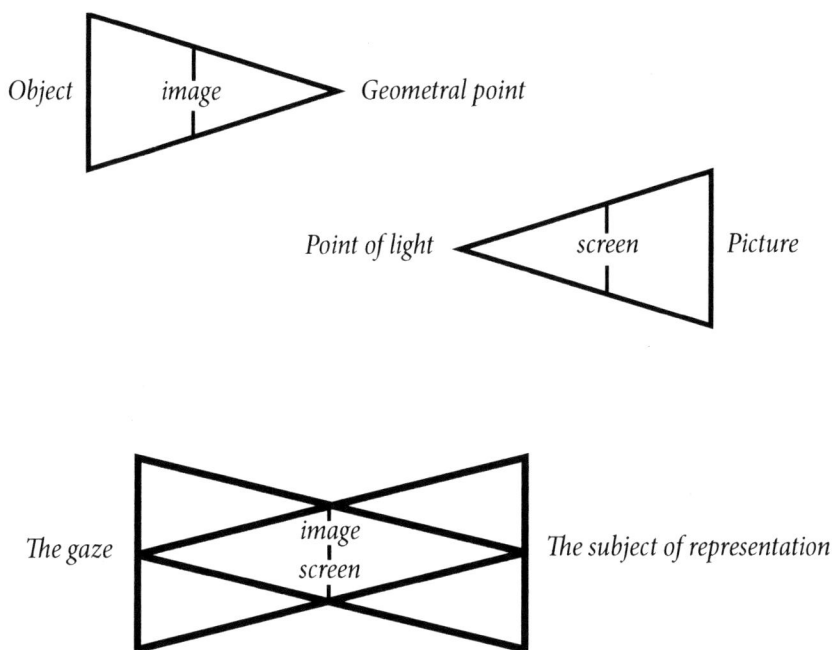

Figure 6.1. The field of vision; adapted from Jacques Lacan, *The Four Fundamental Concepts of Psychoanalysis*, ed. Jacques-Alain Miller (New York: Norton, 1998), 91, 106.

Psychically speaking, geometrical space leaves desire unaccounted for. In order to account for desire we must add the insubstantial supplement of the gaze, the inscrutable "point of light" that prioritizes passive visibility over the volitional act of seeing. On the more mundane level of experience, light is what cannot be looked upon directly, what threatens to overwhelm the ocular apparatus with overstimulation. *Before I see I am always already made visible.* The gaze is immanent to, yet not localizable within, the realm of appearances as they are engineered by perception. In this way the human subject is haunted by a disembodied agency of seeing that refuses to divulge itself to sight.

By placing it on the base of the isosceles triangle on which the point of light is located at the apex, Lacan means to connect his idea of the picture to the subject of the unconscious, to the excess of fantasy that comes to be as an effect of desire's nonsatisfaction in the field of vision. The power of the gaze makes us visible as a tableau. The unconscious responds to this uncomfortable visibility by unfurling a screen in an attempt to mediate our non-mastery of the visual field. The screen, like the stain, is the visual display that we give off like Caillois' butterflies in an attempt to coax the gaze into manifesting itself as a particular look. This explains why the gaze—or rather "something of" it, to quote Lacan exactly (101)—can always be found somewhere on the tableau that the painter will produce on his canvas. Note, however—this is where things get a bit confusing—that Lacan also claims that the painting is offered not to the gaze, but rather to the eye, coming close to contradicting, if he does not do so outright, the previously formulated definition of the tableau as "trap for the gaze."

> The function of the *tableau*—in relation to the person to whom the painter, literally, offers his canvas to be seen—has a relation with the gaze. This relation is not, as it might at first seem, that of being a trap for the gaze. It might be thought that, like the actor, the painter wishes to be looked at. I do not think so. I think there is a relation with the gaze of the spectator, but that it is more complex. The painter gives something to the person who must stand in front of his painting which, in a part of the painting at least, might be summed up thus—*You want to see? Well, take a look at this!* He gives something for the eye to feed on, but he invites the person to whom this picture is presented to lay down his gaze there as one lays down one's weapons. This is the pacifying, Apollonian effect of painting. Something is given not so much to the gaze as to the eye, something that involves the abandonment, the *laying down,* of the gaze. (101)

Not without justification, the apparent contradiction and lack of clarity—the tableau both is and is not a trap for the gaze; is "trapping" the gaze supposed to differ from causing it to be "laid down?"—will lead many readers of *The Four Fundamental Concepts* to the conclusion that Lacan has only a tenuous hold on the formulation of his concept. The seminar's original oral form might have some bearing here. The lack of clarity is doubtless also informed by the fact that Lacan's discussion of painting is sometimes framed around the artist's relation to his Other, as it is in the *"Take a look at this!"* quote, while at other times the focus is on the viewer's relation to the canvas, as it tends to be in the better-known analysis of the painterly technique of anamorphosis in Hans Holbein's *The Ambassadors*, for example. Further, Lacan's discourse makes use of the term *regard* to designate both the concept of the gaze as the visual mode of *objet petit a* as well as, less rigorously, simply the viewer's beholding of the painting. Adding even further muddiness to Lacan's discussion is his seemingly categorical yet extremely rough distinction between, on the one hand, whatever art-historical traditions he has in mind in his references to the tableau as trap for the gaze (he seems to want to invoke a general idea of post-Renaissance figural European art), and what he casually calls "expressionism," a tradition that, he argues, provides "a certain satisfaction of what is demanded by the gaze" (101). I will return to this last assertion momentarily, since it will have tremendous bearing on my argument concerning Lucian Freud's nudes.

At this point, however, I want to claim that, awkwardly articulated though they surely are, Lacan's assertions feature a latent rigor. The key to deciphering the quoted passage in my view is to grasp the significance of "the split [*la schize*, a French neologism] between the eye and the gaze," the title, as it happens, of a prior lesson of the seminar and a distinction that Lacan explicitly evokes at the end of the above-quoted segment.

I have claimed that for Lacan what the painter's canvas tries to do is precipitate a manifestation of the gaze, by which I mean a spatially identifiable instantiation of a particular agency of looking. This is the simplest way of grasping what Lacan means to convey through his idea of the eye in its difference from the gaze. The canvas aims to lure the gaze into revealing itself as a particular look, in the process transforming the opaque and ambiguous virtualities of visual space into fully actualized perspectival space, space as it is geometrically constructed. In short, the canvas constructs its own beholder by establishing a point beyond itself from which its illusion of three-dimensionality can be apprehended, delivering in this fashion a semblance of spatial mastery. This mastery is concomitant with the taming or laying down or pacification of the gaze of which Lacan inconsistently speaks.

The canvas as screen is the subject's response in the realm of art to the demand for self-display that this subject unconsciously believes the Other persistently issues (*"You want to see?"*). A compromise formation if there ever was one, this display aims both to satisfy and deceive the Other, to respond to its demand for visibility while at the same time defending against the prospect of the appearance in the social world of our true, irreducibly shameful bodily essence. Moreover, the ambiguity inherent in Lacan's reference to painting's "Apollonian effect"—is this effect had on the painter or the beholder?—can be addressed with the claim that it occurs for both parties equally: both subject and Other are pacified, however tenuously or temporarily, by the erection of the protective screen. The corollary of this is that for Lacan the painter engages in her practice for precisely the same reason that the aficionado goes to a museum: to seek relief from the shaming, self-shattering impact of a gaze that otherwise refuses to divulge the place from which it sees. Finally, it is essential to remark that Lacan attributes the qualities of illusion and necessity to the screen: though shame is the irreducible truth of the body for the subject of the unconscious, no subject can sustain a direct confrontation with the gaze in the absence of the mediation that the screen provides.

We are now in a position to consider Lacan's explicit admission that an exception to this general rule of what he calls painting's function does indeed exist. Though he will eventually offer the work of Edvard Munch, James Ensor, and Alfred Kubin as examples, purely conventional in European art-historical terms, of what he means by expressionism, the overarching vagueness of Lacan's reference—exactly which aspects of expressionist painting furnish the exception? surely not expressionism to the exclusion of all other schools and traditions? surely not expressionism in general?—will not score points with specialists. Nor perhaps should they.

Yet there are precious insights to be gleaned from Lacan's awkward excursus on painting, though they may not be the ones Lacan himself might have anticipated, at least on the properly art-historical level of his intervention. For my purposes, the important feature of these sessions of the seminar is the suggestion, which I wish emphatically to endorse, that in general terms painting does indeed work for both painter and beholder to attenuate the agency of the gaze, to tame the real of desire in an attempt to postpone the encounter with jouissance, the experience of the body. Even more central to my analysis of Lucian Freud's nudes, however, will be the allowance for exceptions to this rule. As Lacan concedes, some paintings do *not* work to shield us from the gaze. Further, the shame we feel as beholders of these paintings is an indication, objective in nature, that our visual engagement with them has delivered a genuine experience of bodily enjoyment.

Shameful Nudes

There is little doubt that on the art-historical level Lucian Freud's nudes are related to Lacan's examples in only the most tenuous of fashions. In fact, the early critical association of Freud's work with the German tradition known as *Neue Sachlichkeit*, however limited the value of this claim might be, puts him in direct aesthetic-ideological opposition to the expressionist precedent. Like Lacan's, however, my own argument is not art-historical in nature. My claim is that Freud's nudes provide the kind of drive satisfaction that Lacan associates with expressionism. A proviso: this provision has no general or necessary consequences for the understanding of any art-historical current with which Freud currently is, or one day may be, associated. A detailed examination of a key early Freud, part of the Canadian Beaverbrook collection in Fredericton, New Brunswick, will help clarify the important modification of the visual dialectic in painting that we can connect with Lacan's underarticulated distinction between those canvases that lure or tame the gaze and those others that furnish an encounter with embodiment. Freud's *Hotel Bedroom* (1954), I submit, is best read as marking the transition from the former to the latter mode.

Clearly not a nude, this painting appears at first glance to be a relatively conventional canvas by a male artist of a female beloved. In fact, it was developed from sketches Freud made while on holiday in Paris with the woman who was then his wife. In the foreground we see an attractive, perhaps aristocratic-looking young blonde resting in bed. Preoccupied or fatigued, she is conspicuously illuminated, exhibiting that peculiarly self-absent absorption so characteristic of Freud's subjects, an absorption into something other than what can be understood in psychological terms. Though we already recognize characteristic techniques with which Freud would later be identified—depthless attention paid to the skin's masklike surface; the strangely abstracted facial expressions; color and shading (in this case around the eyes) suggesting a half-formed, organic, yet somehow inhuman fleshiness—the canvas retains numerous compositional features associated with the long art-historical tradition of portraits of beautiful women by men

Yet, there are other elements that detract from our capacity as beholders to settle into the comfortable Apollonian aesthetic contemplation to which Lacan makes reference in his discussion of painting's psychical function. Most obviously, Freud paints himself into the picture, cast in shadow, standing vaguely ominously in the upper lefthand corner of the frame, surveying us as we observe the woman's rest, but also watching himself as he paints his object of desire.

Straightaway, we find a subversion of the dynamic tending toward voyeurism that very generally characterizes not only the depiction of the female body in painting, but also the familiar construction of classical perspective. In such a construction, the viewer gains mastery over the canvas's represented space by inhabiting a position—the vanishing point—that is only indexed, and therefore not, strictly speaking, included, within it. As a result, this position remains unacknowledged and unseen by the beholder's consciousness. On Freud's canvas, in contrast, the viewer cannot ignore the insistent visual reminder that as he looks he is being watched. From the perspective of the artist at work, it is as if Freud wants to keep an eye on himself as he paints the image of his beloved, reminding himself of his amorous look's circumscription by his own visibility, but perhaps also engaging in a process of self-policing, keeping the idealizing vectors of transference love in check. Similarly, as viewers we are unable to lose ourselves in the image of the woman, a loss that would blissfully dissolve the consciousness of our own visibility in an act of appetitive, desiring looking. In these ways *Hotel Bedroom* makes visible the very act of seeing, wrenching us from our hiding place behind the Sartrean keyhole where we had taken refuge in order, unseen, to see. The canvas forces its viewer into the glare of an open, nonvirtual space dominated by (the representation of) the artist's possessive look.

But I would be quite mistaken to restrict my analysis to the three elements discussed thus far: resting woman, hawkish Freud, painter/ beholder. On the level of perspective, the canvas focalizes neither the woman's brilliant face nor Freud's watchful silhouette, but instead the multiply framed vanishing point that lends a tremendous sense of depth to what would otherwise be an uncomfortably claustrophobic image. The beholder peers through the frame of the painting itself, beyond the next frame of the hotel room window, through a third frame, that of the second window across the street, toward yet another frame, the one surrounding the door at the far end of the shadowy room in the building opposite. The door's faded outline is barely discernible behind a strongly colored bowl resting on a sunlit table some distance inside the room. Positioned directly in front of a vanishing point constructed through thoroughly classical, that is to say geometrical, lines of perspective, this bowl is the object toward which the painting directs our eye with considerable powers of attraction.

Figure 6.2. Lucian Freud, *Hotel Bedroom* (1954); courtesy of the Beaverbrook Art Gallery and Lucian Freud.

It is this empty bowl—or is it a basket?—that solicits our look with the promise of a commanding view over the painting's constructed space. The bowl lures the viewer to project her subjectivity into the canvas's depths. No doubt this is one way to understand what Lacan meant to say by his statement that the practice of painting causes the beholder to "lay down" his gaze. To illustrate the dialectic of vision, Lacan constructs his third diagram by superimposing the first, depicting geometrical space, on the second, portraying visual space, such that the apex of the one triangle bisects the base of the other. We can understand the dynamic of classical perspective in this light as a kind of suturing, a fusing together, of the two spatial modalities. This fusion can be refigured from the third diagram by flipping one triangle over along its center vertical axis in such a way that they become indistinguishable.

This is to say that in classical perspective the point of light, the agency of the gaze, is trapped or tamed through its localization, its immobilization at the geometral point. In short, classical perspective aims to transcend the visual field's dialectic by reducing it to the terms of geometrical construction. This arrangement allows us as beholders through projection to insert ourselves at the vanishing/geometral point in such a way that the painting's pictorial space becomes perfectly transparent to vision, leading us back outward from the origin toward the canvas's spatial *telos*: Freud's image of restful, if strangely abstracted, feminine beauty. In this properly narcissistic way, we gain a comfortable perspective on our own visual contemplation of the painting; we see ourselves seeing, as it were.

As is quite apparent, however, despite its fully conventional construction of perspective, *Hotel Bedroom* departs from its Renaissance forebears in that it looks back at us at least as intently as we look at the canvas. The colored bowl marking the apex of the canvas's pictorial space invites us to immerse ourselves in its virtual depths through the fusion of *a* and I: the rendering of the partial object qua gaze as an identifiable point of vision, of symbolic identification. Comfortably overseeing the cone that takes shape between this spatial apex and the image of the woman, we rest assured as the painting's beholders that no space has been left unrepresented, that no opaque anomaly dissimulates something unseen behind or beyond. Yet Freud's glower disrupts our absorption by fixing us where we actually are—in real space in front of the painting or its reproduction. Freud's painted look short-circuits the dynamic of perspectival projection by splitting us as viewing subjects (recall Lacan's *schize* of eye and gaze) between our immersion into the painting's depth of field and our conspicuous visibility before the canvas to the artist's wary alter ego. The objective effect of this splitting is to render the beholder's look covetous, and therefore *guilty*.

Yet, we cannot go as far as to base this claim on the premise that Freud's look succeeds in manifesting the gaze. Insofar as it unveils the point from which we as observers are observed, it renders, rather, what Lacan calls the eye, which makes us visible to only a privileged point, one that here quite evidently judges us for our visual desire's transgression. Our look has been found out by an identifiable party, whose perspective we adopt unconsciously to witness ourselves experiencing intimations of guilt. In this important early canvas, we find in embryonic form Freud's desire to paint bodies with which it is impossible to identify, bodies that diffract and displace our desiring look, sending it like a boomerang back to us where it ripples through the body in a way that reminds us, shamefully, of our social visibility. But we are not quite there yet. *Hotel Bedroom* attenuates the agency of the gaze by figuring a particular look which, though it disrupts our absorption by subjecting us to visibility before the canvas, still puts on display the point in pictorial space from which we are seen.

Though the painting's figuration of the artist's alter ego makes us guilty, the determinacy of the judgment, the fact that we know whose law we have transgressed, provides some consolation nonetheless. We would much rather that the painting recognize us as guilty, in other words, than not recognize us at all. This latter prospect is more difficult to tolerate because it thrusts us unwilling into an unsettling experience of the body that cannot be witnessed, that abandons us to our shame. Unlike *Hotel Bedroom*, Freud's later work in the nude tradition either withholds the presentation of any identifiable look at all, or else shows a look that is absent to itself, a look so self-absorbed that it could not possibly have the capacity to see us.

In this way, the nudes confront us head-on with a raw body experience that cannot be redeemed, communicated, or identified through visual interrogation. What results is an intense and immediate embodiment, which we are forced to live directly rather than vicariously through an observed figural intermediary. The nudes offer our look no resting point from which we could observe ourselves observing. For all the suffocating intimacy of the corporeal flash that Freud's nudes deliver, however, they still force us into a properly social space. Yet this space

Figure 6.3. Lucian Freud, *Naked Girl Asleep II* (1968); courtesy of the Lucian Freud Archive and Lucian Freud.

can only fail to communicate any knowledge of embodiment. This is to say that our jouissance as beholders of Freud's nudes can find no witness, no addressee within the frame.

Naked Girl Asleep II (1968) is among the earliest of canvases in Freud's oeuvre that signal an important moment in the evolution of his technique, when he began to plan nighttime sessions with his sitters, whom he would sprawl out under unforgiving artificial light in his London studio. In interviews Freud often draws attention to the arduousness of the task of sitting, the deep discomfort and boredom the model experiences as she is forced to remain still, often in awkward positions, for long periods of time. On one level this commentary provides evidence for what we might wish loosely to call Freud's naturalism. Though his statements about his artistic practice tend toward the laconic and recondite, a recurrent theme is his desire simply to paint what is there in front of him, unaltered by both intrinsic and extrinsic influences; to resist, in effect, any hint of symbolism, signification, narrative, or meaning. There has perhaps never been an artist still invested in figuration quite as hostile to allegory as Lucian Freud.[6]

One must certainly add to Freud's view of his own method the concentrated battle he wages against the temptation of idealization, against the demand for regularity of form that is the hallmark of the classical, indeed the entire premodernist, tradition of the nude. In this light, Freud's painterly technique is best conceived as a revolt against transferential demand on the level of the corporeal form. The object of Freud's nudes is not the pacifying, aspirational body—the one by means of which we anticipate a perfected embodiment that will meet with the Other's approval—but rather the body's generic, shapeless, "animal" being; its being, that is to say, stripped of all predication and specification beyond what can be described by way of brute biological fact. Freud's bodies suggest the generic and abstract qualities of the Platonic ideas, I want to say, but made material, brought resolutely down to earth. A Freud nude depicts the being of a particular body—the model's, of course—but only insofar as this body can embody unredeemed, shameful being as such: life stripped of the demand that it signify, provide meaning, serve a purpose, bestow social identity, "bare life," perhaps, but deprived even of its relation of opposition to the Good, that of the state or for that matter any other institution or apparatus.

In *Naked Girl Asleep II,* the subject's pose draws attention to this prioritization of unadorned being over knowledge or consciousness, over the intelligibility of the idea. Here is a brute ontological corporeality rendered at the expense of form and thought. Distressingly, we get the sense that she is "not there," that she is adrift in sleep or daydream, too bored or oblivious to acknowledge our presence. She is not present to us because she is not present to herself. The subject of the painting lies before us merely as a pile of bone and flesh, which flagrantly subverts the classical nude's ambition to furnish the body with harmonious proportion. Her gaze is visible from an angle so sharp that we cannot discern if her eyes are closed in deep sleep, or else open, pupils rolled back in ecstasy or oblivion. The feet and hands are remarkably large and strangely discolored. The angular skeleton beneath the flesh conveys not regularity of structure—the ideal human proportions that would inspire an entire tradition of classical and neoclassical architectural humanism—but rather an anticipation of death and decomposition, a premonition of human remains.

Finally, the viewer cannot fail to notice that her sex is in full indiscreet view, painted as a figureless mass of flesh and hair, a reminder that our eye has nowhere to rest, no one to whom to relinquish the power to know and to judge. In Lacanian terms, the canvas features no stain behind which we can take shelter from the gaze. Or perhaps the whole canvas is a stain, in which case its omnipresent opaqueness sabotages from the first instant our ability to project ourselves subjectively into its represented space. *Naked Girl Asleep II* can neither tell us that it is all right to look at the vulnerable and exposed body that it insists on showing us nor admonish us for our perverse impudence. We are made visible as voyeurs; yet we cannot connect the ambient reproach to any discernible look or point of view.

As we experience the uncomfortable frisson of embodiment to which our engagement with the painting gives rise, the field of vision is transformed into a space of shame. In this space we are subjected to a gaze that, making us visible, nonetheless neither sees us nor can be seen. We are intruders, transgressors, and we are caught; we sense that we are looking at something not meant for public view. But there is nowhere to appeal for sanction or forgiveness, no authority to judge what we have experienced or ascribe some comforting meaning to it. Whereas Freud's shadowy figure in *Hotel Bedroom* casts our look under the sign of guilt, we feel only shame as we behold this sleeping naked girl. "Guilt," writes Jacques-Alain Miller, "is the effect on the subject of an Other that judges, thus of an Other that contains the values that the subject has supposedly transgressed." Shame, in contrast, "is related to an Other prior to the Other that judges, one that only sees or lets be seen."[7] Guilt obfuscates and thereby tames the experience of jouissance by imposing on it a determinate moral judgment. In contrast, shame provides no refuge from the disorienting excess that disjoins the experience of the body from the symbolic order, from the realm of possible social meaning. Freud's nudes demonstrate that though authentic satisfaction can be derived from the body—indeed, even certain representations of the body can deliver such satisfaction—this satisfaction remains by nature *objectively* obscene.

Lucian Freud's refusal to grant us psychological access to the bodies he paints creates the impression that what we are viewing is too intimate for public view. Naturally, this has the effect of opening us up to the gaze, of reminding us that we are on view, in public, but that this public can have no knowledge of what we have just lived in the body. The argument of Freud's nudes—art does finally make an argument—is that body and consciousness are non-simultaneous. There is a fundamental disharmony between embodied experience and intentional thought. "Thinking through the body," if I am allowed a retro '80s feminist moment, is precisely what cannot be done. This neurotic phrase nicely conveys the ambition to which our insistent and uncreative demand for love bears witness. With scant few exceptions, the human interest in the image, in the figuration of the body, works symptomatically to shield us from, to postpone, the encounter with actual, genuine embodiment. We can be conscious, we can think, we can formalize, we can represent. And then we can have the experience, the jouissance, of the body. But we will never live as embodied beings so long as we insist on having both at the same time.

The Object of Art

In the midst of his discussion of the gaze in *The Four Fundamental Concepts of Psycho-Analysis,* Lacan revisits the same old problem of the relation between artistic production and social value that Freud generally discussed under the rubric of sublimation. Lacan's commentary provides an occasion to address a fundamental difficulty inherent in my claim about the significance of Lucian Freud's nudes. To recap, I have argued that these nudes subvert the dynamic of idealization that underlies the figuration of the human body in Western art. Further, they undermine the function of painting as Lacan generically defines it as a taming of, or defense against, the gaze.

Assuming that these arguments are valid, how then are we to address the phenomenon of the nudes' spectacular, some might say outrageous, commercial success? What can explain the massive attribution of exchange value to canvases that, I have claimed, go strongly against the grain, work against the function of painting as such? Does the fact that Freud's nudes have been so readily "co-opted" by the art market not call into question my argument that they substitute the unsettling self-expropriation of genuine embodied experience for the reassuring ideality of aesthetic absorption and the commodity form?

In May 2008, Lucian Freud's canvas *Benefits Supervisor Sleeping* (1995), a nude portrait of a very fat London civil servant whom the artist affectionately calls Big Sue, made headlines when it set a record for the largest sum ever paid at auction for an artwork by a living artist—US$ 33.64 million, to be precise. Sue Tilley had been introduced to the artist by Leigh Bowery, the London-based Australian performance artist, also remarkably corpulent, who had previously and quite famously posed nude for Freud. No doubt it is safe to conjecture that the conspicuously bulbous bodily forms of both sitters and their general deviation from historically operative standards of beauty would have disqualified them as acceptable for representation in the tradition of the nude over the widest swathes of the history of art.

One way of approaching the conundrum posed by the massive valuation of Freud's nudes is through the lens of the "society of enjoyment" thesis developed in the last decade or so by a number of prominent Lacanian theorists.[8] Jacques-Alain Miller's "On Shame," the essay from which I quoted earlier, makes reference to Lacan's response to the complaints of the unruly and discontented students of 1969 Paris documented in *The Other Side of Psychoanalysis.*[9] This response saw him admonish the impudence of these crypto-Maoist would-be subversives for falling prey to what, he then suggested, was a nascent modification of the general libidinal principle underlying the social link. Recalling the Frankfurt school repressive desublimation thesis, the general idea here is that whereas previously (the temporality is no doubt necessarily vague) adherence to the rules and constraints of civilization required a perceived renunciation of pleasure or satisfaction—through integration with the bourgeois-patriarchal nuclear family structure or internalization

of the "protestant work ethic," for example—a generalized injunction
to enjoy now permeates the dynamic of social life. The transformation
in this view has had the effect of attenuating the force of authority
figures' prohibitions and undermining the influence of the passion of
shame that once buttressed the imperative of at least outward conformity
with the values of social modesty, obedience, and respect.

Arguments in this stream tend to stress the contradiction between
the tenets of the outward social prohibition and the actual behavior that
occurs. The recent American television series *Mad Men*, for example,
draws attention to the coexistence in the world of late 1950s and early
'60s Madison Avenue of what appear to today's viewer as remarkably
rigid social conventions, in particular with respect to gender norms,
with a by now quite shocking tolerance for heavy smoking and drinking, including at the office and in front of children. In contrast, what
characterizes social life today is the exact reverse. On the one hand, we
have witnessed a proliferation of alternative lifestyles, the loosening or
outright suppression of cultural and social taboos, and the efflorescence of
an ideology of enjoyment conceived as a sort of human right. In short,
there are fewer and fewer prohibitions on the surface of the social text.
On the other hand, however, a generalized ambient neo-puritanism is
increasingly palpable. In this latter atmosphere, secondhand smoke on
an outdoor terrace violates the sanctity of a neighbor's personal space,
and a suggestive or awkward remark in a delicate professional situation
can lead to an investigation into workplace safety. Though enjoyment
is everywhere visible on the surface of social relations, it seems to be
getting harder and harder simply to have a good time.

Against this backdrop, it would seem perfectly natural to turn a
cynical eye toward the commercial success of Freud's nudes, particularly
the ones figuring bodies that early-twenty-first-century medical discourse
has stamped morbidly obese. From this standpoint, the significance of
the nudes can be summed up by indexing their symptomatic value:
they simply render the latent logic of a society without shame and
anaesthetized to provocation, a society in which the self-consciously
avant-garde or antibourgeois thrusts and parries of radical modernist
aesthetics fail even to cause the enemy to shirk. When taboo and prohibition, custom and convention, are reduced to objects of ridicule, it
is no longer possible to create art imbued with an intrinsic power to
resist its own transubstantiation into pure exchange value. In this view,
the formless stains of Big Sue's ungainly pounds of flesh and the sleek

airbrushed holograms of today's hygienic cyborg bodies exhibit the same more or less absolute complicity with capital's design to forestall embodied experience. Engagement with either brand of image can only fail to lead us onto the threshold of jouissance—that resolutely asocial corporeal use value that can be neither valuated nor exchanged.

One of the reasons why I find myself unable to endorse this pessimistic view relates to the classroom, no doubt the aspect of academic experience that most closely resembles the analyst's experience of the clinic. As one might expect, the responses of my students to Freud's nudes have varied considerably, particularly in accordance with the relative depth of their prior engagement with visual art, especially of the modern variety. By and large, however, it is fair to say that a general feeling of discomfort has taken hold in the classroom when I have solicited student views. One day, for example, a woman student, visibly perturbed by one of Freud's young female nudes, pointedly asked me why I had chosen to show this particular painting. I understood the question to be in part an expression of skepticism about both the pedagogical and psychological values of studying such images in an academic setting. In her intervention the student made explicit reference to the notion of self-image, which I assumed she had picked up either through popular or academic psychology discourse. I could not help but think that this student wished to reproach me for publicly displaying representations that threatened to do violence to her own self-image, and maybe that of each of her classmates, especially perhaps the women among them.

It is difficult not to interpret this student's reaction as a classic manifestation of the transference. From the psychoanalytic perspective, a student's classroom anxiety is inextricably bound up with his uncertainty about the desire of the professor. Armed with "expertise" and aglow with the prestige of the university's aggressive idealization of knowledge, the professor in the classroom, like the analyst in the session, functions as the subject-supposed-to-know. Every university teacher, no matter how modestly experienced, knows that a student's demand can take many forms: for reassurance that an answer or view is "correct," for entertaining audiovisual enhancement of lectures, for exemptions from late penalties for work handed in, or, now more than ever in today's instrumentalist world of higher education, for clear and concise information about what they are meant to know.

In this instance, however, the student seemed to be demanding alternative, more pleasing representations of the body, not necessarily those of high fashion or mainstream advertising—too "unrealistic," I often heard (soap brand Dove's "Campaign for Real Beauty" was popular at the time I offered the course)—but rather for comfortable, recognizable bodies, bodies with which one can spontaneously identify, bodies perhaps like those of her fitter friends in the gym changing room. The student-subject demands from the professorial Other a sign—I—that will buttress her ideal ego—*i(a)*. In this transferential dynamic I am called to supply an image-sign that can demonstrate that my desire qua Other is for an object that can function as such an ego ideal. The prospect that I might desire other kinds of objects—obscene, repulsive, dehumanized, or vaguely pornographic ones, for example—has the effect of frustrating the student's demand and dislodging me from my role in the transference as an adequate subject-supposed-to-know. Contrary to conventional "teaching and learning" wisdom, this ruination of the Other issues to students the challenge to assume their desire as subjects, an assumption which, from the perspective of psychoanalysis at least, holds tremendous—though impractical and unquantifiable, and therefore in the current climate unrecognizable—pedagogical value.

My classroom experience taught me that for many students Lucian Freud's nudes do not qualify as acceptable ideal egos. What disturbs and unsettles is not merely the fact that the paintings are prone to tarnish our self-image. More importantly, they also confront us with the sometimes traumatic realization that the Other, and therefore we ourselves ("man's desire is the desire of the Other," remember), might derive enjoyment from their contemplation. Hence, the affects of shame, discomfort, and even disgust that surface in the classroom when the encounter with jouissance occurs in an overtly public space, especially one overseen by an Other—the university—that holds within itself vast quantities of social, cultural, and economic capital. My classroom experience therefore suggests that the sale of Freud's Big Sue nude for more than $30 million does not appear to have blunted its capacity to incite a decidedly discomfiting embodiment. An alternative explanation for this phenomenon must therefore be sought.

On the day he presented the commentary on trompe l'oeil in his seminar, Lacan may have startled some of his auditors when his discourse abruptly adopted an explicitly social register, addressing what he called "the position of the painter in history" (*Fundamental*, 112). Lacan had just advanced the no doubt counterintuitive claim that the ambition of trompe l'oeil—that technique of perspective that dissolves the boundary between pictorial space and its surround—is not to pass convincingly for a real, that is to say unrepresented, appearance. Rather, it aims to incarnate "what Plato designates to us beyond appearances as being the Idea" (112). The objective of trompe l'oeil for Lacan is therefore to render not the appearance itself, but rather its origin: that from which the appearance appears. Trompe l'oeil works to make the purely intellectual idea available to sense perception. If you assume that the mural on that South Beach hotel is meant to make the real building invisible to the observer by causing the representation to meld seamlessly with the appearances around it, then you are sadly mistaken, Lacan would want to insist.

The pleasure, the "jubilation" to be derived from the apprehension of trompe l'oeil stems not from the illusion of reality that it creates, but rather from the subsequent realization that we have been deceived. Altering her position in space causes the observer to perceive that the lines of perspective in the image do not shift as they should in accordance with her movement. It is at this moment that the image "appears as something other than what it seemed," Lacan says, "or rather it seems to be that other something" (112 TM). In Lacan's view, trompe l'oeil creates the illusion of the thing that gives off appearances, the thing-in-itself from which appearances originate and that should never itself appear. The jubilation that trompe l'oeil delivers—note that Lacan uses the term associated in his earlier teaching with the mirror stage's imaginary plenitude and not the disorienting self-expropriation delivered by the more sinister jouissance—accrues not from the phenomenon itself, but rather from the knowing distance from which we experience the illusion it compellingly delivers; the retrospective knowledge, that is, that we have been duped.

This elusive thing beyond appearances to which Lacan refers is naturally *objet petit a*, and he goes on to say that the artist in society accumulates cultural capital, and his art its exchange value, through the perception that the artist shares a sort of exotic intimacy with this object in which the observer cannot, or rather chooses not, to partake. The link between trompe l'oeil and the artist's social role is no doubt left underargued in the seminar. But Lacan's point gains in clarity if we compare the gratifying reassurance experienced by the undeceived beholder of trompe l'oeil with the edifying satisfaction to which an ordinary, mediated, or secondhand engagement with the artwork can give rise. In both instances, pleasure arises from the gap that separates the subject from an experience that vaguely hearkens an undoing, a loss of self: the disorienting fusion of "real" and represented space in trompe l'oeil, or the fall into "mad," all-consuming, and purposeless creative passion in artistic practice.

Lacan will say that the artwork "comforts" its public by demonstrating that "there are a few people who can earn a living from the exploitation of their desire," which naturally excuses the others from having to do it themselves (111). In short, the artist's mystique and her object's inflated value derive from a defensive idealization of the jouissance that we would rather encounter in the indirect, reified form of the display, connoisseurship, criticism, and collection of art. These secondary practices effectively tame the enjoyment inherent in creating or genuinely engaging with an art object through an act of mystification, which elevates art's status above its libidinal function as a "mere" avenue for drive satisfaction. The artwork becomes a fetish as it is refashioned as an object coveted by the Other's desire. Inserted into the market's networks of valuation, the art object's worth then increases in direct proportion with the extent to which it is seen as desirable. In short, the consumption of art provides a sort of alibi which defends us from the traumatic mystery of desire; it allows us to "renounce" desire, as Lacan says, by giving a comforting answer to the unanswerable question it poses. The rich connoisseur buys that expensive painting simply because its ridiculous price is an index of its value, that is to say, to its general desirability, a quantity abstracted absolutely from any intrinsic feature or concern.

In this sense, the function of the art object in late capitalism is not fundamentally different from that of the religious icon in the medieval period, for example. Both derive their value from the estimation that they please the Other: God in the latter case, the market in the former. Like the patient in the transference who manufactures a discourse meant to secure a position as a good object for the analyst's desire, the art scene operator aims to create or acquire objects that will be desired in the marketplace, objects whose essence is thereby quantified as exchange value. The system is designed to forestall a genuine encounter with art, an encounter that would upset the workings of the network of exchange by instigating the unsettling eruption of enjoyment.

And yet, the logic of this argument would seem to imply as well that the high market value of artworks such as Freud's also serves as evidence of the immanence of the danger they pose. Could there be a more or less proportional relationship between the market valuation of a work of art and the magnitude of the threat it presents for the stability of a given hegemonic social formation, in this instance the economy of bodily representations that forestall the experience of the body? One wonders what would it mean not only for today's advertising industry, for the health and beauty markets, for the diet and pharmaceutical sectors, but also more generally for our collective political investments, if we began en masse to tarry with the scandal of Freud's nudes by allowing them to transform the nature of our collective libidinal engagement with the field of vision. To alter the valences of desire that draw us toward and repulse us from particular bodies, both represented and "real." To engage with the body not as an object of the Other's desire but on the level of the drive, that is to say, as a cause of libidinal interest that subverts our very identity. Finally, to become aware of the criteria, the preconditions, the Freudian "stereotype plates" that set the agenda for the judgments we mercilessly impose on bodies, including most significantly our own.

Notes

I. The Refusal of Love

1. I will develop in this chapter's last section why this term is not the best one to describe the analyst's preferred role in the transference. Indeed, it tends to forestall inquiry into the problem of what precisely the analyst is meant to remain neutral toward.

2. Butler develops her understanding of this relation in *The Psychic Life of Power: Theories in Subjection* (Stanford: Stanford University Press, 1997). I discuss some of the problems that mar Butler's engagement with psychoanalysis in general and Lacan in particular in *The World of Perversion: Psychoanalysis and the Impossible Absolute of Desire* (Albany: State University of New York Press, 2006), 190–201.

3. Badiou, *Logiques des mondes. L'être et l'événement 2* (Paris: Seuil, 2006), 334; my translation.

4. Readers of French will know that *les non-dupes errent* and *les noms du père* (the names of the father) are homonymic phrases.

5. Lacan, *Le Séminaire, livre XVI. D'un Autre à l'autre* (Paris: Seuil, 2006), 84; my translation.

6. See for example Toril Moi's "Representation of Patriarchy: Sexuality and Epistemology in Freud's Dora," as well as the other essays in the collection edited by Charles Bernheimer and Claire Kahane *In Dora's Case: Freud, Hysteria, Feminism* (New York: Columbia University Press, 1990), 181–99.

7. See for example Lacan, "Critique du contre-transfert," in *Le séminaire, livre VIII. Le transfert*, 2nd ed. (Paris: Seuil, 2001), 219–36. Incidentally, Lacan also argues in this section that no analyst, no matter how thorough her analysis, can fully immunize herself against the effects of transference, can in effect liquidate the contents of her unconscious.

8. "The Dynamics of Transference," in *The Standard Edition of the Complete Psychological Works of Sigmund Freud* (*SE*), trans. James and Alix Strachey (London: The Hogarth Press and the Institute for Psycho-Analysis, 1953–74), vol. 12, 99. Further references are incorporated into the text.

9. "Observations on Transference Love" (1915), in *SE* vol. 12, 168. Further references are incorporated into the text.

10. Lacan, *The Four Fundamental Concepts of Psycho-Analysis*, trans. Alan Sheridan (New York and London: Norton, 1981), 145.

11. *SE*, vol. 12, 151. Further references are incorporated into the text.

12. *SE*, vol. 12, 106.

13. Lacan, *Four Fundamental Concepts*, 169–70.

14. *SE*, vol. 12, 135n-6n.

15. *SE*, vol. 20, 92.

16. Lacan, *Le transfert*, 207. All translations from this seminar are my own; further references are incorporated into the text.

17. See Jacqueline Rose, "The Imaginary," in *Sexuality in the Field of Vision* (London: Verso, 1986), 166–97. Rose's concise presentation of the experiments is keyed to Freud's notions of primary and secondary narcissism and Lacan's concepts of the imaginary and symbolic. The original experiment is linked to primary narcissism/the imaginary and Lacan's reconfiguration to secondary narcissism/the symbolic. While I don't take issue with these associations, Rose's qualification of the former as "prior and resistant to symbolisation" (178) leaves unspecified that this priority is strictly logical, as opposed to chronological, in nature. There is no primary narcissism that is unmarked by the symbolic function, even at the famous mirror stage of early infancy. Further, Rose's discussion does not set itself the task of interrogating the agency of the real in the structures of narcissism. By linking Lacan's discussion of the experiments to the concept of transference, my own discussion attempts to do precisely this, since the transference is an effect of the real. This task is facilitated by the fact that my reading focuses on Lacan's later discussion of the experiments in Seminars VIII (1960–61) and XI (1963–64), whereas Rose's pioneering reading, featured in a paper originally published in 1977, is confined to Lacan's first two seminars (1953–55).

18. Though the conceptualization is his own, Lacan actually derives this expression, usually translated into English as "unary trait," from a direct translation of Freud's "*ein einziger Zug*." This derivation underlines how close to the Freudian texts Lacan's "innovations" tend to remain. What Lacan himself brings to the equation is an explicit consideration of this *Zug* as a signifier. I think "unique trait" is a preferable English translation.

19. "A Short Study of the Development of the Libido, Viewed in the Light of Mental Disorders," in *On Character and Libido Development: Six Essays*, trans. Douglas Bryan and Alix Strachey (New York: Basic Books, 1966), 101. Further references are incorporated into the text.

20. The scare quotes are a reminder that Lacan shifts our understanding of these stages from the chronological to the logical planes. Abraham's work is beset by the badly normative implications of the former understanding.

21. *SE*, vol. 21, 92–93.

22. The discerning seminar reader may sense that Lacan's use of the symbol Ⴝ to mark the place in the Other (A for Autre) where absence, if I can put it this way, makes its presence felt only underscores the "idealist" underpinnings of the conceptual distinction between subject and Other on the level of their intersection in the real. One wonders, plainly put, why Lacan in this instance does not use the symbol Ⱥ. In my view, the latter would make for a more coherent argument. On the other hand, there is a more basic point to be made here: the subject and the Other fail, you could say, in the same place. The subject of the unconscious, in other words, effectively *is* the failure of the signifying chain, of the social Other: the piece of the Other, that is to say, excised from consciousness as the price paid for access to language, to desire.

II. Socrates, Analyst

1. Jacques Lacan, *Le séminaire de Jacques Lacan, livre VIII. Le transfert,* 2nd ed. (Paris: Seuil, 2001), 26. Further references are incorporated into the text; all translations from this seminar are my own.

2. Leo Strauss, *On Plato's* Symposium, ed. Seth Benardete (Chicago and London: University of Chicago Press, 2001), 5.

3. Plato, *Symposium,* trans. Christopher Gill (London: Penguin Books, 2003), 191d. Further references are incorporated into the text.

4. For my own consideration of Lacan's important reading of *Antigone* see "The Guardian of Criminal Being," in *The World of Perversion: Psychoanalysis and the Impossible Absolute of Desire* (Albany: State University of New York Press, 2006), 139–72. For further work on Lacan and ethics see Joan Copjec, *Imagine There's No Woman: Ethics and Sublimation* (Cambridge: MIT Press, 2003); Marc de Kesel, *Eros and Ethics: Reading Jacques Lacan's Seminar VII* (Albany: State University of New York Press, 2009); and Frances Restuccia, *Amorous Acts: Lacanian Ethics in Modernism, Film, and Queer Theory* (Stanford: Stanford University Press, 2006).

5. Martha Nussbaum, *The Fragility of Goodness: Luck and Ethics in Greek Tragedy and Philosophy* (Cambridge: Cambridge University Press, 1986), 176. Further references are incorporated into the text.

6. For background on *agalma* I have relied primarily on C. D. C. Reeve, "A Study in Violets: Alcibiades in the *Symposium,*" in *Plato's* Symposium: *Issues in Interpretation and Reception,* ed. J. H. Lesher, Debra Nails, and Frisbee C. C. Sheffield (Cambridge: Harvard University Press, 2006), 124–46; and Marie-Claire Galpérine, *Lecture du* Banquet *de Platon* (Lagrasse: Éditions Verdier, 1996), 42–45.

7. See K. J. Dover, *Greek Homosexuality* (Cambridge: Harvard University Press, 1978), 4–8.

III. Like a Pack of Rats

1. Lewis R. Gordon, T. Denean Sharpley-Whiting, and Renée T. White, eds., *Fanon: A Critical Reader* (Cambridge, MA: Blackwell, 1996), 5–7.

2. Pierre Kalton writes that Ernesto Guevara, during a visit to the Cuban embassy in Paris in April 1964, expressed to François Maspero, publisher both of Fanon's works and of the French translation of Guevara's own *Guerilla Warfare*, a desire to author a preface to a Spanish translation of *The Wretched of the Earth* to be published in Havana. In his classic text *Pedagogy of the Oppressed*, Paulo Freire cites Fanon's description in *Wretched* of the tendency of colonized populations to indulge in "a type of horizontal violence" targeted at "their own comrades." And finally, though Hannah Arendt's reading of Fanon is complex, and features the claim that Fanon's own endorsement of strategic anticolonial violence is more nuanced and qualified than the one Sartre expresses in his preface to Fanon's book, she nevertheless makes reference to "Fanon's rhetorical excesses" in the context of a critique of existentialism's (and Fanon's) endorsement of the cathartic effects of violent struggle on the oppressed. See Kalton, *Che. Ernesto Guevara: une légende du siècle* (Paris: Seuil, 1997), 95, 380–81; Guevara, *Guerilla Warfare* (New York: Praeger, 1961); Freire, *Pedagogy of the Oppressed*, trans. Myra Bergman Ramos (New York: Continuum, 1993), 44; and Arendt, *On Violence* (New York: Harcourt, Brace and World, 1969), 20.

3. The most recent additions to the list of biographical works on Fanon include David Macey, *Frantz Fanon: A Life* (London: Granta Books, 2000) and Alice Cherki, *Frantz Fanon: A Portrait* (Ithaca: Cornell University Press, 2006).

4. The editors refer to two works: Emmanuel Hansen, *Frantz Fanon: Social and Political Thought* (Columbus: Ohio State University Press, 1977); and Renate Zahar, *Frantz Fanon: Colonialism and Alienation, Concerning Frantz Fanon's Political Theory*, trans. W. F. Feuser (New York: Monthly Review Press, 1974).

5. Henry Louis Gates Jr., "Critical Fanonism," *Critical Inquiry* 17 (Spring 1991): 458.

6. My reading of the Gordon et al. anthology contrasts with that of Anthony C. Alessandrini, who objects to its "explicitly teleological bent." While Alessandrini wants to read Fanon for insights that "might contribute to future cultural, political, and intellectual work," I am more interested in how a faithful reading of Fanon disrupts the contemporary field of postcolonial theory. See Alessandrini, *Frantz Fanon: Critical Perspectives* (New York: Routledge, 1999),

5. For additional overviews of Fanon's work see Reiland Rabaka, *Forms of Fanonism: Frantz Fanon's Critical Theory and the Dialectics of Decolonization* (Lanham, MD: Lexington Books, 2005) and Nigel C. Gibson, *Fanon: The Postcolonial Imagination* (Cambridge: Polity Press, 2003).

7. Badiou, *Logiques des mondes. L'être et l'événement, 2* (Paris: Seuil, 2006), 389, 393; my translations.

8. See Sartre, "Black Orpheus," *What Is Literature? and Other Essays* (Cambridge: Harvard University Press, 1988), 289–332.

9. *Black Skin White Masks*, trans. Charles Lam Markmann (New York: Grove Press, 1967); *A Dying Colonialism*, trans. Haakon Chevalier (New York: Grove Press, 1965); *The Wretched of the Earth*, trans. Richard Philcox (New York: Grove Press, 2004); *Toward the African Revolution*, trans. Haakon Chevalier (New York: Grove Press, 1994).

10. David Macey, *Frantz Fanon: A Life* (London: Granta Books, 2000), 28.

11. For a detailed development of this argument, see my "Passing into the Universal: Fanon, Sartre, and the Colonial Dialectic," *Paragraph: A Journal of Modern Critical Theory* 27, no. 3 (November 2004): 49–67.

12. Lazarus, *Nationalism and Cultural Practice in the Postcolonial World* (Cambridge: Cambridge University Press, 1999), 81. For examples of Bhabha's work on Fanon, see "Of Mimicry and Man: The Ambivalence of Colonial Discourse," *October* 28 (1984): 125–33; "Remembering Fanon: Self, Psyche, and the Colonial Condition," in *Remaking History*, ed. Barbara Kruger and Phil Mariani (Seattle: Bay Press, 1989), 131–48; and "Interrogating Identity: Frantz Fanon and the Postcolonial Prerogative," in *The Location of Culture* (New York: Routledge, 1994).

13. Bhabha, "Foreword: Framing Fanon," in *The Wretched of the Earth*, xvii, xxxii. Further references are incorporated into the text.

14. Taylor, *The Narrative of Liberation: Perspectives on Afro-Caribbean Literature, Popular Culture, and Politics* (Ithaca and London: Cornell University Press, 1989), 35.

15. Mannoni, *Prospero and Caliban: The Psychology of Colonization*, trans. Pamela Powesland, intro. Maurice Bloch (Ann Arbor: University of Michigan Press, 1990), 42. Further references are incorporated into the text.

16. *Black Skin*, 84. Further references are incorporated into the text.

17. See Anna Freud, *The Ego and the Mechanism of Defense*, trans. Cecil Barnes (New York: International Universities Press, 1946).

18. Ousmane Sembene's film *Camp de Thiaroye* (1988) tells a similar tale, possibly inspired by the events on which Fodeba's work is based, or else on Fanon's account of Fodeba's work.

19. In its portrayal of the Algerian anticolonial war, Gillo Pontecorvo's classic film *The Battle of Algiers* (1966) provides evidence that the insurrectionary activists in the capital did not adopt this strategy. On the contrary, it shows

how FLN discourse deemed the "wretched of the earth"—drunks, prostitutes, addicts, pimps, petty criminals—a symptom of counterrevolutionary impurity which required elimination as a means of buttressing the force of the popular national will. The danger here is to avoid not only such ideologies of purification, but also the related thematics of redemption, which would have the abject lifted up by the architects of a revolutionary program dictated from above.

20. See Spivak, "Can the Subaltern Speak?" in *Marxism and the Interpretation of Culture,* ed. Cary Nelson and Lawrence Grossberg (Urbana and Chicago: University of Illinois Press, 1988), 271–313.

21. Hallward, *Absolutely Postcolonial: Writing between the Singular and the Specific* (Manchester: Manchester University Press, 2001), 30.

22. Sekyi-Otu, *Fanon's Dialectic of Experience* (Cambridge: Harvard University Press, 1996), 162.

IV. Loving the Terrorist

1. The liberal commentary on this film has tended to congratulate Spielberg for his humanization of the Palestinian resistance and his linkage, through the concluding scene framed around the Manhattan skyline, of Israeli (and by extension American) vengeance to the horrific events of 9/11. While I have no problem with this latter point, I take issue with Spielberg's depiction of the Palestinian resistance of the early 1970s' as a mirror image of the political Zionist project to secure a national homeland, as represented for example in the sequence in and around the Athens safe house. The logic runs as follows: "They are just like us (liberal Zionists); all they want is a nation-state of their own where they can feel secure." As Genet repeatedly emphasizes in *Prisoner of Love,* however, this was not the primary objective of any major Palestinian faction at that time. Indeed, the Palestinians' main target, at least officially, was not even Zionist colonialism, but rather the corrupt, neo-feudalist, Western-allied regimes of the main Arab states, especially Jordan, Saudi Arabia, and post-Nasserite Egypt. Spielberg's film participates in a general tendency to erase the secular, non-nationalist ("nationalist" here understood in the non-Fanonian ethnic-substantialist sense), properly Marxist contexts of the Palestinian resistance from the historical record.

2. In fact, the Palestinian group that claimed responsibility for the Munich Olympics murders called itself Black September in reference to the massacres.

3. Ilan Pappe, *A History of Modern Palestine: One Land, Two Peoples* (Cambridge: Cambridge University Press, 2004), 223.

4. Robert Fisk, *The Great War for Civilization: The Conquest of the Middle East* (London: Fourth Estate, 2005), 505, 604. Further references are incorporated into the text.

5. Underscoring the intimacy of today's U.S.-Israeli alliance, Fisk also claims that Donald Rumsfeld quashed a developing Belgian judicial consideration of a suit filed by Sabra and Shatila survivors—which under Belgian law could very well have produced an indictment for war crimes against Sharon and other senior Israeli military officials—when, during a 2001 visit to Brussels, he threatened to move NATO headquarters out of Belgium (624).

6. The impact of the massacre on the Arab psyche cannot be underestimated. Fisk quotes Osama bin Laden, who names during their secret 1996 Tora Bora rendezvous the events of Sabra and Shatila as one of the motivations for the al-Qaeda attack on the U.S. Air Force housing complex in Saudi Arabia, which had then just recently taken place. "The explosion in al-Khobar," bin Laden reportedly said, "did not come as a direct reaction to the American occupation [of Saudi Arabia], but as a result of American behaviour against Muslims, its support of Jews in Palestine and of the massacres of Muslims in Palestine and Lebanon—of Sabra and Shatila and Qana—and of the Sharm el-Sheikh conference" (22). The fact that the Sabra and Shatila massacres carry such tremendous weight in the Arab and Muslim worlds while remaining largely a historical footnote in North America and the United Kingdom (and to a lesser extent in continental Europe) only underscores the extent of the marginalization of the Arab perspective in dominant Western media, a phenomenon, of course, not unrelated to the activities of what is known as the Israel lobby.

7. This important text is available in English as "Four Hours in Shatila" in Genet, *The Declared Enemy: Texts and Interviews*, ed. Albert Dichy, trans. Jeff Fort (Stanford: Stanford University Press, 2004), 208–28.

8. Edmund White, *Genet: A Biography* (New York: Vintage Books, 1994), 558. Further references are incorporated into the text.

9. Naturally enough, Genet himself was acutely aware of the difficulty of criticizing Israel in a climate—the Arab perspective in French political discourse of the 1970s was, in comparison with today, more obscure and the memory of Vichy more intensely alive—in which such criticisms lead instantaneously to charges of racism. Responding to Said's question about his reaction to the publication of *Saint Genet,* Genet made the following comment about Sartre's post-1967 support for Israel: "He's a bit of a coward for fear that his friends in Paris might accuse him of anti-Semitism if he ever said anything in support of Palestinian rights." Edward Said, "On Genet's Late Works," in *Imperialism and Theatre: Essays on World Theatre, Drama, and Performance,* ed. J. Ellen Gainor (London: Routledge, 1995), 233.

10. For Fanon, "national culture is the collective thought process of a people to describe, justify, and extol the actions whereby they have joined forces and remained strong." Doubtless, Genet would endorse Fanon's valorization of the transformation of cultural forms resulting from the counter-imperial struggle for sovereignty. Yet Fanon's contention that it is a "mistake" to "miss out on

the national stage" of cultural development emphasizes the importance of the state form in a way that is foreign to Genet's thinking, despite his late, likely strategic, endorsement of Soviet communism. This is so even when the state is defined, as it is in Fanon, in rigorously nonethnicizing and anticulturalist terms. Frantz Fanon, *The Wretched of the Earth*, trans. Richard Philcox (New York: Grove Press, 2004), 168, 179.

11. Said himself sets Genet apart from this familiar orientalizing motivation when, reflecting on their 1972 meeting in Beirut, he writes that in West Asia "Genet was no ordinary visitor, no simple observer or Western traveler in search of exotic peoples and places to write up in some future book." Thus, "in the context of a dominant Orientalism that commanded, codified, articulated virtually all Western knowledge and experience of the Arab/Islamic world, there is something quietly but heroically subversive about Genet's extraordinary relationship with the Arabs" (232, 235).

12. Though there is of course much insight in Hardt and Negri's work, in my view Palestine, or more specifically Israel's behavior within it, bespeaks precisely the kind of classical or territorial imperialism that the authors claim has been (mostly) superseded by the new biopolitical immanentism of empire. I would add that in my view their approach vastly underestimates the political power of international trade law and the international financial institutions, or more specifically the kind of postnational territorializing sovereignty that these structures continue to exert over everyday life among the multitude. Michael Hardt and Antonio Negri, *Empire* (Cambridge: Harvard University Press, 2000).

13. I strongly agree with Badiou when he writes, "Genet's literary efforts culminate in what is to my eyes his masterpiece, *Prisoner of Love*, a work of prose . . . which eternalizes a crucial moment of the Palestinians' war against Israel." See Badiou, *Le siècle* (Paris: Seuil, 2005), 9; my translation. Further references are incorporated into the text.

14. In some respects my analysis of antiredemptive ethics in Genet and Fanon resonates with Leo Bersani's important critical discussion of the thematics of redemption in modern European culture. See *The Culture of Redemption* (Cambridge: Harvard University Press, 1990).

15. Alain Badiou, *Ethics: An Essay on the Understanding of Evil*, trans. Peter Hallward (London: Verso, 2001), 11.

16. Badiou argues strongly and convincingly against the cordoning off—indeed, sacralization—of the Jewish holocaust as unthinkable absolute Evil in contemporary thought, as well as the ensuing logic of victimhood and moral-political exceptionalism that undergirds today's Israeli *Realpolitik*. This text provoked a predictable outcry in the French intellectual field after its publication in the fall of 2005, as exemplified by Frédéric Nef's piece in *Le Monde*. Like Said in his final years, Badiou comes down resolutely on the side of the one-state solution, concluding provocatively that "if we wish to

solve the problem of unending war in the Middle East, we will need to forget the holocaust." The idea here is obviously not to erase the Jewish holocaust from the historical record—indeed, Badiou's passionate 1996 intervention at a Collège international de philosophie conference against negationism figures prominently in the volume—but rather wholly to reconfigure the rigidly sedimented discourse in the region so as to create a new field of empty universality in which the names "Jew" and "Arab," "Israeli" and "Palestinian"—"Fatah" and "Hamas," one should add—are evacuated of their overdetermined identitarian and substantialist contents. Alain Badiou, *Circonstances 3. Portées du nom « juif »* (Paris: Éditions lignes et manifestes, 2005), 98; my translation. For Nef's response, see "Le « nom des juifs » selon Alain Badiou," *Le Monde des livres*, 23 December, 2005.

17. Genet, "Violence and Brutality," in *The Declared Enemy*, 172. Further references are incorporated into the text.

18. Jean Genet, *Prisoner of Love*, trans. Barbara Bray (New York: New York Review Books, 2003), 60. Further references are incorporated into the text.

19. The turn of phrase betokens my debt to the title of Slavoj Žižek's *Organs without Bodies: Deleuze and Consequences* (New York: Routledge, 2004).

20. In the terms of Freud's classification, which takes the repressed content as the chronological point of reference, the "Hamza and his mother" screen memory is at once "retroactive" and "pushed ahead." In the first sense, Genet's recollection of his 1970 visit to the Irbid camp at the height of the resistance on one level tries to mask the difficulty of his later encounter: the screen memory is "retroactive" with respect to that which it screens. In the second, Genet's representation of the maternal-filial bond refers back to the psychical manifestation of the childhood trauma occasioned by his mother's abandonment: here the content is "pushed ahead" to the time of the Palestinian sojourns. But the screen memory analogy is only partly satisfying, not only because its details—the mother's serving of the coffee, the hole in the bedroom wall, for example—are only arguably "indifferent" (Freud's main criterion for the concept's application), but also because Genet's insight into its symptomatic dimension is signaled more or less consistently throughout the text well before its ultimate dissection in the concluding pages—this is what I called its pre-analyzed feature. Freud, "The Psychopathology of Everyday Life," *SE*, vol. 3, 63–64.

V. For the Love of Cinema

1. The *locus classicus*: "The link between signal [signifier] and signification [signified] is arbitrary," Saussure says. "Since we are treating a sign as the combination in which a signal is associated with a signification, we can express

this more simply as: *the linguistic sign is arbitrary.*" Ferdinand de Saussure, "Nature of the Linguistic Sign," in *Modern Criticism and Theory: A Reader,* ed. David Lodge (London and New York: Longman, 1988), 12.

2. Peirce defines his iconic sign as one that is "determined by its dynamic object by virtue of its own internal nature," stressing in this way a relation of similarity or likeness. Quoted in Robert Stam, Robert Burgoyne, and Sandy Flitterman-Lewis, *New Vocabularies in Film Semiotics: Structuralism, Post-Structuralism and Beyond* (London and New York: Routledge, 1992), 5.

3. Christian Metz, *The Imaginary Signifier: Psychoanalysis and the Cinema,* trans. Celia Britton, Annwyl Williams, Ben Brewster, and Alfred Guzzetti (Bloomington and Indianapolis: Indiana University Press, 1975–1982), 3–4. Further references are incorporated into the text.

4. For the so-called post-theoretical contingent in film studies led by David Bordwell and Noël Carroll, Metz would qualify as a representative of the allegedly doctrinaire "Theory" tradition that emerged in the 1970s under the influence of Barthes, Lacan, and Althusser. For Joan Copjec, Metz's work left its mark on the "film theory"—both Bordwell's and Copjec's monikers appear to target the same "usual suspects" linked to *Screen* in the 1970s—that misread Lacan through the lens of Foucault's panoptical model of the apparatus of power. Slavoj Žižek's work in cinema theory sidesteps Metz by going directly to the French sources—Jacques-Alain Miller and Jean-Pierre Oudart—of the original application of the suture concept to film. Though I consider Copjec's and Žižek's work infinitely more valuable than that of Bordwell/Carroll and company, it is worth noting that none of these figures has engaged with the substance of Metz's argument about the properly psychical dimension of the cinematic apparatus. See David Bordwell, *Post-Theory: Reconstructing Film Studies* (Madison: University of Wisconsin Press, 1996); Copjec's classic essay "The Orthopsychic Subject: Film Theory and the Reception of Lacan," in *Read My Desire: Lacan against the Historicists* (Cambridge: MIT Press, 1994), 15–38; and Žižek's "Back to the Suture," *The Fright of Real Tears: Krzysztof Kieslowski between Theory and Post-Theory* (London: BFI Publishing, 2001), 31–54.

5. Todd McGowan's otherwise excellent *The Real Gaze: Lacan and Film Theory* (Albany: State University of New York Press, 2007) also fails to move beyond the commonplace criticisms of Metz's psychoanalytic theory of cinema.

6. Mary Ann Doane, for example, reduces Metz's argument in *The Imaginary Signifier* to the screen-mirror analogy in *The Desire to Desire: The Woman's Film of the 1940s* (Bloomington and Indianapolis: Indiana University Press, 1987), 128.

7. The earliest manifestation of this conflict was likely the infamous *Screen* debate of the mid-1970s, during which psychoanalytically influenced film

theorists, including Stephen Heath, were effectively ejected from the journal's editorial board. This incident is briefly recounted in John Mowitt, *Re-Takes: Postcoloniality and Foreign Film Languages* (Minneapolis: University of Minnesota Press, 2005), 4–5.

8. For example, Metz's understanding of the perversity of spectatorship (the role of scopophilia and fetishism in particular) is marred by his failure to distinguish between desire and drive. He goes as far as to qualify what he considers the two drives privileged by the cinema—the scopic and the invocatory—as "being on the side of the imaginary" (58). For Lacan, the drives belong to the register of the real, and for this reason can only be said to have a destructive effect on the forms of identification of which Metz speaks in his analysis of spectatorship. My reading of Akerman's *The Captive* aims at an understanding of precisely this failure of spectatorship in its relation to the real of desire.

9. Contemporary cinematic phenomenology can be subdivided into two main tendencies, the first of which draws inspiration from the philosophical canon (Husserl and Merleau-Ponty, primarily), the other from Gilles Deleuze's cinema books: *Cinema*, 2 vols., trans. Hugh Tomlinson and Barbara Habberjam (Minneapolis: University of Minnesota Press, 1986–89). The most influential examples of the former tendency are doubtless Allan Casebier's *Film and Phenomenology: Toward a Realist Theory of Cinematic Representation* (Cambridge: Cambridge University Press, 1991) and Vivian Sobchack's *The Address of the Eye: A Phenomenology of Film Experience* (Princeton: Princeton University Press, 1992). For the Deleuzian tendency, see for example Steven Shaviro, *The Cinematic Body* (Minneapolis: University of Minnesota Press, 1993) and Laura U. Marks, *The Skin of the Film: Intercultural Cinema, Embodiment, and the Senses* (Durham: Duke University Press, 2000).

10. I develop a detailed argument against cinema-theoretical technologicism in "You Never Look at Me from Where I See You: Postcolonial Guilt in *Caché*," *New Formations* 72 (Summer 2010).

11. Peter Wollen, "Godard and Counter-Cinema: *Vent d'est*," in *Film Theory and Criticism*, 6th ed., ed. Leo Braudy and Marshall Cohen (Oxford: Oxford University Press, 2004), 525.

12. I distinguish in detail, via Lacan, between generic and structural understandings of perversion in the psychoanalytic tradition in *The World of Perversion: Psychoanalysis and the Impossible Absolute of Desire* (Albany: State University of New York Press, 2006).

13. Freud, "On Narcissism: An Introduction," in *The Standard Edition*, ed. and trans. James Strachey, vol. 14 (London: Hogarth Press, 1953–1974), 100. Further references are incorporated into the text.

14. Freud, "The Ego and the Id," *SE*, vol. 19, 31.

15. Citing transitivism—the phenomenon that sees an infant respond to stimuli received by others as if received by itself—Jacqueline Rose argues that this aspect of Metz's discussion mistakenly distinguishes the spectator's identification with a character from the mirror stage structure as outlined by Lacan. Though the implication of the imaginary in adult affective life—empathy, for example—draws our attention to the lingering effects of such identificatory transitivity, in my view Metz's development of the construction of point of view (secondary cinematic identification), in particular its dependence on the creation of a subjectivized perspective *in front of the screen* which must be distinguished from that of the spectator, properly speaking, not only features a triangulated complexity at odds with the dyadic intimacy that Lacan associated with the imaginary, but also remains medium-specific, secondary also to the symbolic mediation at work in so-called secondary identification outside the cinema. In short, Rose underestimates the purchase of Metz's contention that the cinematic apparatus indeed reproduces the mechanism of human perception, but does so by *redoubling* or *reframing* it, by adding an additional dimension. *Sexuality in the Field of Vision* (London and New York: Verso, 1989), 196.

16. In work subsequent to *The Imaginary Signifier*, Metz elaborates on this notion of enunciation in the cinema, which he distinguishes from both a vaguely auteurist notion of an image engineer who arranges the shots and a deictic function which, like the demonstrative pronouns for example, would signal a contextually determined referent. "In film, when enunciation is indicated in the utterance, it is by *reflexive* constructions," he writes. "The film talks to us about itself, about cinema, or about the position of the spectator." Metz, "The Impersonal Enunciation, or the Site of Film," in *The Film Spectator: From Sign to Mind*, ed. Thomas Elsaesser (Amsterdam: University of Amsterdam Press, 1995), 145–46. The analysis I develop of the first sequence of Akerman's *The Captive* assumes that it functions as an instance of enunciation in the precise Metzian sense. See also John Mowitt's work on Metz's notion of cinematic enunciation in *Re-Takes*, 1–45.

17. Mulvey, "Visual Pleasure and Narrative Cinema," in *Feminism and Film Theory*, ed. Constance Penley (New York and London: Routledge and BFI Publishing, 1988).

18. See for example *What is Cinema?* trans. Hugh Gray (Berkeley: University of California Press, 2005).

19. Plato, *Republic*, trans. G. M. A. Grube (Cambridge: Hackett, 1992), 514.

20. Kant defines transcendental apperception as the "transcendental ground of the unity of consciousness in the synthesis of the manifold of all our intuitions." *Critique of Pure Reason*, trans. Norman Kemp Smith (New York: St. Martin's Press, 1965), 135.

VI. Naked Love

1. For a notable exception to this rule see Chris Venner, "Roger Caillois's *Mask of the Medusa*," *Psychoanalysis and Contemporary Culture* 20 (1997): 545–65.

2. Lacan, *The Four Fundamental Concepts of Psycho-Analysis,* trans. Alan Sheridan, ed. Jacques-Alain Miller (Paris: Seuil, 1973), 100; translation modified. Further references are incorporated into the text; henceforth, TM signals that I have modified Sheridan's translation.

3. Roger Caillois, *Méduse et cie* (Paris: Gallimard, 1960), 120. All translations from this text are my own; further references are incorporated into the text.

4. Kenneth Clark, *The Nude: A Study in Ideal Form* (Princeton: Princeton University Press, 1990), 3. Further references are incorporated into the text.

5. Georges Didi-Huberman, *Ouvrir Vénus. Nudité, rêve, cruauté* (Paris: Gallimard, 1999), 15. All translations from this work are my own; further references are incorporated into the text.

6. "I think portraiture is an attitude," Freud has said. "Painting things as symbols and rhetoric and so on doesn't interest me." Bruce Bernard and David Dawson, *Freud at Work: Conversations with Sebastian Smee* (London: Jonathan Cape, 2006), 33.

7. Jacques-Alain Miller, "On Shame," in *Jacques Lacan and the Other Side of Psychoanalysis: Reflections on Seminar XVII,* ed. Justin Clemens and Russell Grigg (Durham: Duke University Press, 2006), 13.

8. Todd McGowan provides a useful overview of the argument and makes a significant contribution to it in *The End of Dissatisfaction: Jacques Lacan and the Emerging Society of Enjoyment* (Albany: State University of New York Press, 2003).

9. Lacan, "Analyticon," in *The Seminar of Jacques Lacan, Book XVII: The Other Side of Psychoanalysis,* trans. Russell Grigg (New York: W. W. Norton, 2007), 197–208.

Index

Abbot of Cluny, 149
Abraham, Karl, 40–49
Adler, Alfred, 99
agalma, 74–83
Agamemnon, 61
Agathon, 53, 59–67, 68, 73, 76, 85–87
AIDS. *See* HIV/AIDS
Akerman, Chantal, xii, 162, 179–91, 239n8, 240n16
Alcibiades, 30, 53–54, 56, 60, 65–66, 68, 73–89
Alessandrini, Anthony, 232n6
Althusser, Louis, 161, 179
Andrieu, René, 140
Antigone, 61, 130
Aphrodite, 69
Apollodorus, 64, 72, 84
apparatus, of the cinema, 161–91
Arafat, Yassir, 129
Arendt, Hannah, 96, 232n2
Ares, 63
Aristodemus, 84
Aristophanes, 56–60, 71

Baader, Andreas, 141
Baader-Meinhof, 134, 140–41
Badiou, Alain, 4–7, 19, 94, 120, 137, 138–39, 236n13, 236–37n16
Barbey, Bruno, 131

Bataille, Georges, 195, 204
Bazin, André, 164, 174
Bentaga, Abdalla, 135
Bersani, Leo, 236n14
betrayal, 145, 150–51, 153
Beauvoir, Simone de, 104
Bhabha, Homi, 99–100
Black Panthers, 129, 134, 143
Bloch, Maurice, 102
Bourdieu, Pierre, 2
Bordwell, David, 161, 238n4
Bowery, Leigh, 222
Butler, Judith, xi, 3

Caillois, Roger, 195–201, 205, 208
Canguilhem, Georges, 14
Cantor, Georg, 8
Capécia, Mayotte, 117
Carroll, Noël, 238n4
Casebier, Allan, 239n9
castration, 9, 60, 74, 175
Castro, Fidel, 91
Clark, Kenneth, 201–205
Copernicus, Nicolaus, 58
Copjec, Joan, 238n4

Deleuze, Gilles, xi, 239n9
Derrida, Jacques, xi
Dichy, Albert, 140
Didi-Huberman, Georges, 202–204

243